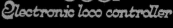

Electronic loco controller

The most comprehensive range of high quality
model figures available across lots of scales

28085 £2.65   **28090** £2.20   **10550** Pregnant Women £10.25

PR10529 Babies   £6.75

10545 Railway Enthusiasts £10.25

Preiser Catalogue	£5.50
HO GAUGE	
PR10371 BR Police Shirt Sleeved	£10.25
PR10410 BR Railway Personnel	£10.25
PR10420 Workers in Safety Vests	£10.25
PR14050 Women Hanging Washing	£5.00
PR14058 Wedding (Catholic)	£5.00
PR14155 Cows (5)	£5.00
PR14167 Ducks, Geese & Swans	£5.00
PR16328 Unpntd Seated People (120)	£16.50
PR28008 Railway Worker in Hi Vis Vest	£2.20
PR28009 Railway Shunter	£2.20
PR29070 British Policeman	£2.20
N GAUGE	
PR79087 Cyclists	£6.75
PR79155 Cows	£5.00
Huge Range Available, contact for lists	

High Quality Range of
kits in HO & N - many
suitable for UK outline

FA130339 ALDI Supermarket
£22.25

FA130932 Office Block
£79.00

Faller Catalogue	£5.50
HO GAUGE	
FA120157 Diesel Fuelling Facility	£23.75
FA130213 Small Market Garden	£14.25
FA130347 BP Petrol Station	£15.75
FA130470 Old Coal Mine	£23.75
FA130472 Municipal Gas Works	£47.50
FA130945 Coal Mine	£36.50
FA130947 Workers Hut	£11.00
FA130948 Oil Tank	£11.00
FA140312 Ferris Wheel	£56.00
N GAUGE	
FA222131 Oil Tanks	£10.25
FA232206 Garden Centre	£27.75
FA232208 Container Set	£7.00
FA232218 Shell Petrol Station	£12.00
Huge Range Available, contact for lists	

Vast range of scenics, figures and accessories in all
scales. Huge range in stock now!

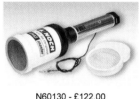 

N60260
£81.00

N60130 - £122.00

Noch Catalogue	£6.00
HO GAUGE	
N11342 Cemetery Plots	£7.00
N11580 Playground	£8.75
N11700 Assorted Tents	£10.25
N15571 Photographers	£6.25
N16106 On The Job (24)	£19.25
N GAUGE	
N32528 Snow Covered Fir Trees	£13.75
N33260 Rowing Boat	£6.50
N35846 Pallets	£8.50
ALL SCALES	
N60130 Gras-Master Flocking Device	£122.00
N60260 Steam Sound Box	£81.00
Huge Range Available, contact for lists	

Of most interest to UK
modellers will be their
catenary and lamp ranges

VN4100 - £43.00

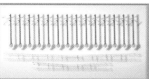  

VN6070
£5.65

VN6090
£5.65

Viessmann Catalogue	£4.75
HO GAUGE	
VN4100 Catenary Starter Set	£43.00
VN6070 Black Park Gas Lamp	£5.65
VN6072 Green Park Gas Lamp	£5.65
VN6090 Modern Street Light	£5.65
VN6363 Double Yard Lamp	£8.50
VN6396 Single Gas Lamp	£6.95
N GAUGE	
VN4300 Catenary Starter Set	£83.00
VN6470 Black Park Gas Lamp	£5.65
VN6472 Green Park Gas Lamp	£5.80
ALL SCALES	
VN4551 Motion Drive for Signals etc	£11.50
Huge Range Available, contact for lists	

Gaugemaster Controls plc
Gaugemaster House
Ford Road
Arundel
West Sussex
BN18 0BN

Tel - 01903 884488

Fax - 01903 884377
E Mail - engineshed@gaugemaster.co.uk
Web - www.gaugemaster.com

RANGES STOCKED INCLUDE

**Antex - Aristocraft - Bachmann -
Berko - Brawa - Busch - Classix -
Cooper Craft - Corgi - Dapol -
Deluxe Materials - Dornaplas -
Eckon - Faller - Fleischmann -
Gaugemaster - Graham Farish -
Harburn Hamlet - Heljan -
HMRS Transfers - Hornby -
Ian Allen Books - Jordan -
Kestrel Designs - Kibri - Knightwing -
LGB - Mailcoach - Marklin - Metcalfe -
Middleton Press - Modelscene -
Noch - Oxford Diecast -
Parkside Dundas - Peco - Piko -
Pola - Preiser - Railmatch - Ratio -
Roco - Rotacraft - Scenix - Seuthe -
Slaters - Smiths - Springside -
Superquick - Tiny Signs -
Tracksetta - Trix - Viessmann -
ViTrains - Vollmer - Wiking - Wills -**

VISIT OUR LARGE SHOWROOM
IN WEST SUSSEX

Right next to **FORD** railway station
OPEN 7 DAYS A WEEK
Mon to Sat 0900 -1730
Sundays/Bank Holidays 1030-1530
Full Product Range Carried
Ample Free Parking
Friendly, Knowledgeable Staff
Second Hand Bought & Sold

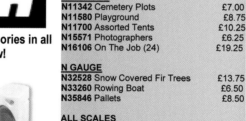

PLEASE CONTACT US FOR YOUR FREE PRICE LIST
Just specify the gauge you model in and we will do the rest

Modelfair.com

New, Pre-owned & collectable model railways
Mail Order with confidence
Tel: 0161 748 8021
Email: info@modelfair.com
Talbot House, 95 Crofts Bank Road, Urmston, Manchester M41 0US

ACE trains, quality gauge 0 tinplate range

E/3	'Celebration Class' 4-4-0 Loco, BR Black, LMS black, GC black, LMS red, LNER green.	£245.0
E3/S	Celebration Set, LNWR Loco + 2 LNWR coaches- stock	£345.0
C1	Extra LNWR coach (all 3rd) stock	£60.00
E3/S	Celebration Set, Caledonian Loco + 2 Caledonian coaches-stock	£345.0
C1	Extra Caledonian coach (all 3rd) -stock	£60.00
	Q Class 0-6-0 Tender Loco, BR Black, SR Black, SR Green	£295.0
E7	Castle Class 4-6-0 Locomotive & Tender, available in British Railways and Great Western liveries, with a number of special order names available, please call for more information. Due Nov/Dec	£750.0

E7/2	Castle 4-6-0 , 'Dudley Castle'/Banbury Castle/Restormel Castle BR Exp light green –Special edition	£750.0
E/6	A3 Class, BR green Smoke deflectors Late crest	£750.0
E6	A3 Class, BR Green without smoke deflectors, BR Blue and LNER green	£685.0
G4/1L	Brake van, with working tail light and interior light- 3 rail	£47.50
C/14	Pullmans, Set of 3: with & without white roofs	£275.0
C/14	BR Pullman Hadrian's bar – white roof. -few	£85.00
C/14	BR Pullman car Full Brake- white roof & grey roof	£85.00
C/13	A & B Set of 3 BR Mk1 coaches, SR, MR, & WR	£245.0
C/13	BR MK1 Buffet car in BR, SR, MR & WR	£80.00
C/13	BR MK1 Full brake coach in BR, SR, MR & WR	£80.00
C/10	6 coach LNER 'Excursion' set in Green and Cream	£525.0
C/11	7 coach LNER Silver Jubilee set in silver and grey	£575.0
C/9	6 coach LNER west riding set-few	£495.0
C/8	7 car LNER Record breaking set' -1 only	£575.0
C/6	Set 2 LNER teak articulated sleeper coaches	£140.0
C/5	B Set / 3 red & cream coaches, full 1st, full 3rd, brake 3rd	£210.0
C/4	B Set of 3 LNER teak coaches, 3rd,1st & 3rd brake	£210.0
C/1F	ETAT, PO & SNCF French Suburban coaches in green set of 3	£175.0
G/1	Set of 3 SWB tinplate tankers Set 1,3,4,5,6,7 & 8	£99.00
G/1M	Set of 3 SWB tinplate Milk Tankers , set A,B & C	£99.00
A/C	Station (terminus/through) set (now with extension set inc)	£250.0

Bassett Lowke trains, gauge 0 tinplate range

BL9931	J39 class Tender loco, 64744 BR late black-	£499.9
BL9941	Rebuilt Patriot, 45534 'E.Tootal Broadhurst' BR late green	£699.9
BL9924	A3 , 60103 'Flying Scotsman' BR green, smoke deflectors	£575.0
BL9940	A1 Class, 4475 'Flying Fox' LNER apple green- DEC 07	£699.9
BL9933	For Range of wagons and tankers please call set of 3's from £99.00 per set	£
	For range of station buildings please call.	

ETS trains, gauge 0 tinplate range

ETS193	WD Austerity 2-8-0 , 90149 BR early black (2 or 3 rail)	£599.0
ETS194	WD Austerity 2-8-0 , 90385 BR late black (2 or 3 rail)	£599.0
ETS195	WD 2-8-0 , 7199 W/D desert Sand livery (2 or 3 rail)	£599.0
ETS187	Garrett 2-6-6-2 locomotive, No 51 plain black	£549.0
ETS203	Steeple cab electric loco, NE green (2 or 3 rail)	£349.0
	We are Stockists for the Atlas 3 rail Track system, full range in stock please call for a price list.	

Skytrex RTR finescale 7mm Gauge O rolling stock

SMR400	Sentinel Y3 Steam Shunting Engine	£145.0
SMR506	BR Mark 1 Suburban's Maroon/green/blue	£162.0
	Large range of Coaches and wagons in stock –call for prices	

Fine Scale Gauge O Locomotives

RR	LMS 10000 Co-Co Diesel Prototype –black & silver	£975.0
Heljan	Class 47, 47635 'Jimmy Milne' BR Large Logo	£650.0
RPR	V2 Class 2-6-2 Loco, 60800 'Green Arrow' BR late green	£795.0
	Aspinal Pug 0-4-0 Tank, 51218 BR black	£395.0
	S14 -0-4-0 Tank, 147 in LSWR pea green (Walshart) valve gear	£625.0
	Fowler 3F Jinty 0-6-0T 47558 BR early black	£325.0
Ace/P	K3 Class 2-6-0 Loco, 61832 BR early Black.	£725.0
MSC	Robinson A5, 4-6-2 Tank, 69806 BR early black	£625.0
MSL	EM2 Class 77 DC Electric, 27000 in BR black	£925.0
	Class 20 Diesel, D8158 BR green (Headcode Boxes)	£575.0
	We are stockists for Parkside Dundas O gauge wagon kits, please phone for competitive prices	

Silver Fox Models, Ready to Run 00 gauge Classic Diesel & Electrics

	Irish C Class Diesel- all liveries *NEW*	£132.0
SF105	Gloucester Motor Parcels Van (Gangwayed) , BR blue	£135.0
SF109	Cravens Single (Motor Parcels Van) BR green	£135.0
SR112	Derby Lightweight single Car DMU unit, BR green	£135.0
SF110	Derby Lightweight 2 Car DMU unit, in BR blue	£175.0
SF111	Derby Lightweight 2 Car DMU unit, in BR green	£175.0
SF117	Cravens 2 Car DMU unit, BR blue livery	£175.0
SF116	Cravens 3 Car DMU unit, BR green livery	£195.0
SF150	AL6 Bo-Bo AC Electric Loco-original	£132.0
SF140	AL1 Bo-Bo AC Electric Loco, BR 'Electric Blue'	£132.0
SF090	Class J70/Y6 0-4-0 Steam Tram Engine, LNER/BR	£75.00
SF097	Class 05 0-6-0DS Diesel Shunter BR black	£95.00
SF10080	Irish A Class Met-Vic Co-Co diesel –in all liveries	£132.0
SF123	Brown Boveri Gas Turbine, 18000 BR black & Silver	£132.0
SF124	Brown Boveri Gas Turbine, 18000 BR green	£132.0
SF120	Metro Vic Gas Turbine 18100 BR black & silver	£132.0
SF121	Metro Vic-AC test Loco E1000 BR black & silver	£132.0
SF122	Metro Vic-AC test Loco E2001 BR black & silver	£132.0
SF0001	4000HP Co-Co , No HS4000 ' Kestrel' in brown/yell	£132.0
SF0002	Co-Co prototype diesel, D0260 'Lion' in white	£132.0
SF0006	SR 1Co-Co1 , diesel, 10203 BR black and silver & green	£132.0
SF0010	Co-Co Diesel, 10000/1 LMS/Plain black&silver, BR black & silver & BR gr	£132.0
SF0016	EE Co-Co diesel, No 'DP2' BR plain green syp	£132.0
SF0017	EE Co-Co diesel, No 'DP2' BR 2 tone green with syp	£132.0
SF0020	Class 22 Diesel, D63xx in all liveries Boxes/Discs	£132.0
SF0030	Class 41, Diesel "Warship" in all liveries Boxes/Discs	£132.0
SF0040	Co-Bo Metro-Vic Diesel D57xx BR plain green, green syp, blue	£132.0
SF0050	Class 23 'Baby Deltic' Diesel, D59xx 2 tone green SYP, boxes	£132.0
SF0051	Class 23 'Baby Deltic' Bo-Bo Type 2 Diesel, D59xx in BR blue	£132.0
SF0070	Class 76 (EM1) Bo-Bo Electric, in Black, Green, Blue	£132.0
SF0060	Class 77 EM2 Co-Co DC Electric, 27xxx BR Early black	£132.0
SF0062	Class 77 EM2 Co-Co Electric BR green syp	£132.0
SF0061	Class 77 EM2 Co-Co DC Electric, BR Electric Blue	£132.0

** NEW** ViTrains Models **NEW**

V2027	Class 37/0, 37378 Railfreight grey	£49.50
V2018	Class 37/4, 37416 Royal Scotsman claret livery	£49.50
V2048	Class 37/0, 37371 Mainline Blue	£49.50
V2028	Class 37/0, 37229 ' John T Jarvis' DRS dark blue	£49.50
V2019	Class 37/4, 37427 'Bont Y Bermo' EW&S maroon	£49.50
V2026	Class 37/0, 37156 'British Steel Hunterston' civil engineers	£49.50
V2022	Class 37/4, 37421 'Strombidae' Petroleum triple grey	£49.50
V2024	Class 37/4, 37430 'Eisteddfod Genedaethol' Triple grey	£48.50
V2024	Class 37/4, 37430 'Cwmbran' Transrail (big T) grey	£48.50
V2021	Class 37/4, 37401 'Mary Queen of Scots' large logo blue	£48.50

Bachmann Murphy Models Irish Loco's

MM143	Class 141 Bo-Bo Diesel, 143B, Irish Rail (CIE)	£74.50
MM156	Class 141 Bo-Bo Diesel, 156B Irish Rail (IR)	£74.50
MM181	Class 181 Bo-Bo Diesel, B181 Irish Rail (CIE)	£74.50
MM188	Class 181 Bo-Bo Diesel, B188 Irish Rail (CIE)	£74.50

New Hornby 2007 Steam Locomotives

Rxxx	A3 , 60039 'Sandwich' BR late green- from set	£59.50
Rxxx	A3 , 2569 'Gladiateur' LNER green-from set	£59.50
Rxxx	Patriot (un-rebuilt) 45515 'Caernarvon' BR green – from set	£59.50
Rxxx	Castle, 5006 'Tregenna Castle' GWR green-from set	£59.50
R2679	Terrier , 'Portishead' GWR Shirt button green	£41.99
R2637	Stanier 4P 2-6-4 Tank, 42437 , Late BR (W)	£59.99
R2637X	Stanier 4P 2-6-4 Tank, 42437 , Late BR DCC Fitted (W)	£69.99
R2636	Stanier 4P 2-6-4 Tank, 42468 , Early BR	£59.99
R2636X	Stanier 4P 2-6-4 Tank, 42468 , Early BR DCC Fitted	£69.99
R2635	Stanier 4P 2-6-4 Tank, 2546 , LMS Black	£59.99
R2635X	Stanier 4P 2-6-4 Tank, 2546 , LMS Black DCC Fitted	£69.99
R2634	Rebuilt Patriot, 45512 'Bunsen' BR early green (W)	£70.99
R2634X	R/Patriot, 'Bunsen' BR early green (W) DCC Fitted	£79.99
R2633	Rebuilt Patriot, 45545 'Planet' BR late green	£70.99
R2633X	R/Patriot, 45545 'Planet' BR late green DCC Fitted	£79.99
R2632	Rebuilt Patriot, 45531 'Sir Fred Harrison' early green	£70.99
R2632X	R/Patriot, 'Sir Fred Harrison' early green DCC Fitted	£79.99
R2631	Rebuilt Scot, 6133 'Green Howard's' LMS black	£70.99
R2631X	R/Scot, 'Green Howard's' LMS black DCC Fitted	£79.99
R2630	Rebuilt Scot, 46146' rifle Brigade' late BR green	£70.99
R2630X	R/Scot, 46146'rifle Brigade' late BR green DCC Fitted	£79.99
R2629	Rebuilt Scot, 46140 'King Royal' late green	£70.99
R2629X	R/Scot, 46140 'King Royal' late green DCC Fitted	£79.99
R2628	Rebuilt Scot, 46102 'Black Watch' early BR green	£70.99
R2628X	R/Scot, 46102 'Black Watch' early BR green DCC Fitted	£79.99
R2627	A1X 'Terrier' Class, 32640 BR early black-	£36.50
R2626	M7 Class 0-4-4 Tank, 30023 Late BR black	£62.50
R2626x	M7 0-4-4 Tank, 30023 Late BR black- DCC fitted	£72.50
R2625	M7 Class 0-4-4 Tank, 111 SR lined green	£62.50
R2625x	M7 0-4-4 Tank, 111 SR lined green- DCC fitted	£72.50
R2658	Class 3F 0-6-0 Jinty Loco, 1670 LMS Black	£34.00
R2657	Class 3F 0-6-0 Jinty, 47294 BR black	£34.00
R2624	61xx Class 2-6-2T Tank, BR early black- (W)	£47.50
R2619	Britannia, 70037 'Hereward the Wake' Early	£79.50
R2619x	Britannia, 70037 'Hereward the Wake' Early DCC fitted	£89.99
R2618	Britannia , 70045 'Lord Rowallan' late	£79.50
R2618x	Britannia , 70045 'Lord Rowallan' late – DCC fitted	£89.99
R2616	Princess Royal , 46211 'Princess Maude' BR early	£79.99
R2515	A4 Class Loco, 60021 'Wild Swan' BR early	£79.99
R2609	Rebuilt WC Class, 'Westward Ho!' BR late green	£82.50
R2608	Rebuilt WC Class, 'Yes Tor' BR late green	£82.50
R2607	Rebuilt B of B Class, '213 Squadron' BR late green	£82.50
R2606	Rebuilt B of B, 'Sir Trafford Leigh Mallory' late green	£82.50
R2605	'Terrier' 0-6-0 Tank loco, No 44 'Fulham' in LB&SCR	£41.99
R2587	Battle of Britain (Rebuilt) '17 Squadron' BR late green	£82.50
R2586	Battle of Britain (Rebuilt)'Sir Keith Park' BR early green	£82.50
R2585	Rebuilt W/C Class, 34045 ' Ottery St Mary' BR green	£82.50
R2584	Rebuilt W/C Class, 34003 'Plymouth' BR late green (W)	£82.50
R2582	King Arthur, 'Sir Harry Le Fise Lake' BR early green	£72.50
R2581	King Arthur class, 'Sir Gawain' BR early green (W)	£72.50
R2561	Black 5, 4-6-0 Locomotive, 5036 LMS lined Black	£69.99
R2559	Princess , 46203 'Princess Margaret Rose' BR Maroon	£79.50
R2558	County , 1007'County of Brecknock' Early BR Black	£69.99
R2556	J94 0-6-0 Tank, 'Wimble Bury' PO – 1st quarter	£39.50
R2555	Black Five , 45156 ' The Ayrshire Yeomanry'	£69.99
R2553	Duchess Class, 46237 'City of Bristol' Early BR Blue	£79.50
R2551	Castle Class, 5077 'Fairey Battle' BR Green early	£69.99
R2550	Class A1X 'Terrier' 0-6-0 Tank loco, 32678 BR black late	£36.50
R2549	A1 Class, 4475 'Flying Fox' LNER Apple Green	£79.50
R2548	Grange, 6816 'Frankton Grange' BR Black early (W)	£74.50
R2547	Grange , 6877 'Llanfair Grange' GWR shirt button	£74.50
R2546	Class J52 0-6-0 Tank loco, 68878 in BR black early crest	£31.99
R2545	Class 4F Tender Loco, 43990 in BR (W) black, late	£42.50
R2544	King 4-6-0 , 6006 ' King George I' GWR	£69.50
R2543	Castle class , 4081 'Warwick Castle' BR Green early	£69.50
R2542	West Country Class , 34092 'City of Wells' BR green early	£82.50
R2541	Class J83 0-6-0T , 68472 'BR' Doncaster Green	£29.99
R2540	Class J83 0-6-0T , 68480 BR lined late Black (W)	£29.99
R2539	14xx Class 0-4-2T Tank loco, 1464 BR early green	£36.99
R2538	Q1 Class 0-6-0 Tender loco, 33002 in BR (W) black early	£59.99
R2537	Q1 Class 0-6-0 Tender Loco, 33023 BR Black late	£59.99
R2535	A4 Class 4-6-2 loco, 60029 'Woodcock' BR Green late	£79.50
R2533	J94 Class 0-6-0T Tank loco, 68035 in BR Black late (W)	£36.25
R2532	B17/4 class 4-6-0 loco, 61648 'Arsenal' BR Green early	£65.50
R2530	King Class 4-6-0 loco, 6007 'King William III' BR late Green	£69.99
R2528	M/N Class Rebuilt 4-6-2 loco 35019 'French Line C.G.T.'	£82.50
R2527	2P Class 4-4-0 Loco, 40604 BR lined black early emblem	£49.99
R2504	M7 Class 0-4-4T Tank Loco, 30479 BR Black Early	£59.99
R2483	Terrier 0-6-0T, No 41 'Piccadilly' LBSC brown	£41.99
R2465	28xx Class ex GWR 2-8-0 loco, No 2836 in BR (W) black	£69.00
R2463	8F Class Loco, 48739 BR plain black (W) Late	£69.00
R2461	County Class 4-6-0 loco, 1005 'County of Devon' BR green	£67.00
R2460	King Class 4-6-0 Loco, 6008 'King James II' GW Green	£65.00
R2459	Castle Class , 5075 'Wellington' GWR green	£74.00
R2456	Patriot, 45543 'Home Guard' BR Early Green (W)	£69.50
R2441	A3 Class , 4472 'Flying Scotsman' LNER gr, NRM	£82.50
R2405	A3 Class 4-6-2 loco, 4470 'Great Northern' LNER green	£76.50
R2403	Grange Class 4-6-0 loco, 6862 'Derwent Grange' BR Black	£69.50
R2396	4F Tender loco, 43924 'British Railway' black	£59.49
R2394	8F Class 2-8-0 Loco, 8453 unlined LMS Black	£65.00
R2339	A4 Class 4-6-2 loco, 4468 'Mallard' in LNER blue	£79.50
R2319	B17/4 , 61661 'Sheffield Wednesday' BR green	£75.00
R2315	West Country Class, 34027 'Clovelly' BR malachite gr	£79.50
R2227	8F class 2-8-0 loco, 7675 in N.E. plain un- lined black	£67.00
R2219	W/C Class, 21C123 'Blackmore Vale' SR malachite	£79.00

Hornby 2007 Diesels & Electric Locomotives

Rxxx	Class 47 , 47709 'Dionysus' FM Rail Blue from set	£39.50
R2297D	Class 110 3 Car DMU, BR green 'Speed Whiskers'	£65.00
R2668	Class 121 'Bubble Car' in British Rail blue	£46.50
R2644	Class 121 'Bubble Car' 55020 in chocolate and cream	£46.50
R2509A	Class 121 Bubble Car, BR green-	£46.50
R2508A	Class 121 'Bubble Car' 55031 NSE-	£46.50
R2656	Class 73 Electro Diesel, E6001 BR green	£44.99
R2655	Class 73 Electro Diesel, 73235 South West Trains	£44.99
R2654	Class 73 Electro Diesel, 73204 GBRF	£44.99
R2653	GWR Railcar in British Railways green-	£46.50
R2652	Class 66, 66702 'Blue Lightning' GBRF	£46.50
R2651	Class 66, 66042 'Lafarge Buddoy Wood' EWS	£46.50
R2650	Class 66, 66709 'Joseph Arnold Davies' Medite	£46.50
R2649	Class 31 Diesel, 31165 British Rail (Pristine) blue	£72.50
R2648	Class 56 Diesel, 56059 EWS	£72.50
R2648X	Class 56 Diesel, 56059 EWS DCC Fitted	£82.50
R2647	Class 56 Diesel, 56128 'West Burton Power Station' Coal Sector	£72.50
R2647X	Class 56 Diesel, 56128 Coal Sector DCC FITTED	£82.50
R2646	Class 56 Diesel, 56049 Railfreight Large Logo	£72.50
R2646X	Class 56 Diesel, 56049 Railfreight Large Logo DCC FITTED	£82.50
R2645	Class 56 Diesel, 56013 Rail Blue	£72.50
R2645X	Class 56 Diesel, 56013 Rail Blue DCC FITTED	£82.50
R2642	Class 31 Diesel, Sub sector Grey Weathered	£72.50
R2641	Class 50 Co-Co Diesel, 50020 'Revenge' LL Blue	£72.50
R2640	Class 60 Co-Co Diesel, 60066 Transrail triple grey	£72.50
R2639	Class 60 , 60014 'Alexander Fleming' EWS triple grey	£72.50
R2611	Class 142 Pacer , Regional Railways yellow	£48.50
R2596	Class 86/9 Electric , 86901 'Chief Engineer' NR Yellow	£44.00
R2594	Class 08 Diesel Shunter, 08871 in Cotswold Rail Silver	£41.99
R2593	Class 08 Diesel Shunter, 08847 in Cotswold Rail Silver	£41.99
R2592	Class 08 Shunter 08530 in Freightliner green	£41.99
R2591	Class 08 Shunter 08419 in BR blue (W)	£41.99
R2590	Class 08 Shunter 08528 in BR blue silver roof	£41.99
R2588	Class 90 loco, 90005 'Vice-Admiral Lord Nelson' One	£44.25
R2579A	Class 101 3 Car DMU, British Rail Blue	£59.50
R2578A	Class 101 3 Car DMU, British Railways Green	£59.50
R2577	Class 60 Diesel Loco, 60077 'Canisp' in triple grey	£69.50
R2575	Class 50 Co-Co Diesel Loco, 50027 'Lion' in NSE Blue	£69.50
R2573	Class 31 Diesel, 31452 'Minotaur' in Fragonset Black	£69.50
R2571	Class 31/0 31111 in BR blue	£69.50
R2570	Class 35 'Hymek' B-B diesel, D7092 BR green (W)	£39.99
R2524A	GWR Railcar in GWR chocolate and cream-	£46.50
R2523	Class 67 , 67005'Queens Messenger' Royal train	£52.99
R2522	Class 67 Bo-Bo , 67005' Rising Star' EWS maroon	£52.00
R2521	Class 59 Co-Co Diesel, 59102 ARC	£44.99
R2520	Class 59 Co-Co Diesel, 'Vale of York' EWS	£44.99
R2519	Class 59 Co-Co Diesel, 59004 Yeoman	£44.99
R2518	Class 73 Electro Diesel, 73107 'Spitfire' Fragonset	£44.99
R2517	Class 73 Electro Diesel, E6003 BR green	£44.99
R2516	Class 73 Electro Diesel, 73101 'Royal Alex' Pullman	£44.99
R2513	Class 156 2 Car, 156425 North West Regional	£59.99
R2512	Class 156 2 Car, 156430 Strathclyde PTE	£59.99
R2511	Class 156 2 Car DMU, 156401 Central Trains Green	£59.99
R2490	Class 60 Diesel, 60078 in Mainline blue	£65.00
R2489	Class 60 Diesel, 60007 in Load Haul black & orange	£65.00
R2xxx	Class 50 Co-Co diesel, full range in stock	£64.00
R2419	Class 09 Diesel Shunter, 09012 'Dick Hardy' 2 tone grey	£41.99
R2413A	Class 31 Diesel Loco, 31174 BR Blue (W)	£67.00

Hornby Digital

R8213	DCC Select Digital Control unit,	£46.50
R8214	DCC Elite Digital Control unit,	£109.5
R8216	Digital Points Decoder	£23.50
R8215	Digital Locomotive decoder (chip)	£ 7.95

New Train Packs/Sets

R2610	Caledonian single 123 and 3 Caledonian coaches	£ 95.50
R2599M	Royal Wessex pack, M/N Class 'Lamport & Holt Line', + 3 green coaches	£145.0
R2445	Silver Jubilee Train Pack, A4 Quicksilver (new ver) 3 silver coaches	£145.0
R2598M	Queen of Scots, A3 'Gladiator' LNER green + 3 Pullmans	£79.00
R2600M	Cheltenham Flyer, Tregenna Castle, GWR green + 3 Collett coaches	£74.00
R2569	Talisman. A3 'Sandwich' BR green + 3 coaches	£74.00
R2612	HST GNER 4 car pack	£77.50
R1076	Pendolino Train set – DCC FITTED – with Digital controller	£142.5
R2467X	Pendolino Train Pack DCC FITTED	£95.00
R2467	Pendolino Train Pack – DCC Ready	£79.50
R2437	Serco Train Pack, Class 47 + 3 Serco test coaches in red	£69.00
R2568	Devon Belle Train Pack, W/C Class loco & 3 Pullmans	£115.0
R2427A	GNER 225 refurbished 4 car train pack	£79.50
R2376A	Midland Mainline High Speed Train (HST) train pack 4 car	£75.00
R2372M	Royal Duchy Train Pack, Trematon Castle BR, 3 coaches	£89.99
R2347M	Manxman train pack, Patriot class loco 3 coaches	£89.99

New Hornby Coaches

	NEW Maunsell coach range –in stock	£19.99
R2569	Set of 3 Mark 1 coaches BR maroon-split from set	£39.50
R2598M	Set of 3 Collett GWR coaches- split from set	£39.50
R2598M	Set of 3 Pullman coaches- split from set	£39.50
	Gresley (ex LNER) BR Maroon full range in stock	£22.50
	Gresley (ex LNER) BR Carmine & Cream full range in stock	£22.50
	LMS/BR Stanier coaches most in stock	£22.50
	BR Pullmans (w/lights) Most in stock	£24.50
	BR Mark 1 coaches, in Maroon, Green, Chocolate & Cream, Carmine & Cream large range in stock	£15.99
	BR Mark 2's, Mark 3's and Mark 4's , FGW, Virgin, GNER, ONE, Midland Mainline, Network South East, Inter-City, large range in stock	£15.49
	GWR, Southern, LMS and LNER coaches – large range in stock	£15.49

New Hornby Coach Packs

R4310	Blue Pullman Coach Pack 3 x Mark 2 Pullmans	£48.50
R4252	Talisman Coach pack, 3 maroon mark 1's ** BARGIN**	£29.99
R4254	VSOE Car Pack	£87.50
R4255	Master Cutler Coach Pack	£56.99
R4251	The Devon Belle Coach Pack – 3 x Pullmans- stock	£59.99
R4228	Northumbrian Coach pack, 3 x Gresley's blood and custard	£48.99

New Hornby Wagons

R	6 wheel tankers all 3 liveries	£ 6.75
R6xxx	Seacow/Sealion Ballast Hoppers Most in Stock	£14.50
R6336	100 ton bogie tanker 'EWS' grey	£15.49
R631x	CCT Utility Vans – maroon & blue	£ 7.99
	We have a large range of other Hornby wagons in stock please ring for prices	
	Skaledale buildings and other accessories please call for prices.	

New Hornby *Special Offer*

R2395A	8F Class 2-8-0 Loco, 48062 BR black early emblem (W)	£57.50
R235xx	Q1 Class 0-6-0 Tender loco, 33037, 33017, 33013 & 33009 – each	£49.00
R2350	Class 50's, Achilles, Ark Royal, St Vincent & Agincourt- all £57.99 each	£57.99

New Heljan O & OO Gauge Locomotives

53xx	Class 53 'Falcon' all 3 liveries available – only a few left	£94.50
17xx	Class 17 'Clayton, BR Green - orders now taken on all liveries	£TBA
26xx	Class 26 Diesel, - all liveries inc new green versions.	£59.99
27xx	Class 27 Diesel, - all liveries inc new green versions.	£59.99
33xx	Class 33/0, 33/1, 33/2 Diesel, all liveries	£59.99
4xxx	Class 47 –few left – Original range-	£
47401	Class 47- BR Two tone green, unnumbered- with transfers	£47.50
47411	Class 47- BR Blue unnumbered- with transfers	£47.50
47421	Class 47- Large Logo Blue unnumbered-with transfers	£47.50
47431	Class 47- Triple grey unnumbered-with transfers	£47.50
	Class 52 Westerns, please call for availability (Last Few)	£65.00
5800	Class 58 Diesel, 58004 Railfreight Triple grey	£71.50
5801	Class 58 , 58014 'Didcot Power Station' coal sector grey	£71.50
5802	Class 58 Diesel, 58001 Red stripe grey (preserved)	£71.50
5803	Class 58 Diesel, 58037 Railfreight Red Stripe	£71.50
5804	Class 58 Diesel, 58047 EWS maroon	£71.50
5805	Class 58 , 58051 'Toton Traction Depot' Mainline blue	£71.50
3580	O Gauge Class 35 Hymek, BR Blue	£364.0
4880	O Gauge Class 47 Diesel BR blue & Green	£420.0
	O Gauge Class 37 orders now being taken , (Blue & Green)	£TBA
5xxx	Cargowaggon available in a variety of liveries - Stock	£20.00
	Dogfish Hopper Wagon 'Dutch 'Grey & Yellow /Green	£11.00
8900	Container Crane set- remote control DCC stock	£350.0
8901	HO Gauge Turntable 32cm (90') DCC- Stock	£125.0

Pre-owned Hornby OO Gauge

R2494	A4 Class, 60020 'Guillemot' BR early green	£84.50
R312	A4 Class, 2509 'Silver Link' LNER grey	£89.00
R649	A4 I/E, 'Sir Ronald Matthews' LNER blue + Doulton plate	£125.0
R1041	A4 Class 'Mallard' LNER blue – Live Steam Set	£179.0
R353	A4 Class, 60006 'Sir Ralph Wedgwood' BR late green I/E	£79.50
R2536	A3 Class, 60073 'St Gatien' BR early green	£69.00
R2036	A3 Class 4-6-2, 60071 'St Frusquin' BR blue I/E	£82.50
R2146	A3 'Flying Scotsman' LNER green I/E Gold plated	£175.0
R075	A3 'Flying Scotsman' LNER green, I/E 2 x green tenders	£145.0
R2017	B17, Manchester United LNER green + 3 coaches	£110.0
R2155A	J83 0-6-0 Tank, 68474 BR early Black.	£29.00
R2444	Duchess Class, 46238 'City of Carlisle' BR late maroon	£125.0
R2231	Duchess Class, 46228 'Duchess of Rutland' BR early green	£85.50
R459	Duchess I/E, 'City of St Albans' LMS black + Doulton plate	£130.0
R2176M	Duchess, 46221 'Queen Elizabeth' BR green + 3 coaches	£110.0
R2426	Princess, 46201 'Princess Elizabeth' BR black I/E	£125.0
R318	Princess, 46208 'Prin Helena Victoria' BR blue	£65.00
R2215	'Princess Elizabeth' LMS maroon I/E Gold plated	£175.0
R553	Caly single 4-2-2, 123 Caledonian Blue.	£85.00
R796	Rocket set, Loco & 3 Liverpool & Manchester coaches	£150.0
R2301	Castle Class, 'Hogwarts Castle' Gold plated edition	£175.0
R2432A	Castle, 7005 'Sir Edward Elgar' late green, from set I/E	£85.00
R2280	Castle Class 4-6-0, 5073 'Blenheim Castle' BR green	£65.00
R2133M	Sudley Castle, BR early green, + 3 coaches.	£100.0
R2294	M/N (Rebuilt) 35029 'Ellerman Lines' BR late green	£89.50
R2204	M/N (rebuilt) 35020 'Bibby Line' early BR green	£64.50
TMC254	W/C Class, 34043 'Coombe Martin' BR late green I/E	£110.0
TMC481	W/C Class, 34033 'Chard' BR Malachite I/E	£110.0
R2316	Streamlined B of B Class, 34061 '73 Squadron' BR early green	£75.00
R2355	Q Class 0-6-0, 33037 BR early black	£42.00
R2165A	A1X Terrier Tank loco, 32670 BR late black	£43.00
R2016	9F Class, 92001 BR late black	£65.00
R2139	9f Class, 92099 BR late black	£79.00
R2422	Class 47 Diesel, D1733/47853 Experimental XPT blue	£35.00
R2408	Class 50 Diesel, 50007 'Sir Edward Elgar' BR green	£65.00
R2604	Class 60, 'IKB' GWR green I/E	£135.0
R2120	Class 86, 86218 'NHS 50' Anglia livery	£54.50
	Please note Modelfair carry large stocks of Pre-owned Hornby Loco's coaches, wagons and accessories, please call with your wants.	

Pre-Owned Bachmann Locomotives OO Gauge

31-952A	A4 Class, 2512 'Silver Fox' LNER grey	£110.0
31-950	A4 Class, 4489 'Dom of Canada' LNER blue, I/E in case	£145.0
31-960	A4 , 60017 'Silver Fox' BR late green 6 coaches I/E	£275.0
31-550	V2 Class, 4771 'Green Arrow' LNER green L.E	£145.0
31-558	V2 Class, 4844 'Coldstreamer' LNER Doncaster green	£69.50
31-610	J39 Class, 64838 BR early Black	£63.50
31-852	J39 Class 0-6-0 Tender Loco, 64967 BR late black	£57.00
31-275	Parallel Boiler Scot,6100 "Royal Scot". LMS maroon I/E	£150.0
31-203	Rebuilt Patriot, 45528 'R.E.M.E' BR early green	£69.50
31-225	Rebuilt Scot, 46102 'Black Watch' BR early green	£67.50
31-279	P/ Boiler Scot,6130 "West Yorkshire Regiment". LMS maroon	£72.50
31-150x	Jubilee Class, 45682 'Trafalgar' BR early green I/E in case	£130.0
32-576	Ivatt 'Flying Pig' 43047 BR lined late black	£54.00
32-575	Ivatt Class 4, 2-6-0, 3001 LMS black	£54.00
32-875	Fairburn 2-6-4 Tank, 2691 LMS black	£58.00
32-228	Class 3F Jinty tank, 47266 BR late black	£36.00
31-777	Hall Class, 6962 'Soughton Hall' GWR	£68.00
31-307	Manor Class, Cookham Manor, BR early black	£72.50
31-300	Manor class, 7816 'Frilsham Manor' BR green I/E	£120.0
31-308	Manor, Lechlade Manor BR late green	£58.00
31-778	Modified Hall Class, 6969 'Wraysbury Hall' BR green	£72.00
32-854	9F Class 2-10-0 loco, 92006 BR early black	£90.50
32-855	9F Class 2-10-0 loco, 92249 BR late black	£90.50
32-852	9F Class 2-10-0 loco, 92116 BR early black	£90.50
32-500	Standard Class 5MT 73068 BR late green	£63.00
32-504	Standard Class 5MT 73014 BR late green	£68.00
32-108V	Class 08 Diesel Shunter, 08410 First Great Western I/E	£85.00
32-113	Class 08 Diesel Shunter, D3032 BR plain green	£39.99
32-105	Class 08 Diesel Shunter, 08800 Intercity Swallow livery	£37.00
31-080	I/E Class 46 Peak Diesel .D172 "Ixion" BR green	£90.00
	Please note we have a large quantity of Wrenn, wagons & coaches in stock.	

Modelfair stock a large range of pre-owned loco's, coaches and wagons, inc : Airfix, Bachmann, Dapol, Dublo, Farish, Hornby, Lima, Mainline, Triang, Trix, Wrenn and many more. We have an extensive range of catalogues & shop display items, please call 0161 748 8021

All the above Locos are boxed and in excellent condition. Call 0161 748 8021 for availability or visit our web site www.modelfair.com for a larger selection.
(Hundreds of locos to choose from)UK Postage & Packing £3.00 per order up to 2KG, over 2KG £10.00, Insured next day£6.50. Visa, Delta, Master Card, Switch & Amex accepted.
Talbot House, 95 Crofts Bank Road, Urmston, Manchester M41 0US. Mail Order only please

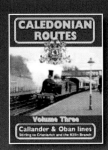

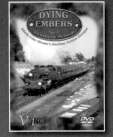
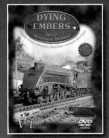
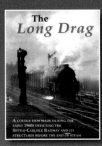

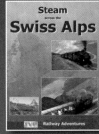
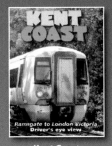

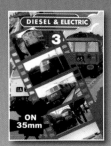

Email us on
midsussexmodels@btinternet.com
www.midsussexmodels.co.uk

OPENING HOURS
Monday - Saturday
9.00 am - 5.30 pm

Mid Sussex Models

VISA MasterCard **Mail Order** SWITCH SOLO

EXPORT A SPECIALITY

13 Junction Road, Burgess Hill, West Sussex RH15 0HR
Tel: (01444) 232972 - Fax No: 01444 239723

ALL GOODS IN STOCK OR ON ORDER MAIL AND TELEPHONE ORDER DISPATCHED SAME DAY SUBJECT TO CHEQUE CLEARANCE IMMEDIATE REFUND ON ANY OUT OF STOCK ITEMS OR OPTION TO FOLLOW ON. PLEASE GIVE EXPIRY & START DATES & SECURITY CODE ON ALL CARD ORDERS. OVERSEAS P&P & INS. AT COST. MAIL ORDER ONLY. PRICES SUBJECT TO ALTERATION WITHOUT NOTICE. UK POSTAGE £3.75 (except where otherwise stated) INSURANCE OPTIONAL 75p

We stock products of all major suppliers - Price match for unlisted items. Bachmann, Wills, Ratio, Scalextric, Woodland Scenics etc. (Subject to availability)

PECO
PECO 00

SL100 25Yds N/ Silver Track £56.00
SL102 25Yds Concrete N Silver £56.00
SL10/11 Metal Ins. Rail Joiners £1.64
SL50 Track Underlay £6.40
SL80 Single Slip £21.90
SL86/87 RH LH Curved Pt. £8.85
SL88/89 RH LH Large Rad. Pt. £8.53
SL90 Double Slip £23.50
SL91/92 RH LH Small Rad. Pt. £6.64
SL93 Short Crossing £6.50
SL94 Long Crossing £7.35
SL95/96 RH LH Med. Rad. Pt. £7.40
SL97 Small Y Point £7.51
SL98 Large Y Point £7.95
SL99 3 Way Point £18.45
Pair Point Underlays £3.22
Add 10p Per Point For Electrofrog

PECO FINE SCALE 00

SL100F 25Yds N/Silver £56.50
SL110/111 Metal/Ins.Rail Joiners £1.65
SL180 Single Slip £26.32
SLE180 Single Slip £26.00
SLE186/187 RH LH Curved Pt. £9.05
SLE188/189 RH LH Lg. Rad. Pt. £9.05
SL190 Double Slip £27.87
SLE190 Double Slip £28.40
SLE191/192 RH/LH Small Rad. Pt. £7.65
SL193 Short Crossing £7.05
SL194 Long Crossing £7.45
SLE194 Long Crossing £8.25
SLE195/196 RH LH Med. Rad. Pt. £8.18
SLE197 Small Y Point £8.45
SLE198 Large Y Point £9.70
SLE199 3 Way Point £21.05

PECO 00 SETRACK

ST100 Starter Track Set £44.50
ST200 Std. Straight 91p
ST201 Double Straight £1.46
ST202 Short Straight 81p
ST203 Extra Short Straight 81p
ST204 Long Straight min by post 10 £2.53
ST205 Isolating Track £2.10
ST220 Std.Curve 1st Rad. £1.15
ST221 Double Curve 1st Rad £1.54
ST222 Half Curve 1st Rad £1.10
ST225 Std Curve 2nd Rad £1.29
ST226 Double Curve 2nd Rad. £1.82
ST227 1/2 Curve 2nd Rad. 95p
ST230 Std. Curve 3rd Rad. £1.43
ST231 Double Curve 3rd Rad. £1.95
ST235 4th Radius Std. Curve £1.57
ST238 Curve For Y Point £1.60
ST240/241 RH LH Point £6.72
ST244/245 RH LH Curved Pt. £11.26
ST247 Y Point £7.64
ST250 Diamond Crossing £6.40
ST271 Uncouping Ramp £1.02
ST273 Power Clip £1.63
ST280 Fixing Nails £1.42

PECO 00 ACCESSORIES

PL10/PL10E Point Motor £3.70
PL12 Adaptor Base £1.33
PL13 Accessory Switch £2.24
PL26B/R/W/Y Point Switch £4.37
PL27 Switch Console £2.91
PL28 Mounting Plate Pkt 6 £1.90
LK55 Turntable £35.00

HORNBY
COLLECTORS CENTRE

2007 Hornby Catalogue £7.00

TRAIN SETS

R1036 Smokey Joe £76.00
R4254 VS Pullman Car Pack £75.50
R1068 The Rover £48.00
R1069 Old Smoky Passenger Set £62.00
R1070 Goods Master Digital Freight £60.00
R1071 Eurostar £93.00
R1072 Flying Scotsman £102.00
R1073 Digital VSOE British Pullman £238.00
R1075 Mixed Goods Digital £110.00
R1076 Pendolino 4 car Digital £138.00
R1077 GWR Western Pull. Digital £190.00
R1080 Hornby Virgin Cross Country £90.00
R1092 City Freight £83.00
R1093 Blue Pullman £93.00
R4310 Blue Coach Pack £48.00
R1094 The Royal Scot £140.00
Train Set Postage £6.00

TRAIN PACKS

R2568 The Devon Belle Pullman £112.00
R4251 Devon Belle Pullman Car Pk. £64.00
R2569 Talisman Train Pack £89.50
R2610 Caledonian Single Train Pack £120.00
R2663 Caledonian Sleeper Train Pk £89.50

HARRY POTTER

R1095 Order Of The Phoenix Set £81.00
R2662 Hogwarts Castle Loco £56.00
R4308A/B Hogwarts Comp £15.40
R4309A/B Hogwarts Brake £15.40

STEAM LOCOMOTIVES

R782 Smokey Joe £24.00
R2339 LNER Mallard £79.60
R2392 BR County of Salop £69.95
R2405 LNER A1 Great Northern £79.60
R2441 LNER NRM Flying Scotsman £79.60
R2450 BR Black 5 Weathered £71.45
R2456 BR Patriot Home Guard Wea £71.45
R2465 BR Black 2800 No.2836 Wea. £71.45
R2468 BR 3F Black Wea. 47281 £32.50
R2483 LBSC Terrier Piccadilly £44.00
R2530 King William III 6007 L/C £71.45
R2533 BR J94 Weathered 68035 L/C £43.00
R2534 GWR Pannier 2738 £32.00
R2535 BR A4 Woodcock L/C £79.60
R2537 BR Q1 33023 L/C £64.00
R2538 BR Q1 33002 E/C Weathered £64.00
R2540 BR J83 68480 L/C Wea. £31.00
R2541 BR J83 Lined Apple Green 68472 £31.00
R2547 GWR Grange Llanfair 6877 £76.70
R2548 BR Grange Frankton EC Wea. £76.70
R2549 LNER A1 Flying Fox £79.60
R2551 BR Castle Fairy Battle E/C £71.45
R2553 BR City of Bristol £79.60
R2555 BR Cl5 Ayrshire Yeomanry L/C £71.45
R2561 LMS Black 5 Lined Black 5036 £71.45
R2584 BR WC Plymouth E/C Wea. £79.60
R2585 BR WC Ottery St Mary E/C £79.60
R2586 BR BB Sir Keith Park £79.60
R2587 BR BB 17 Squadron £79.60
R2605 LBSC Terrier £44.00
R2606 BR Late BB Sir T Leigh Mallory £85.00
R2607 Late BB 213 Squadron £85.00
R2608 BR Late WC Yes Tor £85.00
R2609 BR Late WC Westwar Hoe £85.00
R2615 BR A4 Wild Swan EC £85.00
R2616 BR Princess Queen Maud £79.60
R2617 BR A3 Ladas £85.00
R2618 BR Cl7MT Lord Rowallan L/C £79.60
R2619 BR Cl7 Hereward The Wake E/C £79.60
R2619X BR Cl7 Hereward The Wake E/C £96.00
R2620 SR N15 Pendragon £75.00
R2621 BR N15 Sir Ironside Wea. L/C £75.00
R2622 BR N15 Sir Pelleas L/C £75.00
R2623 BR N15 Kingwither E/C £75.00
R2624 61XX Wea. E/C £48.00
R2625X SR M7 DCC Fitted £85.00
R2626 BR M7 Cl £76.00
R2626X BR M7 E/C DCC Fitted £85.00
R2627 BR Terrier EC £44.00
R2628 BR Scot Black Watch E/C £72.00
R2628X BR Scot Black Watch E/C £82.00
R2629 BR Scot The Kings Royal Rifle £72.00
R2630 BR Scot The Rifle Brigade EC £72.00
R2631 LMS Scot The Green Howards £72.00
R2632 BR Patriot Sir F Harrison EC £76.00
R2633 BR Rebuilt Patriot Planet £76.00
R2634 Patriot Bunsen L/C £76.00
R2635 LMS Stanier 4P 2-6-4T £61.00
R2636 BR Stanier 4P 2-6-4T E/C £61.00
R2637 BR Stanier 4P 2-6-4T L/C £61.00
R2657 BR 3F 47294 £36.00
R2658 LMS 3F 1670 £36.00
R2664 LMS Royal Scot Crimson £90.00
R2678 LSWR M7 £79.00
R2679 GWR Terrier £44.00

DIESEL & ELECTRIC LOCOS

R2376A Midland Mainline HST £77.00
R2413A Cl31 BR Blue Wea. 31270/17 £65.00
R2421 Cl31 Civil Engineer No.31110 £65.00
R2428 BR Cl 50 Illustrious £65.00
R2467 Pendolino Pack £88.00
R2467X Pendolino Pack DCC Fitted £103.00
R2486 BR Cl50 Agincourt £57.00
R2487 BR Cl50 St Vincent £57.00
R2508A BR Cl121 NSE £49.00
R2509A BR Cl121 Green £49.00
R2510 BR Cl121 Blue £49.00
R2512 New Strathclyde PTE Cl156 £61.00
R2513 Northwest R.R Cl156 £61.00
R2516 BR Cl73 Pullman Royal Alex £53.00
R2517 BR Cl173 Green £49.00
R2518 Fragonset Cl73 Spitfire 73107 £49.00
R2519 Foster Yeoman Cl59 £48.00
R2520 EWS Cl59 Vale of York £48.00
R2521 ARC Cl59 59102 £48.00
R2522 EWS Cl67 Rising Star £54.00
R2523 Cl67 Royal Train £54.00
R2524A GWR Rail Car £49.00
R2570 BR Hymek Green D7092 Wea. £46.00
R2571 BR Cl31 Blue £72.00
R2573 BR Cl31 Fragonset £72.00
R2575 NSECl50 Lion £72.00
R2576 BR Trainload CL56 56063 £46.00
R2577 BR Trainload Cl60 Canisp £65.00
R2578A BR Green Cl101 £61.00
R2579A BR Blue Cl101 £61.00
R2612 GNER HST 125 4 Car Pack £78.00
R2613 BR Inter HST 125 Exec. Livery £78.00
R2639 EWS/Trainload Cl60 A Fleming £72.00
R2640 Trainload Cl60 John Logie Bair £72.00
R2641 BR Cl50 Revenue Large Arrow £72.00
R2644 BR Cl121 Choc/Cream £50.00
R2645 BR Cl56 Rumanian Sub Sector £84.00
R2646 BR Cl56 Railfreight (1987) £84.00
R2647 BR Cl56 Large Arrows £84.00
R2648 EWS Cl56 £84.00
R2649 BR Cl31 Blue £84.00
R2650 Medite Cl66 J A Davis £50.00
R2651 EWS Cl66 £50.00
R2652 GB Cl66 Blue Lightning £50.00
R2653 BR Diesel Railcar W22W Green £49.00
R2654 Cl73 GB Railfreight £50.00
R2655 Cl73 SW Trains £50.00
R2656 BR Cl73 Green £50.00
R2668 BR Cl121 Blue £49.00

COACHES

R446 GWR 4 Wheel Coach £8.40
R468 LMS 4 Wheel Coach £8.40
R4086G Virgin Mk2 Standard £15.40
R4087G Virgin Mk2 Brake £15.40
R4088D Virgin Mk.2 First £15.40
R4095C LMS 68ft Dining Car £15.40
R4095D LMS Restaurant Car £15.40
R4096D/E Virgin Mk3 1st 11040 £15.40
R4097D Virgin Mk3 Open £15.40
R4100E BR Autocoach Maroon £15.40
R4109B BR Mk1 Brake Blue/Grey £15.40
R4114C BR Mk1 Brake Coach £15.40
R4115D BR Mk1 Comp £15.40
R4116B BR Mk1 Parcels Green £15.40
R4117C BR Mk1 Buffet £15.40
R4135 SR Olive 4 Wheel Coach £8.40
R4143B Pullman Rosemary £26.50
R4144A Pullman 3rd Parlour No.34 £26.50
R4146A Pullman 3rd Kitchen No.168 £26.50
R4150B Pullman Brake £26.50
R4153A Network SE Mk.2a Open 2nd £15.40
R4154/A Network SE Mk.2a Brake 1st £15.40
R4155 LMS TPO £27.50
R4160C GWT Mk3 First £15.40
R4161A/B GWT Mk3 Second £15.40
R4162A Pullman 1st Parlour Leona £26.50
R4164A Pullman 1st Kitchen Argus £26.50
R4165 Pullman 3rd Kitchen No164 £26.50
R4166A Pullman 1st brake No.54 £26.50
R4171 LNER Corridor First £28.00
R4172 LNER Corridor Third £28.00
R4173 LNER Corridor Buffet £28.00
R4174/A LNERCorridor Sleeper £28.00
R4179/A BR Corridor First Ex LNER £23.00
R4182/A BR Corridor Sleeper Ex LNER £23.00
R4183A/B GWT Mk3 Buffet £15.40
R4188B BR Restaurant Car £15.40
R4200A BR Mk1 Brake Mar. Wea. £15.40
R4202A BR Mk.1 Sleeper Mar. Wea £15.40
R4203A BR Mk.1 Buffet Maroon £15.40
R4204A BR Mk.1 Parcels Maroon £15.40
R4205A BR Mk.1 Brake C/Cream £15.40
R4206B BR Mk.1 Comp C/Cream £15.40
R4207A BR Mk.1 Parcels C/Cream £15.40
R4208A BR Mk.1 Brake WR £15.40
R4209B BR Mk.1 Comp Choc/Cream £15.40
R4210 BR Mk.1 Sleeper WR £15.40
R4211A BR Mk.1 Buffet WR £15.40
R4212A BR Mk.1 Parcels WR £15.40
R4213A Midland Mainline Mk.3 First £15.40
R4214A Midland Mainline Mk.3 Std. £15.40
R4215A BR Mk2D First Intercity £15.40
R4222A GWR Clerestory 3rd £15.40
R4223A GWR Clerestory Brake £15.40
R4224A Mk2 FGW 1st £15.40
R4225B Mk2 FGW Open 2nd £15.40
R4226A/B One Mk.3 Open first £15.40
R4227A One Mk.3 Standard £15.40
R4232 LMS Corridor Brake 3rd £23.25
R4233 LMS full brake £23.25
R4240 FGW Mk2 Open Brake £15.40
R4242 BR Ex GWR Comp C/Cream £15.40
R4243/A BR Ex GWR BRK C/Cream £15.40
R4244A BR Ex GWR Restaurant C/C £15.40
R4245 One Anglia DVT £15.40
R4247 Midland Mainline Buffet £15.40
R4256 BR Mk1 Comp S15042 £15.40
R4257 BR Mk1 Brake R34269 £15.40
R4260A BR Maroon Corr. Brake £23.25
R4261A/B BR Maroon Corr. First £23.25
R4262B BR Maroon Corr. Third £23.25
R4263A/B BR Maroon Corr. Buffet £23.25
R4264A Maroon Corr. Sleeper £23.25
R2469 BR Ex SR Comp. Carmine/Cream £15.40
R4270 BR Ex SR Brake Carmine/Cream £15.40
R4271 Pendolino 1st Open £23.25
R4272 Pendolino Trailer Std Open £21.00
R4273 Pendolino 1st Open MFO £21.00
R4274A/B Pendolino Std Open MSO £21.00
R4275 BR Mk3 Trailer Guard 2nd £15.40
R4276 FGW Mk3 Trailer Guard Std £15.40
R4277 Mid Mainline Mk3 Guard Std £15.40
R4278 Virgin Mk3 Guard Std £15.40
R4282A BR Mk3 Sleeper £15.40
R4283A Scotrail Cala. Sleeper £15.40
R4284 Royal Train Sleeper £15.40
R4286 GNER Mallard Mk4 1st Open £15.40
R4287 GNER Mallard Mk4 Tourist £15.40
R4288 GNER Mallard Mk4 Catering £15.40
R4289 BR Centenary Comp £15.40
R4290 BR Centenary Brake £15.40
R4291 GWR Comp £15.40
R4292 GWR Brake £15.40
R4293A/B Suburban B Set £15.40
R4294 BR Intercity MK3 Exec Open £15.40
R4296 BR Intercity MK3 Exec Buffet £15.40
R4297A/B SR Maurnsel Corr 3rd £21.00
R4298A/B SR Maunsell corr 1st £21.00
R4299A/B SR Maunsell Comp £21.00
R4300A/B SR Maunsell 6 Comp Br £21.00
R4301A/B SR Mausell Brake Van £21.00
R4302A/B BR Maunsell Corr 3rd £21.00
R4303A/B BR Maunsell Corr. 1st £21.00
R4304A/B BR Maunsell Comp £21.00
R4305A/B BR Maunsell 6 Comp £21.00
R4306A/B BR Maunsell Brake Van £21.00

HORNBY TRACK

R600 Straight £0.98
R601 Double Straight £1.65
R603 Long Straight Min By Post 10 £2.15
R604 Curve 1st Radius £1.20
R605 Double Curve 1st Radius £1.37
R606 Curve 2nd Radius £1.20
R607 Double Curve 2nd Radius £1.72
R608 Curve 3rd Radius £1.46
R609 Double Curve 3rd Radius £1.78
R610 Short Straight 77p
R614/5 LH/RH Diamond Crossing £6.35
R617 Uncoupling Ramp £2.00
R618 Double Isolating Rail £4.70
R620 Railer Uncoupler £3.20
R628 Curve 33.5" £1.31
R643 Half Curve 2nd Radius 86p
R8072/3 LH/RH Point £5.90
R8074/5 LH/RH Curved Point £10.50
R8076 Y Point £6.65
R8077/8 LH/RH Express Point £10.50
R8206 Power Track £2.90
R8211 Rolling Road £28.50

THOMAS

R9071 Thomas set £50.00
R9072 Percy Circus set £70.00
R9073 James Passenger set £80.00
R9074 Thomas & Bill set £95.00
R350 Percy The Saddle Tank £19.00
R351 Thomas The Tank Engine £29.50
R382 Duck £29.50
R383 Gordon The Big Blue Engine £68.90
R852 James The Red Engine £58.90
R9046 Toby The Tram £23.90
R9047/8 Bill or Ben £18.90
R9049 Henry £58.00
R9064 Diesel Loco £39.00
R9066/7 Bert or Arry Diesel £28.50
R9069 Stepney £42.50
R9070 Oliver £42.50
R9231 Emily £58.00
R9232 Edward £58.00

TRACK ACCESSORIES

R070 Turntable £42.00
R076 Footbridge £9.60
R083 Buffer Stop £1.00
R169 Junction Home Signal £6.85
R170 Junction Distant Signal £6.85
R171 Single Home Signal £5.00
R172 Single Distant Signal £5.00
R394 Hydraulic Buffer £3.20
R406 Colour Light Signal £12.00
R636 Double Level Crossing £11.25
R645 Single Level Crossing £6.70
R8008 Suspension Bridge £28.20

TRACKSIDE BUILDINGS

R334 Station Canopy £13.90
R460 Straight Platform £2.75
R462 Large Curved Platform £2.75
R463 Small Curved Platform £2.75
R464 Platform Ramp £2.75
R495 Platform Subway £2.75
R510 Platform Shelter £7.00
R513 Platform Fencing £4.85
R514 Platform Canopies £7.85
R539 Railway Cottage £10.45
R8000 Country Station £24.00
R8001 Waiting Room £13.90
R8002 Goods Shed £13.70
R8003 Water Tower £10.40
R8004 Engine Shed £12.65
R8005 Signal Box £10.90
R8007 Booking Hall £20.50
R8009 Station Terminus £33.50

CONTROL EQUIPMENT

R044 Point Switch £5.10
R046 On On Switch £5.10
R047 On Off Switch £5.10
R602 Power Clip £1.45
R8012 HM 2000 Controller £48.00
R8014 Point Motor £3.20
R8015 Point Motor Housing £2.40

DIGITAL CONTROL

R8213 DCC Select £54.00
R8214 DCC Elite £107.00
R8215 Locomotive Decoder £8.50
R8216 Accessory Decoder £22.50

SKALEDALE & LYDDLE END
10% off available items

GAUGEMASTER

D Twin Track Controller £57.00
DS Twin Track Inertia Controller £95.00
TS Three Track Plus One Inertia £98.00
Q Four Track Controller £105.00
HF1 Track Cleaner Single Tk. £21.00
HF2 Track Cleaner Double Tk. £31.00
CDU Capacitor Discharge Unit £10.30
SEEP PM1 Point Motor £3.80
SEEP PM2 Point Motor £3.65
SEEP PM4 Point Motor S/Latching £4.60
Controller/Trans. Postage £6.00

BACHMANN LOCOS

30601 Virgin Voyager 3 car set £86.00
30900 Junior 0-6-0T Red £21.00
30920 Junior 0-6-0 ST LNER Green £21.00
31058 J75 BR Black L/C Weathered £37.00
31612 BR V3 Tank Black L/C £45.00
31711 LNER B1 Sir William Gray Green £56.00
31712 BR B1 Springbok Lined Black £56.00
31952 LNER A4 Mallard Blue £80.00
3200DC BR Guild Hall Green L/C £76.00
32204 GWR Pennier Tank green £43.00
32585 BR 2-6-0 4MT Ivatt 43106 L/C £66.00
32586DC BR 2-6-0 4MT Ivatt 43154 E/C £76.00
32853 BR 9F L/C Wea. S/Chimney £110.00
32854 BR 9F E/C S/Chimney £93.00
32855 BR 9F L/C D/Chimney £93.00
32875 LMS Fairburn tank black £57.00
32876 BR Fairburn tank black E/C £57.00
32877 BR Fairburn tank black L/C £57.00
32952 BR 4MT 2-6-0 76079 Blk L/C £67.00
32953DC BR 4MT 2-6-0 76020 Blk E/C £77.00
30915 Junior Diesel Shunter Rusty £21.00
31341 BR 04 Shunter Black E/C £36.35
31342 BR 04 Shunter Green L/C £36.35
32032 Cl20 D8307 BR Blue Box Wea. £43.00
32040DS Cl20 D8113 BR Green Discs £110.00
32041 Cl20 20028 BR Blue Discs £43.00
32042DC D8101 BR Grn. Discs Yellow £54.00
32043DS 20129 BR Blue Boxes £110.00
32375DC Cl37/5 37672 Transrail £61.00
32380DS Cl37/5 37698 Railfreight Coa £118.00
32381 Cl37/4 EWS Ty Hafan £55.00
32400DS Cl25/3 25095 BR Blue £108.00
32726DS Cl66 66522 Freightliner Shan. £128.00
32727 Cl66 66701 GBRF £64.00
32731 Cl66 66407 DRS £64.00
32732 Cl66 66532 Freightliner £63.00
32750 Cl57/0 57008 Freightliner Explorer £63.00
32753 Cl57/0 Freightliner Challenger £63.00
32760 Cl57/3 Lady Penelope Virgin £63.00
32800 Cl47 D1500 Green Half Yell. En £60.00
32800DS Cl47 47404 BR Blue Hadrian £124.00

BACHMANN COACHES & WAGONS
WAGONS 20% OFF
MK1s £17.00 MK2s £18.00
PULLMANS £23.00 OTHERS £15.00

N GAUGE
DAPOL, PECO & FARISH LOCOS, COACHES AND WAGONS
20% OFF AVAILABLE ITEMS

SECONDHAND MODEL RAILWAY PURCHASED AND SOLD
HORNBY DUBLO/HORNBY 0 GAUGE
WE ALWAYS HAVE A LARGE SELECTION
NO LISTS

WANTED

UNWANTED OR UNUSED MODEL RAILWAYS, SLOT CAR, DIECAST, OLD TOYS—ANY SIZE, ANY MANUFACTURER, ANY AGE—BOXED OR UNBOXED - ANYTHING CONSIDERED

OVER 20 YEARS EXPERIENCE

COMPETETIVE QUOTES BY RETURN

DISTANCE NO OBJECT

WE PAY FOR COLLECTION OR DELIVERY

SETTLEMENT MADE IMMEDIATELY

CONTACT BRIAN AT EDWARD JAMES COLLECTABLES

HOME (0114) 2489940

MOBILE (07780) 776682

EdJamCollectable@aol.com

42 BRYONY CLOSE

KILLAMARSH

SHEFFIELD S21 1TF

Dapol (N Gauge)

D022b Class 73 Electro-Diesel 73110 in Civil Engineers Dutch style livery (list £75) .... BARGAIN....£29
Also available
D021a Class 73 Electro-Diesel 73114 "Stewarts Lane" in Mainline blue livery (list £75) .... BARGAIN.....£35

ND035 45xx straight sided 2-6-2 tank loco 4565 in BR lined green with late crest(list £65).. BARGAIN....£29
Also available
ND023 45xx straight sided 2-6-2 tank loco 4527 in GWR livery (list £65) .... BARGAIN..... £37
ND024 45xx straight sided 2-6-2 tank loco 4571 in British Railways livery (list £65) .... BARGAIN..... £32

ND047 45xx Slope sided 2-6-2 tank loco 5531 in GWR green (list £65) .... BARGAIN....£32
Also available
ND059 45xx Slope sided 2-6-2 tank loco in GWR green shirtbutton £35

ND050 Class 66 diesel 66545 Freightliner (list £80) .... BARGAIN....£39
Also available
ND051 to ND056, also Freightliner but different running numbers, all priced at £39 each (RRP £80)

ND073a Class 221 4 car Super Voyager DMU 221109 'Marco Polo" in Virgin trains livery £85
ND073b Class 221 4 car Super Voyager 221110 "James Cook".. £85
ND073c Class 221 4 car Super Voyager 221130 "Michael Palin".. £85
ND073d Class 221 4 car Super Voyager 221144 "Prince Madoc".. £85

Bachmann (OO Gauge)

31-711 B1 1189 'Sir William Gray' LNER apple green £53
Also available
31-712 B1 61000 'Springbok' BR lined black early emblem....... £53

31-954 A4 60007 'Sir Nigel Gresley' BR express blue double chimney £73

32-178 Crab 2-6-0 Mogul 2715 & tender in LMS lined black (list £77.45) .... BARGAIN....£49

32-275 K3 2-6-0 2934 & group standard tender in LNER black (list £78.50) .... BARGAIN....£49

32-300DC Collett Goods 2244 & churchward tender in BR lined green with late crest (DCC on board) £53

32-381 Class 37/4 diesel 37411 "Ty Hafan" EWS livery £50

32-382 Class 37/4 diesel 37410 "Aluminium 100" in BR blue with large logo £59

32-585 Ivatt class 4 2-6-0 43106 BR black with late crest & tablet catcher. £62

32-602 Class 220 Virgin Voyager 4 car unit 220018 'Dorset Voyager' £82

32-726DS Class 66 diesel 66522 in Freightliner/Shanks Waste Solutions livery (DCC sound on board) £119

32-733 Class 66 diesel 66068 in EWS livery £61

32-825 Ivatt Class 2 2-6-0 46521 in BR lined green with late crest £56
Also available
32-827 Ivatt Class 2 2-6-0 6404 in LMS black (with Walscherts valve gear) £56

32-951 Standard class 4MT 2-6-0 76069 & BR1B tender in BR black with late crest £62

32-976DC Class 66/9 diesel DRS 66412 (DCC on board) £69

Exclusive First Editions (OO Gauge)

27702 "London Transport" AEC STL d/deck bus (no roof box) £18

Heljan (OO Gauge)

2600 Class 26 BRCW Sulzer diesel D5335 in BR green with full yellow ends (list £79) ...... BARGAIN....£49

2602 Class 26 BRCW Sulzer diesel D5331 in BR blue with full yellow ends (list £79) ...... BARGAIN....£49
Also available
2603 Class 26 BRCW Sulzer diesel D5340 in BR blue with full yellow ends (list £79).......................... BARGAIN..... £49

3302 Class 33/0 diesel 33035 in Network South East revised livery (list £79) .... BARGAIN....£47
Also available
3303 Class 33/0 diesel 33030 in EWS maroon & gold livery (list £79) .... BARGAIN..... £47
3312 Class 33/0 diesel.33025 "Sultan" in BR blue with grey roof (list £79) .... BARGAIN..... £49

3334 Class 33/2 diesel 33202 "Meteor" in Fragonset livery £63
Also available
3335 Class 33/2 diesel 33207 in West Coast Railway Company Maroon livery £63

3503 Class 35 Hymek D7042 in BR blue with yellow ends (list £79) .... BARGAIN....£44
Also available
3507 Class 35 Hymek D7040 in BR blue with white cab and yellow warning panel (list £79) .... BARGAIN..... £44

5211 Class 52 Western diesel D1041 "Western Prince" in BR maroon (list £89) .... BARGAIN....£54
5203 Class 52 Western diesel D1015 "Western Champion" in experimental golden ochre livery (list £89).......... BARGAIN..... £54
5207 Class 52 Western diesel D1004 "Western Crusader" in green livery (list £89).......................... BARGAIN..... £54
5208 Class 52 Western diesel D1058 "Western Nobleman" in BR blue (list £89) .... BARGAIN..... £54

Hornby Model Railways (OO Gauge)

R2530 King Class 4-6-0 6007 "King William III" & tender in BR green with late crest (list £95). BARGAIN....£53

R2555 Class 5 4-6-0 45156 "Ayrshire Yeomanry" & tender in BR black with late crest (list £95) BARGAIN..£58

R2569 Ltd Edition The Talisman train pack (list £125) .... BARGAIN....£79

R2649 Class 31 diesel 31165 in BR Blue. £74

R4252 "The Talisman" coach pack Ltd Edition (list £55) .... BARGAIN....£30

R4255 Master Cutler coach pack containing 4 Gresley coaches in BR crimson/cream (list £100) BARGAIN .£57

Bassett-Lowke (O Gauge)

BL99022(C) Class A3 4-6-2 Flying Scotsman loco with 2 tenders in LNER green (1928 record breaker livery) (list £900) .... ABSOLUTE BARGAIN....£449

BL99027(C) Class 20 Diesel locomotive in British Railways green with 3 x goods vans (list £700) ..... BARGAIN....£299

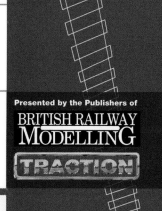

BRITISH RAILWAY MODELLING
THE QUALITY MODEL RAILWAY MONTHLY
INVITES YOU TO

Presented by the Publishers of
BRITISH RAILWAY MODELLING
TRACTION

IN ASSOCIATION WITH
DONCASTER & DISTRICT MRC

16th & 17th FEBRUARY 2008

THE *festival of* BRITISH RAILWAY MODELLING

Yorkshire Event Centre
Harrogate Showground, North Yorkshire

OPENING
Sat 10am - 5.30pm
Sun 10am - 5pm
Doors open 9:45am for pre-booked ticket holders

HOW TO GET THERE
FREE shuttle bus between Harrogate station and the venue. *FREE* car parking. See website for detailed directions and a map.

Disabled Access ♿

Ellerton Road

COME AND ENJOY A SUPERB DAY OF RAILWAY MODELLING
- 29 quality working British layouts to enjoy
- Over 100 trade stands to stock up on all those essentials
- BRM Specialist Trade Village for those harder to source items
- Modelling demonstrations and displays - pick up some great modelling tips!
- Children's modelling area (5-14yrs) Sponsored by Freestone Model Accessories

Book on-line at www.brmodelling.co.uk
or call the ticket hotline: **01778 391180** (Mon-Fri, 8am-6pm)

THE FESTIVAL OF BRITISH RAILWAY MODELLING BOOKING FORM 2008

Title _____ Forename _____ Surname _____

Address _____

_____ Town _____

County _____ Postcode _____

E-mail address _____

Daytime Telephone _____

PRE-BOOKING CLOSES 9am FRI 8 FEB 2008
ALL ADMISSION LETTERS (TICKETS) WILL BE DISTRIBUTED AFTER 1ST FEBRUARY 2008.
ADMISSION IS NON-REFUNDABLE, NON-EXCHANGEABLE
& WE REGRET LOST LETTERS CANNOT BE RE-ISSUED

PLEASE SEND TO (photocopies acceptable): **FBRM TICKETS,**
WARNERS EXHIBITION DEPT, WEST STREET, BOURNE, LINCS PE10 9PH.

ADVANCE ADMISSION RATES - PLEASE SEND ME:
All under 14's must be accompanied by an adult
ONE DAY ADMISSION Letters are valid for use on **EITHER SATURDAY OR SUNDAY**

_____ Adult @ **£6.00**   _____ Senior (60+) @ **£5.00**

_____ Child (5-16 yrs) @ **£3.50**   _____ Family (2+3) @ **£19**

BRM/TRACTION subscribers *receive a £1 discount on pre-booked adult/senior admission (Max.2)*

Subscription No. _____   Magazine_____
Subs No. must be included to qualify for discount.

_____ Subscriber rate adult @ **£5.00**

_____ Subscriber rate senior @ **£4.00**   TOTAL DUE £ _____

On-the-door admission: Adult £8.00, Senior £7.00, Child £4.00, Family £24.00

I enclose a cheque for £ _____ made payable to "WARNERS GROUP PUBLICATIONS PLC"
or please debit my Credit Card   VISA / MASTERCARD / SWITCH

INT REF: DDAY   Switch only

Card No ☐☐☐☐ ☐☐☐☐ ☐☐☐☐ ☐☐☐☐ ☐☐☐

Expiry Date ☐☐☐☐   Start Date ☐☐☐☐   Issue No ☐

Signature _____ Date _____

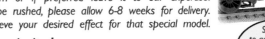

ORDER FORM

I would like to order:

☐ 12 issues of British Railway Modelling for just £36.99 inc Annual
☐ 15 issues of Traction for just £45.00 inc Annual
☐ 6 issues of Traction for just £16.99

Your Details

Mr/Mrs/Miss/Ms _____ First Name _____

Surname _____

Address _____

_____

_____

_____ Postcode _____

Telephone No _____

Email Address _____

☐ I enclose a cheque for £_____ made payable to *Warners Group Publications*

☐ Please debit £_____ from my: ☐ VISA ☐ MasterCard ☐ SWITCH

Card Number   Switch Only
☐☐☐☐ ☐☐☐☐ ☐☐☐☐ ☐☐☐☐ ☐☐☐

Expiry Date ☐☐☐☐   Start Date ☐☐☐☐ Issue No ☐

Signature _____ Date _____

Final closing date for orders is 31st October 2008. This is a UK offer only. Overseas rates are available on request.

 Please return to: <Magazine Name> Subs, Warners Group Publications, FREEPOST PE211, Bourne, Lincs, PE10 9BR

REF: BRM/ANNUAL08

Also included:

● **FREE** delivery direct to the door
● Priority Mailing – receive your copy before the shops
● Protection against cover price increases
● Guarantee your copy each month
● Money back guarantee on all un-mailed copies
● Save on admission to 3 great shows a year

Contents

162

BRM Annual 2008 COMPETITION

1st prize worth £500

£1,400 worth of prizes to WIN!

Your chance to win a share of £1,400 worth of Hornby railway models in this easy-to-enter competition. To enter, correctly answer the question below - or take part at the Warley NEC show, the Festival of British Railway Modelling at the YEC, Harrogate, or the London Festival of Railway Modelling at Alexandra Palace. You'll have the opportunity of winning one of these great prizes:

1st Prize £500 worth of Hornby 'Skaledale' model buildings and accessories

2nd Prize £300 worth of Hornby 'Railroad' sets and individual models

3rd Prize £200 Hornby Digital train set

Plus: There will also be runners-up prizes of Hornby train packs, steam and diesel locomotives and rolling stock totalling £400.

In order to win one of these magnificent prizes, correctly answer the following question:

Which famous model railway manufacturer, mentioned in the BRM 2008 Annual, originally had their main showroom at High Holborn in London?

A) **Bertie Bassett**
B) **Fred Bassett**
C) **Bassett-Lowke**

Send your answer on a postcard or the back of a sealed envelope, together with your name, address and daytime telephone number to:

Hornby Competition (ref BRM0137)
British Railway Modelling
Warners Group Publications,
The Maltings, West Street,
Bourne PE10 9PH

Or enter online at **www.brmodelling.co.uk**
Entries to reach us by closing date March 31, 2008

COMPETITION RULES:
1. Closing date for entries is March 31, 2008.
2. The competition will be drawn on Tuesday April 1, 2008 and the winners will be notified by post/telephone.
3. The prizes must be accepted as offered, there can be no alternative awards, cash or otherwise.
4. All entries become the property of Warners Group Publications
5. The decision of Warners Group Publications is final and no correspondence will be entered into.
6. Competition is open to all UK residents, including the Channel Islands, Eire, and BFPO except for employees of Warners Group Publications or anyone connected with this competition.
7. Entrants must be over the age of 18.

The impressive Hassell Harbour Bridge from the Alsager Railway Association is the setting for this WR freight train - see page 46.

Welcome

to the 2008 *BRM Annual*

It's hard to believe that we are already publishing our third *BRM Annual*. Time has simply flown by since the first Annual was produced back in 2005, and in the intervening years *British Railway Modelling* has gone from strength to strength. In fact, so great has been the success of *BRM* in recent months, the number of pages in *BRM* is in great danger of overtaking the number of pages in the Annual! As part of the continuing growth of the *BRM* 'brand', we are also pleased to announce the publication of the first in a new series of *BRM* modelling books, which we hope will prove to be just as successful as the popular Right Track DVDs. The first, *Lineside Buildings*, written by Paul Bason, is now available, with several other titles also in preparation.

This year's Annual is packed with in-depth articles and features, as well as *BRM* favourites such as 'Layout Focus', 'Classic BRM' and 'Lineside Look'. Michael C Shaw uncovers the history of Bassett-Lowke and celebrates 80 years of the Romney Hythe & Dymchurch Railway, while Steve Knight pieces together the rise and fall - and rise and fall - of Airfix.

Eric Sawford presents another great selection of black and white images featuring BR's freight workhorses in 'Steam Pictorial', Tony Wright looks back at the Woodhead Route, and Garry Stroud remembers the final years of steam at Swindon - post 1968! We discover the delights of up-to-date steam operation with Nigel Burkin, Peter J Page investigates the choices to be made when deciding on a layout, and I take a look at the secrets of the editorial workbenches.

Finally, providing something completely different, Steve Adcock describes his HO scale American short line layout, set in the Chicago connurbation. We hope you like it!

As always, Happy Modelling!

CONTACTS

British Railway Modelling
The Maltings, West Street,
Bourne, Lincolnshire PE10 9PH

Published by
Warners Group Publications plc
01778 391027
Fax: 01778 425437 (editorial)

Printed by
Warners (Midlands) plc

Publisher
John Greenwood
email: johng@warnersgroup.co.uk

Managing Editor
David Brown
email: davidb@warnersgroup.co.uk

Editor
John Emerson
email: johne@warnersgroup.co.uk

Assistant Editor/Photographer
Tony Wright
email: tonyw@warnersgroup.co.uk

Editorial Assistant
Richard Wilson
email: richardw@warnersgroup.co.uk

Group Advertisement Manager
Patrick Raphael Sisko
01778 391114
email: patsisko@warnersgroup.co.uk

Sales Executive
Jane Cottam
01778 395002
email: janec@warnersgroup.co.uk

Designer and Production
Andrianna Curtis
01778 392076
email: acurtis@warnersgroup.co.uk

Head of Design and Production
Jayne Thorpe
email: jaynet@warnersgroup.co.uk

Designer
Ryan Housden

Editorial Secretary
Jean Waterfall
email: jeanw@warnersgroup.co.uk

Track Plan Illustrator
Ian Wilson at Pacific Studio

Website Design
Andy Gilbert
email: andyg@warnersgroup.co.uk

Trade Account Sales
Natalie Cole
01778 392404
email: nataliec@warnersgroup.co.uk

UK/Overseas Newstrade sales
Andrew Stark
01778 391194
email: andrews@warnersgroup.co.uk

Newstrade Distribution
Tom Brown
01778 391135

ISSN 0968-0764

Ideas for future contributions should be sent in outline form to the Editor for consideration. Please clearly mark all material with your name and address, and include sufficient postage if you require material to be returned. Views expressed by contributors are not necessarily those of the Editor or Publisher.

From time to time Warners may lend reputable companies the names and addresses of readers who have responded to offers, services and competitions organised by *BRM*. If you do not wish to receive such mailings, please write to Warners Group Distribution, Dept WD, Manor Lane, Bourne, Lincolnshire PE10 9PH or call 01778 391153.

Manston Airport

Trains and planes at a Southern 'might have been' terminus, modelled in OO finescale by **Andy Hopper.**

Work on the Club layout was substantially completed, and so, in the way of all modellers, my mind was starting to turn to a project of my own. My Isle of Sodor layout (see *Railway Modeller* March 1995) was still doing the rounds, but I was interested in something a bit more serious. But what? Some of the decisions were easy. It should

be portable, as I like exhibiting, and small enough to be manageable in a reasonable timescale. It should be somewhere in the ex-South Eastern & Chatham Railway territory, and set in the 1950s to pander to my nostalgia for the train spotting days of my long lost youth.

Other decisions were more difficult. I was committed

to 4mm scale, and was very tempted by EM, but in the end as the club is firmly wedded to OO, and I wanted to be able to run my stock on the club

layouts too, I eventually decided it had to be OO. I consoled myself with the idea that if the layout was fairly high, which I wanted, then the track gauge would be less noticeable.

The most difficult decision of all was where? I needed a small terminus which would justify a variety of trains. Long hours were given over to this without much result until I borrowed a book from the library on the history of Manston Airport, near Ramsgate. I actually drive across it on a regular basis, and at the time it was in the news, as the RAF were leaving and the airport was being sold to a private operator. A railway branch served the airport during its construction, but was lifted in the 1920s. All of a sudden everything came together. If Sir Herbert Walker had turned his attention to air travel, in the way he had to the ocean liners at Southampton Docks,

then he could have developed Manston in the 1930s. Aeroplanes were small, so trains would be short, there would be mail traffic, and a small amount of freight, and possibly livestock such as racehorses or pedigree cattle. There would also be supplies for the main users who, in the 1950s, were the USAAF. This was what I needed.

Planning

I am a railway modeller for two main reasons. Like most boys of my age I used to go train spotting, and I like making things. This means that I like to make as much as possible of a layout for myself. I find it very satisfying to do things this way, this has the benefit that, when the layout is exhibited, it is different from most others. In one way or another I have built almost everything, except the majority of the coaching stock. I enjoy exhibiting because it gives a point to the modelling (I don't actually play with the trains much at home), and I get to talk to a

lot of interesting people. I wouldn't really be interested in presenting an 'out of the box' layout.

Now I had the basics, much thought was given to the detail. Track plan first. To fit the car, I decided on three baseboards giving a total of 12'0" by 2'0", which would have to include the storage area. Cassettes offered the most space efficient storage method, and could be concealed behind scenic features, so as not to waste any of the length. (Being involved with the club exhibition I know that layouts with long fiddle yards give poor value for the space they occupy.) A platform for three coaches and a small loco was adequate, a Royal Mail facility, and a small goods shed were needed. A fuel depot was decided on to conceal the storage area, and provide another source of traffic. To hide where the trains vanished a large water tower would be sited in front of a hole in the 'sky'. These were all fitted together in a manner that avoided having everything in parallel straight lines, as this can look unnatural.

Baseboards

I had decided that light weight was the key here, I was tired of struggling

O1 Class No.31065 shunts goods wagons as L1 No.31756 prepares to leave.

A glimpse of L1 No.31756 around the end of the goods shed. Post-war neglect leaves the buildings looking distinctly grubby. The new platelayers' hut awaits off-loading.

to move heavy pieces of chipboard around. The frame members are formed from two strips of 3mm ply separated by 18mm square softwood. The frames are 75mm deep, but the front and rear strips are higher, the front to form the edge of the built up scenery, and the rear and ends to support the backscene. The boards are surfaced with 6mm ply, and as the ground is almost level at Manston, a continuous top was used for simplicity. This construction is much lighter than many people use, but seems to be quite strong enough so far. The boards were arranged so that

they all bolt together using squares of ply at the outer ends to form a single package for transport, the scenery of course facing inwards. Care had to be taken at the design stage so that the buildings did not interfere with each other when packed up.

Alignment of the boards is by brass dowels and sockets, they fix together with case clips. I was determined to have a good foundation for the boards after years of problems trying to line up trestles, and eventually built two box beams 12'0" long and hinged in the middle. These are of 150mm deep 3mm ply sides with the top and bottom

of 18mm x 38mm softwood. They have proved to be over engineered, as they will support my not inconsiderable weight. They could obviously have been much smaller and lighter. These are supported by one trestle at each end, and the baseboards simply lie on top, properly levelled every time. The trestles have only three legs so they will always stand firm. This system has attracted a lot of attention from other exhibitors, and I've noticed that it is starting to appear in various guises under a few other layouts.

Track

Plain track is SMP bullhead, with most of the points being of soldered construction. In my view this looks much more like the real thing for my chosen period than the usual flat-bottomed track, which is really designed for HO. As previously mentioned the height to a certain extent disguises the narrow gauge. To exaggerate the difference in standards between the main line and the sidings, the points in the fuel depot are of smaller radius and use the plastic based SMP kits. These were the first points I built, and amazed me by how easy they were. I had really been quite worried about this, but they gave me confidence, and I found that the soldered points were not much more difficult. I have a pet hate of seeing point tie bars the size of sleepers, so decided to adopt the Iain Rice point operating mechanism

USAAF personnel ignore the station pilot, P Class No.31323, as it fusses with a 'dance hall' brake van.

A Grumman Albatross air sea rescue plane being serviced, whilst in the background is a high powered meeting to discuss the F84 Thunderjet going through the perimeter fence.

(see *Approach to Finescale Track in 4mm*, by Iain Rice, published by Wild Swan) which was fitted under the baseboard. I also used his idea of using a foam camping mattress as underlay, which cushioned the track well, and also gave it some height above the baseboard. This worked well at the beginning, but after several years the foam started to disintegrate, giving very uneven track. We started to have regular derailments, which had not happened before. The final straw came at Harrogate, where hot days and cold nights caused such problems that we could not get vans into the goods shed - they

were leaning so far that they hit the doorway. It all had to come up, and a summer was spent replacing it with new track to a similar standard, but laid on cork in a more conventional way. New operating mechanisms were also used, this time from square plastic tube.

At the planning stage I started off by trying to keep the pointwork away from the baseboard joins, but this proved impossible, so in the end two of the points were very firmly fixed right across one join (glued and ballasted with Araldite rather than PVA!), and then just cut across with a razor saw. One of the switch blades

had to be slightly shortened to suit, but, I am somewhat amazed to say, there have been no problems yet.

To operate the points I wanted to use a manual method, as this would avoid unnecessary complication. At first I used wooden push rods, but these proved very temperamental. Any slight change in humidity caused them to swell or shrink and so become either too loose or too tight in their guides. They were replaced with the plastic 'wire in tube' used in model aircraft (I think aero modellers call them 'snakes'), and these work well. They are just brought to the rear of the baseboard and fixed to the inner leaf of the frame, and are reached through a cut-out in the outer leaf.

Electrical continuity at track joints is ensured by using wire jumpers. Brassmasters cosmetic fishplates are soldered on at appropriate intervals. The few electrical sections are operated from switches set into the back of the appropriate baseboard. This simplifies the wiring no end as there are very few wires crossing the baseboard joins. Originally there was provision for one controller, but recently I have added a second, so that on occasions there can be two locos running. This helps with the exhibition ideal of keeping something running for as much of the time as possible. This is what the paying public seem to want, and so it is what we should give them.

Sir Agravaine has the road as R1 No.31047 prepares to place the empty wagons in the goods shed for loading.

Vans of mail freshly arrived from the Commonwealth are ready for their onward journey behind J Class No.31595. The Q1 is an unusual visitor to the branch. This shot gives a good view of the art deco buildings.

Scenery

This is simply expanded polystyrene stuck down with PVA glue and shaped with a Surform tool (with the Hoover pipe in the other hand to reduce the mess!), to give a prototypically gentle slope from one end to the other. Surfacing was with strips of newspaper stuck down with more PVA, the last layer incorporating brown powder paint in case it showed through the greenery. The end result is much lighter than a plaster shell, and doesn't crack. Greenery is from various grades and colours of Woodland Scenics scatter, and carpet underlay, all in accordance with Barry Norman's methods (*Landscape Modelling* by Barry Norman published by Wild Swan). Different areas had different treatments to differentiate them. Being red/green colour blind (as are many men) I have to use a very limited selection of colours which I know, thanks to advice from club mates, look right. (After the layout's first outing I had to redo most of the airport grass as it was too bright a colour). The layout's lights are fed through a dimmer which is adjusted at each exhibition to get the best colour balance. The airport land is well manicured, the railway land very much less so. Fences too are of different types and materials in different places. Recently the fence wires have been added using lycra thread which works well, originally I just used the posts, as oversize fence wire looks worse than none at all.

The track was dry ballasted, again with Woodland Scenics, and well weathered with repeated thin washes of dirty coloured poster paints. Colour

One of the Grumman Albatrosses is being serviced. They were used for air sea rescue before helicopters took over.

Manston Airport Track Plan

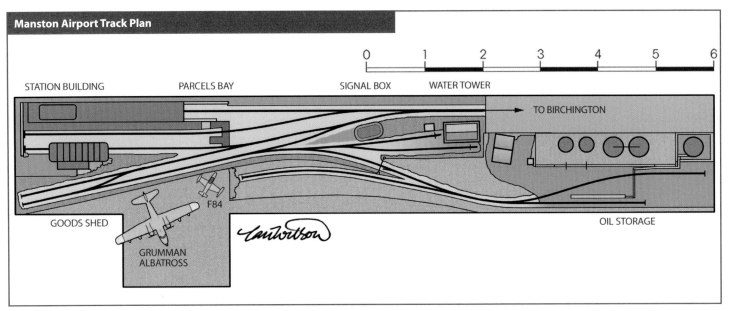

STATION BUILDING   PARCELS BAY   SIGNAL BOX   WATER TOWER

TO BIRCHINGTON

F84

GOODS SHED

GRUMMAN ALBATROSS

OIL STORAGE

blind though I am, weathering with plain black never looks right to me, it is too stark, so I always use a mixture of black, brown and white in varying proportions. Rails and chairs were painted rust, including the cosmetic chairs which were laboriously stuck onto the soldered pointwork. Point rodding is needed, but as yet I haven't had the courage to start.

The backscene is an uneven thin wash of blue watercolour put on a roll of heavy duty lining paper with a 2" brush, and is unrolled around the rear of the layout so that there are no joins. It is fixed with Velcro. It shows only sky to emphasise the flat and bleak nature of the area.

The fuel depot is loosely based on that built at the airport during the last war. Large tanks are set into an earth embankment with a retaining wall at the front. The tanks are altered from a kit, with sundry piping and valves from various sources. At a recent exhibition I was pleased to be told by two visitors who worked for BP that it looked about right. That seems to show the benefit of going out and looking at the real thing before starting a model, there really is no substitute for this. The offices are Nissen huts from kits brought back from the US by a friend.

The gateway across the track to the fuel depot opens and shuts, the hanging stile extends through the baseboard and is turned by another length of the plastic snake. Again simple and effective.

Buildings

Part of the attraction of Manston was that I could design a matching set of buildings in the style that the Southern might well have used for a prestige project. Something modern would have been needed, and art deco would have filled the bill admirably, as it did elsewhere on the Southern. So some time was spent at the drawing board, evolving something that would have echoes of an airport control tower, but be practical for all the buildings. The signal box is based on that at Deal, and some of the detailing on the water tower is taken from Ramsgate. These were then built up in layers from large sheets of varying thicknesses of plastic card. The rounded corners were formed using jigs to hold the card whilst it was boiled in a saucepan of water. Wooden jigs were the easiest to shape, but needed a long cooking time to heat through, a metal jig was more effective at shaping the card. The external string

The fuel depot was originally part of the FIDO fog repellent system in the war, now it stores fuel and oil for the aircraft. Most of the tank wagons are scratch-built to achieve the characteristic uneven look of tanker trains of the time.

General view from the west.

courses and cornices were formed from Evergreen strip, which I found to be of very consistent size. The Crittal windows were formed *in situ* using clear acrylic sheet onto which was stuck the glazing bars, again of Evergreen strip. The strips were cut and carefully placed over a drawing of the window which was taped behind the glazing, and when all was in place the window was flooded with solvent and the strips gently pressed down. The solvent doesn't affect the acrylic glazing, but softens the polystyrene strips enough to make them stick.

Painting was with matt acrylics to give the very slight texture of painted rendering. Once bedded into the layout, all was weathered by spraying over the whole thing with a plant sprayer full of a thin wash of dirty brownish black watercolour. This leaves dirt on all of the ledges, and a suitably shabby look for the 1950s.

I was doing all of this for the enjoyment of it, so didn't hurry and also spent a lot of time thinking about ways of doing things, and so the construction took about four years from first thoughts to first exhibition,

and a lot of further work has been done since. Not for me a new layout every year!

Stock
Inevitably, given my tastes, the locos we use most are all from the old SE&CR which were locally shedded at Ramsgate and Dover, and are those which I saw at the time. There are 4-4-0s of Classes D, D1, L and L1 (the D as preserved No.737 painted in all its glory by Bob Fridd - I know it didn't

ever actually run like this, but I just couldn't resist it); 0-6-0s of Classes C, O1 and Q1; R1 and P 0-6-0Ts, and an H Class 0-4-4T. Finally there is a J Class 0-6-4T for parcels traffic. All of the 4-4-0s have been fitted with home brewed compensated chassis to overcome the usual nose heavy problem. The rear driving wheels are fixed and the compensation beam balances the front drivers and front bogie. This seems to work well. In a belt and braces approach, the tender draw bar is of 1mm square nickel silver, which is quite springy and is arranged to bear down on the rear of the loco. I am undecided on the merits of compensation for the other locos, some have it, others don't, but it seems to make little difference. The chassis for the J Class also needed considerable modification and is still

Is there a problem? While newly arrived tank wagons wait to be unloaded, the staff peer at the maze of pipes.

rather temperamental (as it is getting older, though, it is getting better) - one day I'll get around to building it a new one. As many wheels as possible are fitted with pick-ups, an 0-6-0 tender engine with pick ups on all twelve

General view from the east.

wheels is virtually unstoppable.

At times a Drewry 250hp shunter and a Bulleid 350hp shunter can also appear.

Just squeezing in are two American switchers, Bachmann GE 44tonners as used in Europe (but not actually in the UK) by the USAAF. I couldn't resist the quality of the mechanisms, or the price. They are the only ready to run locos regularly used. They deliver and collect freight for the USAAF.

Sometimes for a change we run

green diesels with Classes 24, 33 and 73 together with a couple of diesel electric units. Most of these are supplied by fellow Canterbury Club member Dennis Prior, who was my mentor and operator at the beginning of our travels; now Jeremy Kennet bears the brunt of the work. Thanks are due to both.

There are three rakes of coaches, including Hornby Pullmans, much altered with bogies and bits from Keen Systems, plus a two-coach pull-push set for the H Class. Parcels and goods stock is a selection from the multitude of kits available, although I have managed some scratch-built wagons, including oil tanks. These were very time consuming, but

enjoyable to make, and allow the very varied aspect of a train of steam era tankers to be modelled. The tanks are rolled from polystyrene sheet to the required diameter before a final wrapper is added, putting on all those rivets is mind numbing. The cradles, saddles, etc. are from more Evergreen strip, and all of the other parts are from wire and suitable bits and pieces. The underframes are from various kits.

Just for fun we sometimes run a bulled up Bulleid Pacific (No.34070 *Manston* of course), which is decorated with the French coat of arms and flags, together with two pristine Pullmans and attendant luggage vans, for a state visit by Monsieur Rene Coty, the French President. To the bemusement of nearby exhibitors, departure is always marked by the playing of *La Marseillaise*. (The train was copied from a photo of the real thing).

Newly delivered road vehicles await unloading. This shot clearly shows that the main station building suggests the appearance of a control tower.

A train of oil empties awaits the dummy and the opening of the gate. The Hillman Minx is a model of my first car.

All stock uses Spratt & Winkle couplings with permanent track magnets, these have given good service, and need very little maintenance. For me these give a better performance when shunting than having to fiddle with three link couplings, which I have to admit I am hopeless with. I don't like to watch people struggling with three links - it creates a bad impression.

A number of road vehicles from the period are used, mainly plastic and white metal kits, and the USAAF is represented by an F84 Thunderjet fighter standing in the corner of the airfield, to remind me of the thrill of their noisy low level passes over my home when they were stationed at Manston. There is also a Grumman Albatross flying boat for air/sea rescue duties, again remembered from childhood. These always arouse considerable interest, and are a great talking point. It's amazing how many people are very knowledgeable about them. A small front extension of the baseboards was needed to make room for them.

Presentation
I wanted a theatre type presentation, so the layout is set quite high. The ply end boards used for transport are left on the ends when the boards are set up and used to support a lighting beam, built in a similar way to the support beams, containing six light bulbs, controlled by a dimmer, to give even lighting, which is adjusted to suit each hall. Front ends and the lighting beam are draped with dark green curtains to present a neat and tidy appearance. Operation

An F84 Thunderjet - these were appallingly unreliable and crashed regularly. There were many fatalities.

The pull-push departs under a bright summer day.

is from the rear with the operator peering over the backscene. None of the usual clutter is visible, but it is possible to talk to the audience, which I like to do. In some ways it would have been easier to operate from the front, but when I'm looking at a layout I find it irritating to have the operator between me and the trains. Wherever we have exhibited, from Yorkshire to the South coast, we have met people who know Manston, and everyone has something new to say. I really enjoy these conversations.

There is much detailing still to be done, and I am quite sure that I won't be able to resist building more stock, even though there is too much already. But then hobbies are all about doing what we like.

On exhibiting

As I've already mentioned I like exhibiting the layout for a number of reasons. I wouldn't, however, want to do it too often, three or four times a year is enough. If I did more, I think it would risk becoming boring, and we've all seen those layouts where the operators are obviously too bored to bother to operate properly, or at all. This is not fair on the paying public, and if they didn't come to exhibitions, we wouldn't have the pleasure of attending them, and our hobby would be so much the poorer for that. I think that I'm lucky to be given expenses paid trips around the country to play trains, the least I can do is to do it as well as I am able.

I seem to have expressed a number of opinions here, but then, this is my railway. They explain why I have done things the way I have, BUT this does not entitle me to tell anyone else how to build or run their railway. We have too much of that in our hobby, as the correspondence columns in the magazines regularly testify. If you don't like my layout, or anyone else's layout, just pass by and find one you do like. As long as the owner is enjoying himself (or herself) then the hobby is serving its purpose.

Finally

Thanks to Tony Wright for the photos, it's fascinating to watch a professional working, and the way he sees different angles and aspects of his subject. He makes the layout look better than I thought, it really cheers me up!

No.34070 *Manston* (which other Bulleid Pacific could it be?) having been bulled up to bring the French President to the airport.

A trip back in time

Paul Rhodes backdates his 7mm scale H Class locomotive.
Photographs by the Author.

This is a wonderful hobby. First, we can learn all kinds of practical skills, and get real fulfilment from using them. Then there is the network of modellers and the fun of meeting up at club nights or shows. Perhaps most important, however, is the opportunity to indulge our dreams. When building a layout, we all have a romantic vision of a landscape. It might be urban or rural, historical or contemporary, but we are creating our own world; we control it and it's a safe place to enter. Of course, in reality the era we model was never as happy as it is in our dreams. It doesn't matter of course, because it is our fantasy. For anyone who doubts that we live in good times, think about the experience of going to the dentist.

Are you like me, constantly prevaricating about what period you wish to model? Until recently I was modelling the Southern Region circa 1955. My build up of stock had been very slow due to the pressures of work, and I was the proud owner of only one working loco in 7mm, a Meteor SECR H Class 0-4-4T. She looked good, with many added details and accurate push/pull gear and piping. The 'H' is a gorgeous little loco, and it was an enjoyable kit to build. Then, quite without warning, I developed a strong desire to go back in time to an earlier period. British Railways suddenly seemed drab and rather monochrome, and I felt nostalgic for an earlier time; one that I couldn't in fact remember. This feeling gradually

became stronger over a period of, well, a day or two, until I decided that I must follow my dreams, and do so before there were more kits built.

There were two possible periods for me; pre-Grouping LBSCR with SECR running powers for the Chatham stock, or the Southern Railway. I chose the Southern Railway in 1938/9. It's a time, just before the war, which fascinates. On the romance scale it should score low as the nation was desperately anxious about the future hostilities, but visually in railway terms it was a treat. There are plenty of good general photographs of the period, and importantly it would allow me to paint locos in Maunsell's beautiful olive green livery. As a final point, if I wished to use the more

The locomotive completed, before weathering.

futuristic Bulleid livery, this was introduced from 1937 and there could be some stock newly out-shopped in the loud bright green.

The SECR H Class tank is a Harry Wainwright design, although it is generally agreed by railway historians that most of the engineering development was done by his Chief Locomotive Draughtsman at Ashford, Robert Surtees. Surtees went on to work under Richard Maunsell for both the SECR and Southern Railways. Wainwright was definitely responsible for what Surtees called 'a weakness for frills'; like the pretty pagoda cab. The class were built between 1904 and 1915, and had a long life, some surviving until 1964. They were popular with crews in 'my' area, the Central Section of the Southern Region where they were employed on push/pull duties on the Oxted lines. My H Class tank was in British Railways lined passenger livery, No.31544. I had presented her in dirty working condition; weathered using the methods so well described by Martyn Welch in his book *The Art of Weathering*. Research around the Weald and further south towards Lewes and Eastbourne showed that,

following the Grouping, the H Class had started to appear here in 1929, and an 'H' tank was a regular duty on a morning Oxted to Eastbourne train from 1937. My loco, which would have been 1554 in Southern days, did not stray westward from SECR lines until much later, so a new identity would need to be created for my model. A search of my railway books turned up a few examples, and I settled on 1182, which in the early '30s was a Redhill-based locomotive.

Another big change would be the removal of the push/pull gear, which was not fitted until 1951. I wasn't sure how I felt about this, ripping off my modelling *tour de force*, but it needed to go in the name of historical accuracy. One other result would be a two-coach push/pull set without a loco, but my great friend Richard Heard has come to the rescue with an offer to build me a D Class tank, No.2626 which can haul the set once it has also been re-sprayed in Southern livery. Also, I have a 'Terrier' kit in the pipeline which will be in Southern unlined black, equipped with push/pull gear appropriate to the time.

Chassis

Making a start, I divided body and frames, and put the body aside. There were various jobs to do on the chassis as well as painting the wheels. I wanted to fit Slater's

plunger pick-ups instead of using wipers, and I also wanted to sort out an annoying noise which emanated from the loco when running forwards. Coupling rods, wheels, motor and gearbox were removed, as was the reservoir tank from between the frames at the front. The motor/gearbox was tested and all ran smoothly and very quietly. I cleaned up the electrical parts underneath; the paxolin cross-pieces which provide a junction for the wiring, and the two longitudinal brass rods which carry the current along each side of the frames. All wires and wipers are connected to these. It's very important to get the position of the plunger pick-ups correct, so this was carefully measured and marked with a CD marker on the frames. Holes were then drilled and reamed out to fit the plastic housing of the pick-ups, stopping regularly to check for size.

Once this was done, I turned to the painting of the frames. As a BR loco, the sides and the wheels had a heavily weathered, textured finish. Although many Southern locos might have looked like this, I wanted my new engine to have a clean appearance, so the frames were rubbed down smoother with emery paper ready for re-painting. Turning again to Martyn Welch's book, I mixed up a concoction of Humbrol paints; Metalcote Gunmetal (27004), matt black (33), leather (62) and tarmac (112). This gave me the colour I wanted, a dark grey but with a hint of a dusty colour from the leather. I masked off the electrical parts and airbrushed the mixture over the old paintwork. The result was as I had hoped; still showing signs of dirt and grot, but a more consistent, less extreme texture and hue. Touches of rust colour weathering powders around the firebox rivets and brake shoes completed the effect I wanted.

Since originally building this loco I have discovered the joys of chemical blackening, so this was applied to the coupling rods using Carr's 'Steel Blackening' with pleasing effect. The wheels were then painted with Phoenix Precision Maunsell Light Olive Green, the tyres in black, and put aside to dry. I now fitted the plunger pick-ups, and soldered wires to the longitudinal brass rods. I left the wiper pick-ups on the rear bogie as they work well and did not need adjustment.

Once dry, the wheels and motor/gearbox were refitted. The rear bogies take their full share of the load, so I spent some time ensuring that all wheels sat squarely on the track. I then fired her up to see how she ran. The electrical connections were excellent, with consistent running even without oiling. So why was there a previous problem with noise when the loco was travelling forwards? To explore this I refitted the body and observed what happened in motion. Suddenly the answer presented itself, and I felt very foolish. The noise I had tolerated for years was nothing more than the motor spindle fouling the loco body behind the boiler backhead. When travelling backwards, the motor rose slightly and ran freely. Running forwards, the motor pressed downwards and scraped against the brass cab front inside the boiler. In five minutes I had sawn 8mm off the spindle with a junior hacksaw and all ran beautifully quiet. Finally, moving parts were lightly oiled and the nuts on the coupling rods touched lightly with a drop of superglue. Part one of the project was over.

Body

Turning to the body, I removed the crew, plastic cab doors and floor, buffers, screw couplings, coal and the plastic frame in the bunker. I prepared for stripping the paintwork with some anxiety. I have used this method before, but there's always the fear that the whole model is going to come apart in your hands. Definitely an outside job, I covered the old garden table thickly with newspaper, and filled an old washing up bowl with cold soapy water. I donned a protective

face mask and rubber gloves. 'Nitro-Mors' (from the green can) was dabbed onto the paintwork with a stippling action. Immediately paint began to bubble up on the surface. After about half a minute the loco body was dipped into the soapy water and gently scrubbed with a clean brush. There was still plenty of paint on the body so the process was repeated a few times, concentrating on the areas still painted. Various loco parts come away or fall off during this process. This is no bad thing, as they are probably telling you that they were vulnerable anyway. In my case this included two lamp irons and most of the rear spectacle plate bars. I removed the rest of these deciding that that it would be easier to start again from scratch. Lost parts collected in the bottom of the bowl of soapy water, so this was carefully scrutinised before emptying.

After drying, I had a thorough review of the situation and made a list of jobs. It was also time to study the prototype. Photos of the H Class loco in Southern livery are not common, but there are enough around to get a clear idea of what was needed to be done. The first job was to strip the loco of all push/pull gear and other bits not there in Southern days, and I attacked it with pliers. Off came the air pipes on the front and rear buffer beams. Next I removed the Westinghouse pump with all its piping, and a pipe running across the right-hand side of the boiler and into the cab. From the left-hand tank side the regulator operating cylinder

came off, as did auxiliary operating cylinder, operating arm and electrical control box. Finally, four narrow pipes were removed which ran the length of the left-hand valance. It was a dramatic half hour.

The next task was to fit or refit those parts which need to be there. First of all, the tank filler caps were removed from the centre of the tank tops and refitted to the front. Photographic study showed some piping along the boiler sides, and this was added as shown on the photos. I thoroughly enjoy adding detail of this kind; it really adds texture and depth to the overall look of the loco. I confess ignorance as to what a lot of these things do, so I go by photographic evidence to make things as correct as possible. I do my best, but if a bit of pipe is the wrong size or goes slightly to the wrong place, well 95% of other modellers wouldn't know whether it was correct either. There are always some parts of a locomotive that never seem to be photographed; tank tops for example.

The two lamp irons were re-fitted, as were two new handrail knobs which I decided needed replacing. The rear spectacle plate bars were then added. These were glued on with two-part epoxy adhesive. Following the example of Gordon Gravett in his article on building Terrier DS377 in *Model Railway Journal* No.63, I didn't worry too much about getting the length absolutely correct at the bottom, knowing that this area would eventually be covered by coal. The loco was now put aside for the epoxy

Before beginning the project. H Class No.31544 on my layout, Duddleswell.

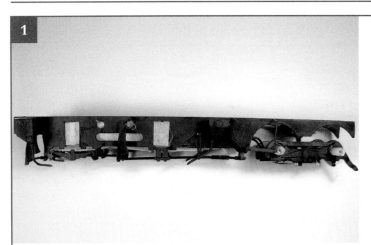

1. The frames masked up and ready to spray.

2. The body with the parts removed in preparation for paint stripping.

3. After paint stripping, showing the push/pull gear which was removed from the model.

4. Primed with Halfords grey primer.

5. The first covering; Phoenix Precision Maunsell light olive green.

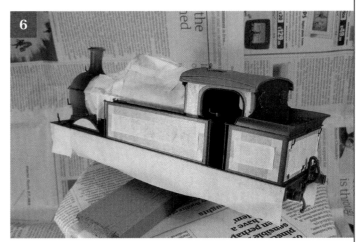

6. Masked ready for the coat of black.

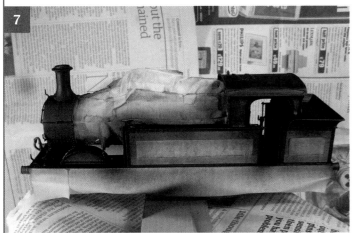

7. After the coat of black.

8. Masking tape removed, the two areas of colour can be seen clearly.

9. Having been lined, lettered and gloss varnished, 1182 is now ready for a coat of satin varnish.

10. The locomotive completed, before weathering.

glue to harden. At the next modelling session, I soldered small pieces of brass underneath the holes created when moving the tank filler caps forward, and filled this and all the other gaps with car body filler.

Painting

My SECR H Class is changing identity; she is to become Southern Railway 1182. To prepare for this I had previously ordered a pair of Ashford plates from Guilplates, and Maunsell Southern Railway loco transfers and white lining from HMRS. For the paint, I used Phoenix Precision Maunsell

light olive green, and dull black. I like to paint my locos pristine first, then use airbrushed weathering techniques to soften the brightness of the finish, in particular the white lining.

The locomotive was prepared for painting in the usual way. Using an old toothbrush dipped in a kitchen cleaner called 'Cif', I gently scrubbed the metalwork over a plastic kitchen bowl, and followed it with a rinse under running water. Once again, the bowl was checked afterwards for wayward body parts, luckily it contained only water. I then gave the loco body a thorough drying with a

hair dryer, and put it aside to cool and become totally dry. For priming, I used Halfords grey primer, my H Class was given two coats of primer and left overnight to harden.

One should never underestimate the importance of well stirred paint. Without good mixing, it has an unpredictable glossiness, and can appear streaky on the painted surface. For many years now I have taken the advice of Robert Shephard in his booklet on painting models, *The Finishing Touch*, and mixed paint using a shaped piece of wire in an electric drill. The Maunsell green paint was stirred in this way and the airbrush and compressor prepared for spraying. After much experimentation, I have arrived at a formula for airbrushing which suits me and gives me consistent results. I mix the paint very thin, using Phoenix Precision 'Quick Drying Airbrush Thinners', and keep the pressure low, at around 12-14 psi. I always wear a facemask and work in a well ventilated room. When airbrushing, it is very important to keep rotating the loco and resist the temptation to overspray in any particular area. Also, it's easy to forget to airbrush from a low and high angle, and find afterwards that there are unpainted areas – very frustrating. This time the airbrushing went well and coverage was excellent. I cleaned the airbrush in the usual way: after running some white spirit in through it, I dipped it in an old beaker filled with more white spirit, and turned it on. This circulates the liquid and gives the airbrush a thorough cleaning. These days I pay the extra to buy low odour white spirit; it makes me much less unpopular in the house.

I was now able to see my loco in Maunsell Southern green for the first time. Yes, I was going to like this loco in its new livery.

After a day for the paint to harden, I turned to the job of masking up. It is important to do this slowly, and to keep checking as you go. As well as the standard cheap masking tape, I use the thin Tamiya tape to mask up small or tricky areas. The mindset here is to cover up everything which needs to stay green. It was time for me to resolve one of my questions about the Maunsell Southern livery on this locomotive. The contentious area was the tank fronts. I'm not an expert on these things, and go by what I can glean from photos. Many tank fronts were in lined green, but my photographic evidence suggests that on the H Class it was painted black. Possibly this is because of the presence of the vacuum brake pump on the right-hand tank front. Having masked up, and checked carefully, I airbrushed black. There are many opinions about using black on models, some arguing that it should be lightened by mixing in white. My system is to paint it black first, then soften the tone later with careful weathering. To me, the sheen is more important in creating the illusion than the lightness or darkness of the colour. I left the mask on for an hour after painting, then carefully stripped

it off and enjoyed the result. All had gone well. After painting the buffer beams I was ready to make a start on the lining and lettering.

Lining

For lining, I used the HMRS General White Lining. The thinner lining width provided is perfect for the job. The only problem with 'Pressfix' lining is that it stands proud slightly, and tends to pick up dust. A piece of advice is to wait right till the end before adding the white lining on the valance. We all tend to pick locos up with our finger and thumb here, and this kind of lining is easily damaged before being preserved under varnish. For the boiler bands I had previously airbrushed a piece of inkjet decal paper black, and used a bowpen to draw the two outer white lines onto it. With careful cutting I was able to recreate the boiler band strips of white/black/white. For lettering I used the HMRS 'Methfix' range. There are different sizes of Southern lettering, and after checking against photos, I chose the smaller lettering appropriate to tank engines, and 16" numbers. The number was also added to the rear of the bunker and the front buffer beam. Once all the lining and lettering was completed, the cab doors were replaced, with one fixed open. I gave the loco a coat of gloss varnish initially, then flattened down the shine with satin varnish. I find that this gives me the level of sheen that I like. I also believe that the initial coat of gloss varnish gives it a tougher finish, but this may be a false supposition.

After a day for the varnish to dry, the buffers, couplings and crew were put back and the coal replaced in the bunker. I had nearly finished my work. I have never actually seen an H Class in Southern livery, as the Bluebell H Class is kept in SECR green, and rightly so. Often, we can only imagine how our favourite locos looked from black and white photographs, and the first time we see them as they actually looked is when we re-create them in model form. I placed her on the tracks and studied her for some time. She was a butterfly emerging from a chrysalis. This really is a very pretty locomotive. In Southern green, the tanks look lower and the boiler seems more prominent than in BR livery. The pagoda cab roof looks delicate and attractive. The yellow lettering is dramatic, and contrasts strongly with the body colour. This locomotive is a visual treat.

As a display model, the project would now be considered complete, and I will leave her like this for a time. There is more for me to do, however. My locomotive is to spend its life on my layout, and needs to be presented with some evidence of a working life. Also, the lettering and white lining are very prominent. I won't want heavy weathering, just enough to soften the contrast and present her as a well kept working locomotive, with some wear and tear and evidence of daily use. I will study contemporary photos before tackling this job; it shouldn't be rushed.

In conclusion, this was a highly rewarding project. I am pleased with the look of SECR H Class 1182. She runs quietly, and does not look over bright. She will take her place alongside my LBSCR E4 0-6-2 No.2475, which is also in Southern green livery, working on my fledgling layout, Duddleswell. My next jobs are to re-spray the two-coach LBSCR push/pull set in appropriate livery, then start on the three-coach birdcage set which is sitting on my 'future projects' shelf. Painting models is a rewarding pastime. I believe that we can all do it if we are patient and take our time. Once this Southern Railway project has run its course, I intend to take a trip further back in time to the pre-Grouping era and build and finish stock for a layout set on the territorial borders of the LBSCR and SECR; the two loveliest of liveries; an H Class in that intricate lined green - gorgeous!

Further reading

Locomotives of the South Eastern and Chatham Railway
D L Bradley (RCTS, 1961)

The Cuckoo Line
A C Elliott (Wild Swan)

The Art of Weathering
Martyn Welch (Wild Swan)

Model Railway Journal No.63
'Brighton Works' by Gordon Gravett

The Finishing Touch
Robert G Shephard (Phoenix Precision Paints)

Locomotives Illustrated No.56
Wainwright Tank Locomotives

'The Jacobite' is a daily return service between Fort William and Mallaig that is operated during the summer season by the West Coast Railway Company. In 2005, two locomotives were used, one of which was LNER B1 No.61264, (TOPS 98564) which was photographed at Fort William Junction on June 24, 2005, on the afternoon return leg, running tender first.

Modelling 'Modern' Steam

Nigel Burkin takes time off from his usual diet of diesel and electric locomotives, to explain the operation of steam locomotives on the modern railway.
Photography by the author.

How can the D&E era modeller enhance layout operations with main line steam? It is not as straightforward as placing a steam locomotive at the head of a train, as I discovered when I investigated the operation of the 'Jacobite' and some recent steam-hauled charters.

Introduction

Steam train operators are faced with a number of practical difficulties and challenges when it comes to organising charter and summer season tourist trains on the main line. The modern infrastructure simply does not readily support steam operations and it is the steam operator that has to adapt to the conditions of the modern railway, using some ingenious solutions to make it all possible rather than it being the other way round, as was the case during the transition period when British Railways was dieselised.

It is also worth considering, as a modeller, the problems faced by the preservation movement when setting up preserved railway societies and rehabilitating long disused lines. Many lines were handed over or sold to preservationists with virtually little of the steam railway infrastructure remaining, often after long battles with British Rail to save the track and therefore what little infrastructure remained was in rundown condition. Much of the former steam infrastructure had been long removed when the lines were dieselised, or left in a poor state of repair. In many instances, restoring large items of steam infrastructure was not possible and other solutions for servicing steam locomotives from the ground have had to be found.

No, life is not easy for the 'modern' steam operator and this article offers a glimpse at the practical issues that full-size steam train operators have to overcome and how such operations can be incorporated on a diesel and electric based layout for added realism.

Modelling steam specials

So, why do so many D&E modellers take an interest in modelling steam operations? It's fascinating when you balance the DEMU 'no kettles' branded mugs and tee-shirts (which suggest that there is little or no interest in modelling the occasional steam train), against the real interest out there, which is gauged by the fact that the subject comes up time and time again on Internet groups and at exhibitions. It may have something to do with the availability of beautifully created and

Another sunny day in the Highlands sees B1 No.61264 being prepared for departure at Fort William in May 2006. Note the extensive use of orange high visibility jackets and a black portable high-intensity head light in addition to the period oil lamps.

Mk.1 coaches can still be found in regular service on the main line thanks to steam-hauled charters and seasonal tourist trains. 'The Jacobite' is made up of a rake of eight Mk.1 coaches and spares which are kept in excellent condition. TSO No.4958 retains its original running number because it was never de-registered from the system unlike the adjacent coach, No.99326 which is a re-registration number.

K1 No.62005, *Lord of the Isles*, (TOPS No.98605) rests between duties at Fort William Yard, where the 'Jacobite' steam locomotives and coaching stock are serviced. Noteworthy is the in-service condition of this locomotive, which is showing signs of superficial rusting to the lamp irons, coupling rods and associated equipment, together with the buffers, footsteps and couplings. Usually, two steam locomotives are allocated to the 'Jacobite' service, the B1 was out on the run on this particular day in June 2005.

Steam locomotives used in main line service frequently rub shoulders with the most modern of traction, such as EWS 66 104, which has been prepared to operate the Fort William-Mossend 'Enterprise' service.

finished models of steam locomotives in N and OO gauge, which has prompted some diesel and electric enthusiasts to actually look at incorporating a charter train, or even a regular seasonal tourist train on their layouts. It is difficult to resist the superb Mk.1 coaches now available from Bachmann and the temptation to incorporate them on a layout otherwise dominated by 'Sprinters' and EMD diesel electric locomotives is rarely resisted.

There is more to 'modelling' modern steam than buying a rake of Mk.1 coaches and slapping the nearest steam locomotive on the front. There are many operational considerations that steam locomotive owners and train operators (such as West Coast Railways Company of Carnforth) have to consider before they venture out on to the main line with a steam locomotive. The logistics of organising a tour like the 2007 'The Great Britain', which used nearly ten or more locomotives of one type or another, mostly steam, must have been a nightmare, for the tour started in Cornwall with No.71000 *Duke of Gloucester* and finished up in Thurso

with 8F No.48151 (which had travelled to the Scottish Highlands earlier in 2007 to operate a private charter).

Think of the logistics and you could start by considering how the steam locomotive(s) are to be serviced and at which location during a tour. After all, on the modern railway, there is a distinct lack of 'elephants' trunks' and associated water towers and other infrastructure located at the platform end of a typical main line station which could be used to replenish water tanks. Overhead electrification also presents safety considerations,

A steam locomotive and a pile of coal at Fort William. B1 No.61264 is serviced ready for its next turn of duty on the following day.

The modern way of filling a steam locomotive's tender with coal.

Servicing a steam locomotive in the modern way is demonstrated by this photograph which shows the use of a hose to fill the tender from a ground level filler pipe (A) and a water supply from a standpipe (C). The tender is nearly empty, which is an interesting detail that should be carefully considered by modellers when modelling steam locomotives, because it is rare for a steam locomotive to have a completely full tender unless it is at the very start of its journey. Note the size of the lumps of coal in the stockpile to the right (D).

Detail for the modeller: but beware, because main line steam today is not exactly the same as in-service steam 50 years ago. Note the use of modern electrification warning notices. Also, many steam locomotives are not in pristine condition when out on the main line – they become dirty very quickly indeed.

especially on the (very) safety conscious railways of today and that has a bearing on the external appearance of steam locomotives used on the main line and how they are operated.

Another question: How is your steam locomotive to be turned at the end of its journey? With the lack of coaling towers and other steam era infrastructure, how do you refill the tender with coal? Then there's the issue of lineside fires in summer, the availability of suitably trained drivers and firemen, signalling systems and safety devices, together with the problems that arise should a steam locomotive fail on the main line. Each of these factors should be looked at in turn, because there are some very interesting 'work-rounds' which make modern steam operations so much different from the time when steam was routine, and indeed taken for granted.

There are details to catch the unwary modeller out, because preserved steam locomotives are not necessarily in the same condition as they were when in service during steam days. The very nature of steam locomotive preservation and restoration means that some modifications may have been made during the restoration process, to account for modern manufacturing processes, which makes them subtly different from the remainder of a particular class when it was in squadron service. This is in addition to modifications to incorporate modern safety equipment such as TPWS and AWS. Is not necessarily safe to model a particular steam locomotive by directly following the instructions in a kit because those kit instructions may actually relate to the locomotive when it was in main line service and not in

Early morning (7.30 am) on April 11, 2007, sees K4 No.61994 *The Great Marquess* (TOPS No.98642) tackling the sharp incline out of Garve station on the 1Z42 06.19 Inverness-Kyle of Lochalsh leg of 'The Great Britain' tour. It was photographed crossing the Ullapool road.

It is the combination of modern and period railway equipment that makes main line steam trains so attractive to the modern railway modeller. Whilst the semaphore signals at Fort William Junction are in keeping with steam era operations, note that the signal box has modern glazing, the coaching stock has orange lines applied to the rain gutters and ends and the rear of the train is marked with a modern flashing tail lamp.

Servicing a steam locomotive on the run – a water hose snakes across the track at Achnasheen as K4 No.61994 *The Great Marquess* takes water. Fortunately, the Kyle of Lochalsh-Inverness service train had passed earlier and there was no risk of the hose being run over!

With no convenient standpipe to hand, cold water is delivered by a road tanker.

its present state. The same applies when choosing a ready-to-run steam locomotive and this was highlighted by Hornby when it released a version of No.4472 *Flying Scotsman* in its modern condition. This makes the use of reference photographs of preserved steam locomotives cleared for modern main line use particularly important, or fundamental detail errors may result.

Servicing steam locomotives

Gone are all of those facilities that were used to service steam locomotives when they were in service under British Railways, before the demise of steam in the 1960s. There are no coaling stages or coaling towers ready and waiting at motive power depots. Ash pits for cleaning steam locomotives at the end of the day, ie: dropping the fire, are not to be found very easily. Steam locomotives also require large quantities of quality cold water for effective operation and that is not easy to obtain at the average railway station without making special provision. The most common method of servicing steam locomotives is to arrange for coal to be delivered to a freight yard or similar location where steam locomotives are to be stabled prior to, or during a tour. In the case of 'The Great Britain' tour, the three locomotives used in Scotland were serviced in Millburn Yard, Inverness, where a large quantity of coal was stocked on hard standing to avoid contamination. The coal was loaded into the tender with a modern loading shovel – carefully so as not to damage the side of the locomotive tenders.

West Coast Railways employs the same method of coaling its engines when stationed at Fort William for the summer-only 'Jacobite' tourist train, that operates between Fort William and Mallaig. Steam locomotives are loaded in exactly the same way on the Strathspey Railway at Boat of Garten too; a common method of loading steam locomotives where the original infrastructure no longer exists. To model this feature would be very simple; you would need a pile of coal and a suitable model of a loading shovel. You can guarantee that it will not be the newest model used on a preserved railway and the loading shovel model may provide an interesting weathering and rusting opportunity.

The next vital ingredient is water and our steam-hauled specials are not going very far without it. It appears that the most common method of watering steam locomotives is to use a standpipe and hose, which is connected to a ground level filler located somewhere on the locomotive tender. Watering in such a way can take time and presents some interesting photographic opportunities, if problems for time keeping. Clearly, with the danger of overhead wires, the use of a ground level filler pipe is considered to be more desirable than any top filler hatch. During 'The Great Britain' tour, mains water from standpipes and similar was mostly used to service the locomotives. It was only occasionally when steam locomotives were supplied with water from a road tanker. Nonetheless, this introduces an interesting modelling feature and an excuse to introduce a modern road tanker onto your layout which could be parked in the station car park!

Part of the job of servicing steam locomotives is disposal of the ash dropped from the firebox at the end of the day. Ash presents environmental problems and probably environmental challenges for the operators as well, if they are to comply with local regulations. It appears that the best way of disposing of ash is to use the same loading shovel used to coal engines to remove it from the area designated for locomotive servicing and load it into a lorry for safe disposal. If dusting is likely to be a problem to adjacent properties, the ash would have to be watered to lay the dust.

Turning locomotives

Unfortunately, turntables are not as common as they used to be. For the photographer, this means that there is a great deal of tender-first running when turning a steam locomotive at the end of its journey cannot be carried out. In some instances, a triangular track formation or junction will be used to turn a steam locomotive. The two steam locomotives used on the Highland main line leg of the tour; A4 No.60009 *Union of South Africa* and K4 No.61994 *The Great Marquess*, ran to and from Inverness boiler first, because the locomotives could be turned on a triangular track formation at Inverness station, which includes the Ross-shire siding.

However, the locomotives used on the 'Jacobite' and also when K4 No.61994 *The Great Marquess* ran to Kyle of Lochalsh in April 2007, could not be turned, so the return journey was made running the locomotive tender first, usually at reduced speed. This is something worth considering

The traditional oil lamps are supplemented with a portable high-intensity head light which is an operational requirement.

To enable the train to be run over lines which are signalled using Radio Electronic Token Block (RETB), the appropriate equipment has to be installed, albeit temporarily. This is RETB unit No.2232 fitted to the inside of the door to the cabinet that protects the locomotive's radio equipment. Without such equipment, tokens could not be issued by or surrendered to the signalman at Inverness Signalling Centre.

For better reception, try the side of the tender!

Support coaches are an important part of main line steam tours and offer the opportunity to model something different.

Loading coal into the tender of 8F, No.48151 *The Gauge O Guild* at Inverness Millburn Yard on April 11, 2007.

8F No.48151 *The Gauge O Guild* crosses the viaduct over the River Shin at Invershin on the run to Thurso. The train ran to Thurso on April 12 and returned on April 13, tender first.

when planning the operation of your steam charter – do you have some method of turning the locomotive, or will you have to consider operating the train tender first on the return leg of its journey?

Running lights
The last thing that steam locomotive owners wish to do is irreversibly modify their charges with equipment that would be completely out of character, at least where the cosmetic appearance of the locomotive is concerned. This would preclude the fitting of a permanent high-intensity headlight which is a requirement of the modern railway. Some requirements cannot be avoided if a locomotive is to be certificated for main line use and those will be discussed a little later on in the article. However, where lights are concerned, operators can use a modern, portable headlamp, which is contained in the same body as a conventional modern flashing taillight used on the rear of freight and passenger trains. Some operators paint the portable high-intensity headlight black to minimise its impact, whilst others are quite happy to leave the casing in the original white colour. The correct marker lights appropriate to the type of train are also usually applied – oil lamps being quite commonly used and of a 'period' design. Modellers can use the 4mm scale lamps from Springside models, including a modern design, to recreate the correct lamp positions. Needless to say, the rear of the train would have to have a contemporary flashing red taillight, no matter which locomotive was in charge.

Signalling systems
Needless to say, operators would have to comply with all of the requirements of modern safety and signalling systems and that, in 2007, would include the fitting of TPWS (Train Protection & Warning System), OTMR devices (On Train Monitoring Recorder) which is all in addition to the older AWS equipment, and together with radio network equipment. Otherwise, your tour may be a non-starter! In the Highlands of Scotland, trains operating over lines north of Inverness or to Oban, Fort William and Mallaig will have to be capable of being signalled using RETB (Radio Electronic Token Block, described by Graeme Elgar in the October 2007 *BRM*). This has resulted in some

Photographed north of Rogart, 8F No.48151 *The Gauge O Guild* works hard to gain speed after a stop for an RETB token.

fascinating operating practices, such as attaching the RETB aerial to a shovel and waving it out of the cab of the leading locomotive at times when reception is particularly poor. Usually, a spare RETB set is loaned for the duration of the tour, and in the case of the 'Jacobite', the locomotives are fitted with RETB for the season. Whichever way you look at it, the contrast between heritage steam locomotives together with their basic equipment (shovels, etc) and modern signalling equipment such as RETB is fascinating. Some effort has to be made to protect sensitive electronic equipment from the harsh environment that is the cab of your typical steam locomotive, which is usually uncompromisingly hot, sooty and pretty unforgiving.

Safety rules

There are always plenty of those to take into account on the full-size railway and some of the more obvious ones can be applied to modelled steam charters for added realism too. Rather than delve into the intricacies of the rulebook, it's sufficient to say that your steam locomotive and coaching stock will have to comply with the trappings of the modern railway such as orange cantrail stripes and warning notices, for example. Steam locomotives have to bear modern electrification warning notices, even if the locomotive did not carry them in regular service. Overhead line electrification equipment (OHLE) presents a particular hazard to railway staff working on steam locomotives, because there is a requirement for climbing over a locomotive when dealing with coal and possibly water. Many steam locomotives do not have a fully enclosed cab either and that too

Main line steam offers the chance to incorporate coaching stock that otherwise could be hard to justify, such as the Mk.1 Pullman stock, currently available in N and OO gauge from Bachmann.

The LMS Club Car would make an interesting repainting project. This coach was used throughout 'The Great Britain' tour together with a pair of Mk.1 Pullman coaches.

can result in a potentially hazardous situation when under the wires.

Whilst modern equipment rarely has footsteps up the outside, which could result in accidental contact with overhead wires, steam locomotives in their heritage condition cannot be modified to remove footsteps from the end of tenders or those provided at the front of the locomotive to reach the smoke box door. One method of preventing accidental access to steps is to use safety wedges, which are placed on each step and present a physical barrier to using the steps. The wedges frequently have a warning sign applied to them, just to reinforce the point.

Another safety feature, which is often the bane of steam photographers, is the orange 'high visibility' jacket or vest. One fact, well-known to hardened diesel enthusiasts, is that the use

8F No.48151 *The Gauge O Guild* was caught on camera working hard up the Strath of Kildonan north of Kinbrace, heading to County March Summit (708') in glorious weather.

RETB reception can be poor, and some low-tech solutions are required to obtain a decent radio signal. It's a good job that the cable is long enough!

of a high visibility vest when out photographing steam specials can be infuriating to the steam enthusiast, who is, usually in vain for most of the reasons described in this article, trying to capture an authentic looking image, usually on film. The last thing they want is an orange vest creeping into the shot! However, no matter what, rail staff have to wear them and usually photographs of steam locomotives being serviced will be enhanced or spoilt, depending on your point of view, with the ubiquitous high visibility clothing. As far as the modeller is concerned, this means that model figures being used to detail a scene will have to wear the obligatory orange, applied with a paint brush!

Support vehicles

Here's an opportunity for more modelling diversity which will bring further interesting variation to your layout operations. Most tours operated today have to have a degree of self-sufficiency because servicing facilities are not always available when things go wrong. Things that can go wrong can include simple defects such as a broken train brake pipe, or total failure of a locomotive, resulting in considerable disruption on a busy main line. Running repairs may have to be made during a long tour, such as the week-long 'The Great Britain' and support coaches are included in most if not all charter trains. Support coaches are the maids of all work in the world of coaching stock, and they can include a canteen, some seating, so that off-duty crew members can 'ride the cushions', a maintenance bay with essential spares (brake pipes, etc) and somewhere to store supplies and the refuse that accumulates during the day. Usually, support coaches are Mk.1 or Mk.2 BSK or BSO vehicles depending on the operator and these are worthy of research and careful modelling because each one is pretty unique, at least internally.

'The Great Britain' tour, operated by West Coast Railways, relied on several of its diesel electric locomotives for support should something have gone wrong, especially on the single track Far North and Kyle Line legs of the tour. The support locomotive for these lines was 47 245, and it ran light engine to Georgemas Junction, preceding the Far North Line leg of the tour to Thurso which was hauled by the company's 8F locomotive, No.48151 *The Gauge O Guild*. 47 245 ran between Georgemas Junction and

Thurso at the rear of the train, so that it would be in a position to pilot the train back to Georgemas because of the lack of a suitable place to service No.48151 at Thurso. At the end of the tour, 57 601 managed the train on its return to London.

Support and 'pilot' locomotives used on the full-size railway present an opportunity to choose a favourite locomotive, which would not otherwise be justifiable in a layout time-frame or geographical location, which could be operated as a support locomotive. Of course, during the operation of your 'tour', you could 'arrange' for something to go wrong and call in the support diesel locomotive to assist.

TOPS numbers

All steam locomotives are registered for main line use and allocated a TOPS number, which is never applied to the locomotive for aesthetic reasons. Some of the Mk.1 coaches favoured for steam charters are usually privately owned and some were removed from the network system after sale, before being returned to main line use. Those coaches sometimes do carry the re-registration number and that should be applied to any models to be authentic.

Conclusion

A search on the internet will reveal a number of locomotives currently passed for main line duties, equipped with OTMR, TPWS and AWS, with tours and seasonal tourist train duties lined up throughout the year. They offer tremendous opportunity to model something different and I hope the accompanying photographs of the 'Jacobite' taken during the 2005 and 2006 seasons, together with images of 'The Great Britain', will provide inspiration for creating the operations surrounding the running and servicing of such trains in model form. As I discovered, there's more to it than choosing a steam loco and a rake of Mk.1s and I have only scratched the surface – further research will reveal more about this little appreciated aspect of modern railway operation. As an aside, there's an opportunity to model the lunatic driving as photographers chase the train – cars could be abandoned all over the layout on the lineside, as was witnessed on the A9 north of Perth and beyond on April 10 and on subsequent days of 'The Great Britain' tour.

Intense activity at Georgemas Junction as 48151 runs round its train for the short hop to Thurso. 47 245 was attached to the rear of the train so it could pilot it back to Georgemas Junction later in the day.

'The Great Britain' tour returned to Perth from Inverness, with A4 No.60009 *Union of South Africa* (TOPS No.98809) and K4 No.61994 *The Great Marquess* on April 14, 2007, to be met by 57 601, which took over at Perth for the long trip back to London Kings Cross. This photograph, taken at Kingussie, appears wintry thanks to the sand on the track which was the result of a flood earlier in the year.

LINESIDE LOOK REVISITED - 1: Vintage Hornby

The Hornby R145 Signal Box (not the one from the infamous advert of some years ago!) is an obsolete model only available via the second-hand box or eBay. With a little TLC – and some brick-embossed plastic sheet – it can be turned into a reasonable model of the 1950s-designed LMR Type 15 signal box for BR (or later) period layouts. For larger installations two (or more) could be spliced together, while the cabin can be removed from the base and used as a shunter's cabin, ground frame or offices.

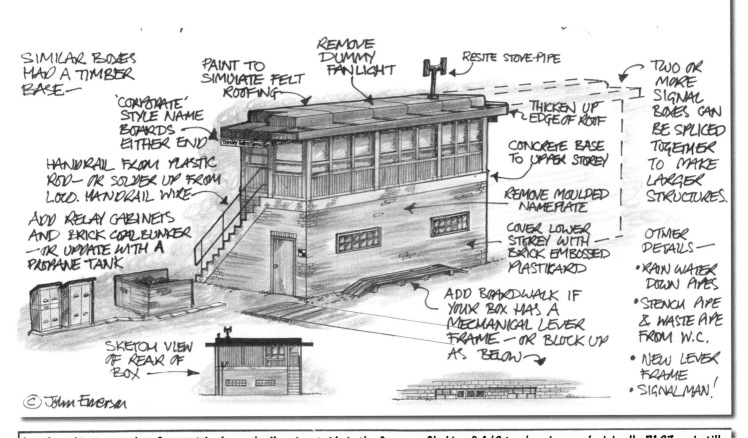

Another old – but rather fine model - from the Hornby stable is the Cowans, Sheldon 6 1/2 ton hand crane (originally R127 and still in the catalogue as R6004!). Several were still in use in the 1990s and, with a bit of work and some added detail, an atractive model results. Use an RTR single-plank, three-plank or 'Bolster' wagon as a runner or match wagon. Just the job for your TMD or CCE yard.

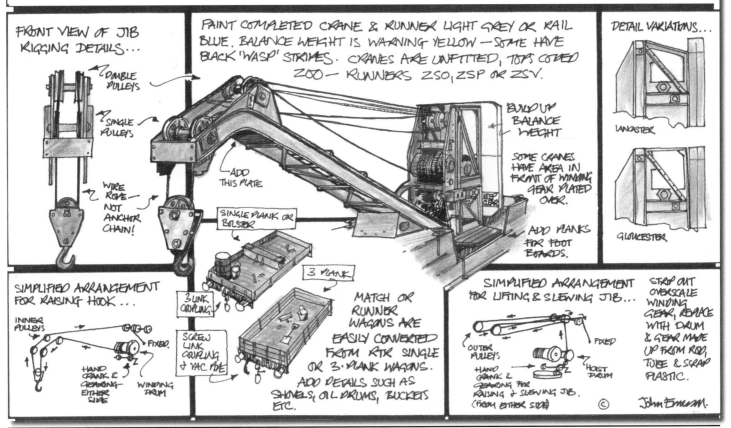

Hassell Harbour Bridge

Mike Sant describes this new O gauge layout built by members of the Alsager Railway Association.

Hassell Harbour Bridge is the new main line O gauge layout from the members of Alsager Railway Association, who are part of the South Cheshire O Gauge Group.

We decided to rise to the challenge set by the Gauge O Guild to produce a new 41' x 15' layout for the 50th Anniversary of the Guild, 2006 celebrations. Thanks go to the Guild, for some funding *via* the Area Rep., to help us get started on this major project.

Our old layout Hassell Rode was getting close to its sell-by date, some boards being 20 years old. We had been thinking about producing another layout, so the prompt from the Guild gave us the final push. This would give us two years to make the layout.

We all started to think what we would like to see on the new layout, and what the viewing public would like to see. After several pub meetings, and many discussions, we finally came up with a plan. I was set the task of drawing the plan of the layout, so everyone could see what the layout would look like. The only part of the old layout we would keep was the ten road storage siding boards and the elevated track at one end going over the bridge.

We then presented the plan and budget requirement to our club Committee for approval, and they gave us the go ahead.

The main frontage of the layout includes two viaducts and a hog's back steel girder bridge spanning the river and harbour scene. The girder bridge alone is 5'6" in length and is loosely based on one at Sunderland, and although not a direct copy, it is constructed as it might have been in the late 1800s. We have had advice on its construction by a retired Civil Engineer, even down to the size of the rivets.

The river and harbour scene is modelled at low tide, exposing the mud banks, upon which rests a coastal steamer, moored to the quay and delivering its goods. A light railway runs along the quay to aid the unloading. Access to the quay is *via* a wagon incline from the exchange sidings, where you can watch a wagon being lowered down to the harbour. The river and harbour board is close to floor level to give it a good visual appearance. Our girder bridge is 3' above the river scene, which is a scale 130',

LNER N2 passing Hassell Rode North signal box with a short mixed goods train.

giving a spectacular and dramatic set piece to run our trains over.

We also have working crossing gates and a canal basin scene, where you can see stone being loaded into a canal barge from the quarry close by.

A small station sits at the back of the layout, receiving local passenger trains and the special train for the coal miners. Ten sidings at the back of the layout are used to hide the stock, and these are covered with boards depicting a Staffordshire coalfield. Most of the wagons to be seen in the mine area are Settle Speakman, since there was a railway wagon works at Alsager, and these wagons transported coal throughout the region.

All the boards are made out of 9mm birch plywood, cross braced with 4mm ply, with access holes cut out for wiring. The ends of the boards use 18mm ply, which connect to the other boards with cabinet makers metal alignment dowels, and coach bolts with wing nuts. On top of this rests the track bed, made out of 12mm ply, the rest of the scenic area is then filled in with 50mm thick sheets of styrene carved to shape.

The viaduct and girder bridge profiles were drawn on a CAD drawing system on my computer at work. These were then sent to one of the suppliers that we use, for them to be laser cut out of 18mm ply, this saves time and is very accurately cut.

All the track is from Peco, except the pointwork, which is hand made from C&L parts. All the pointwork was made by Phil, one of our members who was working in Melbourne, Australia at the time and was then posted to us, so they travelled a few thousand miles to be part of the layout! All the points are operated by Tortoise point motors.

The electrics and control panel were designed by Pete, who works in the electronic industry, Derek and Pete then commenced wiring up the layout, with a few thousand yards of wire and multi-pin 'D' type connectors. We then tested the whole layout to make sure it

worked OK, before starting to ballast the track and doing the scenic work.

Two teams were organised, one to produce the front of the layout with its viaducts and bridge and another team to produce the colliery area.

The hog's back girder bridge on the front of the layout took almost 12 months to complete.

As mentioned earlier, the main spans are cut out of 18mm ply, which are bolted to a base at each end, with a central pivot at the centre top. Support rods were then connected from the girder ironwork to the track base. These are threaded at one end so the tension can be adjusted to keep the track level. The bridge was then

Bulleid Light Pacific *Plymouth* heading 'The Devon Belle' coming off the bridge. This is a Finney kit modified to run on 6' radius track.

weight tested, with six bricks - it didn't even move a millimetre.

Card overlays and plastic truss beams were then added. The jointing plates were put on and then all the rivets were put in one at a time by Bert, (no joke), using small brass pins. This has been well worth the effort, for the realism obtained. (Bert is now known as Bert the Rivet!)

The sides of the viaducts and the girder bridge towers were covered with stone sheets from Slater's, with corner keystones from card, by Mick and Chris.

The landscape areas were made from styrene sheets carved to shape, and then covered over with old net curtains, glued on with PVA. This helps the plaster mix to adhere better. The whole area was then covered with various scenic materials available from Woodland Scenics and Greenscenes. The trees are scratch-built using twisted wire and foilage matt.

All the various buildings have been scratch-built using thick card, plywood and plastic sheet and have been covered with Slater's brick and stone sheets. Some have detailed interiors which are illuminated, including the signal boxes.

Bulleid Light Pacific *Plymouth* exiting the bridge with 'The Devon Belle'.

Hassell Harbour Bridge Track Plan

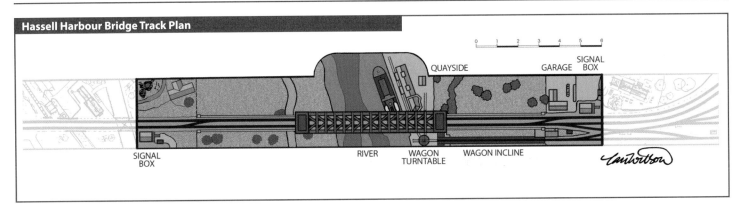

QUAYSIDE   GARAGE   SIGNAL BOX

SIGNAL BOX

RIVER   WAGON TURNTABLE   WAGON INCLINE

The signals all work and have been made from scratch from drawings, with some parts purchased from Model Signal Engineering. They are operated by Post Office relays mounted underneath the layout and operate via a wire in a tube soldered to the base plate with weighted ends, these then rest on arms connected to the relays, which give a movement of 6mm up and down, just enough to operate the signal arms. The signals are all illuminated with small LEDs and have been made removable so they don't get damaged during transit.

The harbour board is an open box, made from plywood, with a quayside added. The river/basin is covered with plaster to represent mud banks, filled in with casting resin to give the impression that the tide is out. The quayside has a railway running alongside it to assist with unloading the boats and to access the quayside warehouse; this will be made operational in the future. A coastal steamer sits on the mud bank having its cargo unloaded, after which it will wait for the tide to come in before departing. There is still a lot of detail

to add to the quayside area.

We are planning to have real water pumped in and out of the river basin, to give the effect of the tide coming in and out. The only reservation we have about this is the amount of water required (about six gallons), which will need to be close to an exhibition floor and the problems caused if it leaked! We might still try this out in the club premises first.

Now we come to the backscene, an area we feel adds considerably to the look of a layout. We all agreed that we would need something

Adams 'Jubilee' Class and M7 shunt the breakdown train into the siding to allow main line trains to pass.

View underneath the bridge, showing truss beams being bolted in position. This also shows the trackbed support rods.

First half of the girders, made out of 8mm ply, with the track support rods in position.

special, especially as the backscene area behind the girder bridge and harbour was very large. This board alone measures 8'0" long by 5'6" high. It is so big that you cannot see through it to the operating side of the layout, which would have distracted the visitor from the view of the girder bridge. The backscene was painted for us by a professional artist, who happened to be a friend of one of our new members. Although it cost us a few pounds, it was well worth it, and if you ever see our layout, I know you will agree with us.

Hassell Hill

And now to what the group consider to be the back of the layout. Many years ago we decided to cover the ten road fiddle yard with a scenic feature, the idea seemed good enough, but the result was a fairly uninspiring flattish area, with some buildings dotted about and a narrow gauge line that no one wanted to operate. So simultaneously with the new bridge feature, plans were drawn up for a revised area over the fiddle yard. A colliery scene was chosen, partly because of the modelling potential created, but also because Alsager is on the edge of the North Stafford coalfield, with historical connections with the coal industry. The North Stafford Railway at

Alsager once boasted a loco shed and marshalling yard for handling coal traffic from the Audley line and Kidsgrove Area, and Alsager was also the location of the wagon shops for colliery owners and coal factors, Settle Speakman Ltd.

Hassell Hill Colliery will feature as a separate article in *BRM* in future months.

The trains running are pre-grouping era, the 'Big Four' and BR, which allows members to run their own stock. We have found this pleases the viewing public, who have their own favourites. You can catch a glimpse of a long train packed with steam lorries from Sandbach, a

LSWR 700 Class 0-6-0 at the head of a main line goods. The loco is a Shedmaster kit with fully working inside motion.

Manchester to Sheffield express, the LNER 'Coronation', coal trains, 'The Devon Belle', The 'ACE', and many more. You are also welcome to join in with the shunting at the front of the layout.

We are a friendly group, when we are at exhibitions and you would like a test run of your stock, or just have your favourite loco photographed on the bridge, please ask. The layout has been designed for expansion and improvements; we will be adding further scenic details to it in the future.

The layout was very well received at the Gauge O Guild's 50th Anniversary Exhibition in September 2006 where we received further invites to exhibit at Macclesfield and York in 2007 and Stafford and Scalerail Bolton in 2008. It was also displayed at our own exhibition in Crewe 2006. We have since exhibited the layout at York over Easter 2007 where we received a lot of good comments, and further invites to Doncaster, Wakefield, Southampton and Warley.

Lastly, we must thank our wives and partners for supporting us in the last couple of years, when we seemed to spend a lot of time down the clubhouse working on the layout. Also thanks to Alsager Railway Association Committee, for their funding and patience.

Please visit our website - www.hassellharbourbridge.com, where you can keep up-to-date with the progress of the layout.

A3 *Papyrus* passes over Hassell Rode South level crossings, watched by a young lady.

An LNER N2 approaches Hassell Rode South level crossings with a mixed goods.

A4 *Dominion of Canada* heads the southbound 'Coronation' past the church, signal box and garage, on the approach to the viaduct.

A3 *Papyrus* again, heading a train of LNER teak coaches over the bridge. The first coach is the Pathe Cinema Coach; this was a converted Dia. 113 passenger brake van. This was the first cinema coach on British railways, introduced in May 1935, it lasted until the outbreak of war in September 1939.

Exeter hauling the 'ACE' formation as it ran in winter between Sidmouth Junction and Exeter. The loco is a much-rebuilt Acorn kit.

A tale of two 'Cities'

Tony Wright produces a pair of ex-LMS OO gauge 'Princess Coronation' Pacifics by two very different means.

pologies must be given to the great Charles Dicken's memory for the plagiarism of his title, but it's just about appropriate for this piece. I say just about, because amongst the numerous epithets describing Stanier's masterpieces, 'Cities' is one, along with 'Princess Coronations', 'Semis', 'Duchesses', 'Big Lizzies' and 'Big-uns'(were there others?). Actually, neither of these 'Semis' has turned out to be named after a city (though both of

them could have been), with one being named after a Duchess and the other after the designer of the original class (though the actual loco carrying his name came out under his successor's stewardship at Crewe).

The 'Duchess'

Some little time ago, at one of the highly successful Missenden Abbey weekends, my good friend Bob Alderman gave me a part-completed,

scratch-built OO gauge model of an original non-streamlined 'Duchess' (actually 'original' isn't quite true, for it had a double chimney). The model had been bequeathed to him after the builder died, with the suggestion that perhaps he'd like to 'finish it'. After many years' ownership (remember, Bob is an O gauge modeller of some distinction), he must have thought completion would never take place (hence his giving it to me). Well,

Even though this picture shows *Sir William A Stanier FRS* in BR maroon, I couldn't ask Ian to paint that disfiguring yellow stripe on the cabside. Supposedly indicating its prohibition south of Crewe (under the wires), nevertheless No.46256 is entering Bletchley on an Up express on August 21, 1964. This was the last year for the 'Big-uns' (though this loco will be cleaner at the end of its life for working enthusiasts' trains). AWS is fitted, but the electric lighting is now removed. **Alec Swain, The Transport Treasury**.

not being one to miss out on an opportunity, I thought I'd give it a go. The basic model looked well put together and worthy of completion, providing (my decision), as much as possible of the late builder's work was retained. Which one should it be? The tender was built as an original non-streamlined type, so for my chosen period (mid '50s) it could be 46232/33/34. I'd already produced 46232 (*BRM*, December 2005), so the choice was between *Duchess of*

Sutherland or *Duchess of Abercorn*. The latter got the nod, largely because of its relative rarity for me. Despite its Scottish title, No.46234 was never based north of the border, though it might just as well have been as far as I was concerned, continually evading being a 'cop'. The Polmadie 'Semis' were always rare birds to Cestrians (the only one I never saw came from there). Though Crewe was near, the Scottish locos usually went there in darkness (unless on works running-in turns). 5A 'Duchesses' were very common, as were the London-based ones, so 46234 should have been seen regularly up to 1959, but she wasn't. In 1959 she went to Upperby, and was less likely to be spotted - how frustrating? Sometime in 1960 (if my memory serves) she was in Crewe works, and the local bush telegraph reported that fact to those of us on the 'Walls' at Chester. Needing 46234 as a 'cop', I duly wrote off to the works for a permit. It duly arrived and off I went, but she'd gone. However, whilst spotting at Crewe station after the works visit, the loco turned up - on a running-in return trip to/from Chester! My non-travelling chums on that day told me she'd gone onto 6A after being turned and was on view for ages before returning. The only other time I saw her was on the scrap road in Crewe works, adjacent to the Chester-Crewe line, bereft of front numberplate and nameplates. A sad spectacle indeed.

The 'Man'
Coincidentally, just as I was contemplating finishing the scratch-built 'Duchess', two further 'Princess Coronation' items arrived in the editorial office. One was Hornby's current *City of Leeds* and the other Comet's modification kit to turn just such a model into one of the two Ivatt 'Duchesses'. Serendipity? Perhaps, but an ideal opportunity to put together an article for our latest *Annual*. Which to choose, 46256 or 46257? I suppose the fact that *Sir William A Stanier FRS* received BR maroon swayed it, something *City of Salford* never did. Also, though I don't want to offend Salfordians (is that the right description for a native of this bit of Manchester?), surely a much better case could have been made for naming the last 'Big-un' *City of Bath*, *City of York* or *City of Aberdeen*? All were served directly by the LMS, and all are cities of great architectural merit.

Oddly enough, I have no recollection

of when I saw 46256 or 46257 for the first time - just memories of very frequent sightings of them both. Also, why the former was never preserved (the zenith of British express steam?) remains a puzzle, especially as she was the last in service.

How to proceed
As always, source material was gathered first. This consisted of the usual loose pictorial material, and two 'definitive' books - *The Book of the Coronation Pacifics* (and its accompaniments) by Ian Sixsmith (Irwell Press, 1998) and *Profile of the Duchesses* by David Jenkinson (OPC, 1982). I also used the Roche/Ian Allan book of 4mm drawings as a guide. Though substantially inaccurate in many of its other images, I don't think the 'Semi' drawings are that far out, and both provided a useful guide for the basic dimensions.

So, with a decent idea of what I had in mind, I set to work to finish one and modify another model of (arguably) the most impressive British Class 8P Pacific. The following pictures explain how I got on.

Duchess of Abercorn

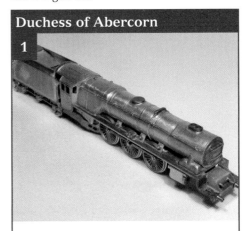

1 The 'Duchess' as received - substantially complete and crying out to be completed. No bogie, no pony, no motion, no front steps, no lamp brackets and no buffers, but enough there to stimulate the creative energy.

2 I really don't know whether the original builder became too infirm to carry on or that someone else had a go at finishing the model, but some of the detail soldering was very crude - the handrail pillars' fixing, for instance.

3 A hand-made gearbox had been installed in the chassis, driven via a flexible tube by a gutsy Pittman motor. Wheels were ancient nickel silver-tyred Romfords, shorted out one side.It ran, just!

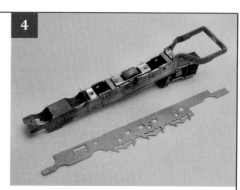

4 I took the wheels off and considered a complete Comet replacement chassis. However, after cleaning up, the drive arrangement worked beautifully, so I retained the original chassis. Cross wires have been soldered on to take the brakes.

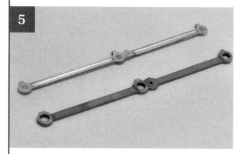

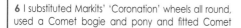

5 The original rods were fashioned from brass, and were much too coarse in my opinion. Comet rods were substituted - at least the original builder's chassis wheel centres were the same as Comet's.

6 I substituted Markits' 'Coronation' wheels all round, used a Comet bogie and pony and fitted Comet

brakes from their frame kit. The original chassis relied on the 'American' pick-up system - I used nickel silver wipers.

7 Markits' latest bespoke sprung 'Coronation' buffers were used, along with the same firm's smokebox dart. Lamp brackets were fashioned from scrap etched-brass.

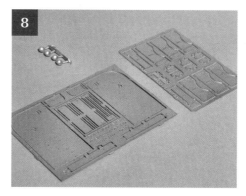

8 I don't know whether the builder was going to finish his model as in BR days but it was certainly my intention - hence the need for smoke deflectors, courtesy, as usual, of Comet.

9 All the boiler-side handrails and pillars were replaced with Alan Gibson items, after the grotty originals were removed. Fixing of the deflectors was achieved by solder, and great care!

10 It says a lot for the original builder's ability that I had to do very little remedial work on the basic body. I completed the cab roof detail with brass/nickel silver and added odd pipe-runs from fusewire. The body sits on the Roche drawing.

11 The basic tender platework was excellent and, apart from cleaning up and adding extra detail (coal pusher, from Comet), little extra in the way of finishing was necessary.

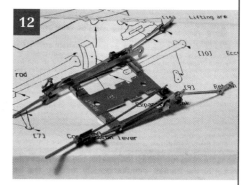

12 I use a lot of Comet's valve gear frets, and the tackle for this 'Semi' proved to be no different. Minor modifications were needed to the motion support bracket to ensure it fitted the chassis.

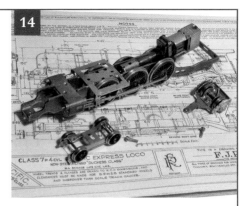

13 The original scratch-built cylinders were retained, and the Comet motion and gear fitted as appropriate. Cylinder drain cocks were formed from 15A fusewire.

14 As mentioned, the Roche drawing for this loco is pretty good and was used extensively. Comet's extra add-on bits (bogie, pony, etc.) are a real boon for the modeller. Imagine making these bits from scratch!

15 Complete and ready for Ian Rathbone to work his magic. I hope I've remained true to the original builder's ideals in completing this loco. In the main, all I've added are the bits to complete and numerous detail bits and pieces. She now looks good and runs well. As mentioned, Comet provided much in the way of add-ons, enabling me to finish this model to the standard (forgive the arrogance), I believe, expected of the builder.

What a wonderful sight, as freshly out-shopped *Duchess of Abercorn* leaves Shrewsbury and returns to Crewe in the winter of 1955. This is probably her final running-in duty for she's in charge of a cross-country express (for Manchester or Liverpool) which she'll take as far as Crewe (having replaced a WR loco). No AWS is fitted (even though this is over two years after Harrow!) and the sanders are in operation. **The Transport Treasury.**

Sir William A Stanier FRS

1 Hornby's current 'Princess Coronation' as supplied (minus one front step - goodness knows where that went). In short, an exceptional model needing little in the way of 'fiddling' to bring it into the 'scale' class.

2 Comet give you a host of bits for improvement in the 'Ivatt' pack. The first job was to shift the inadequate inside cylinder cover, best achieved using a piercing saw after first drilling some pilot holes.

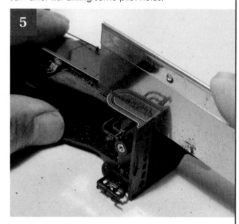

3 Final cleaning up of the gaping aperture was achieved using a craft knife and fine files. Beware, don't dig too deeply, and remember, especially with the utility front end, you've now made this area very weak.

4 Quite why the original Hornby inside cylinder cover is so puny, I don't know, but Comet's cast metal substitute does make a difference. I fixed it in place using viscous super glue.

5 To make the Ivatt 'Duchess', the original Hornby cabsides had to be shortened, best achieved by the careful use of a razor saw, first horizontally (like this) and then vertically from below.

6. Great care was taken not to damage the moulded pipework under the cab, nor the bottom edge of the cab roof. The etched-brass overlay was simply fixed on with superglue.

7. I retained both Hornby's rear handrail assemblies (they have to be removed before cutting) and fixed them back after the new cabsides were glued in place. Comet give you some etched replacements - those went on the 'Duchess'.

8. The replacement 'City' deflectors are different from the 'Duchess' ones, having no extended bit at the bottom to match the curved front end. Soldering on the supports was achieved using a beech mitre block.

9 I didn't change Hornby's handrails (they look all right to me), merely adding one more handrail pillar each side. Comet's design for fixing on the deflectors at the top is excellent - just finally cut off the excess strips and turn over the ends.

10 There was a 'mile' of extra pipework to add at the back end, mainly made from fusewire of different thicknesses. I found the easiest way of securing this was to glue on some pads of PCB - 4mm sleeper material.

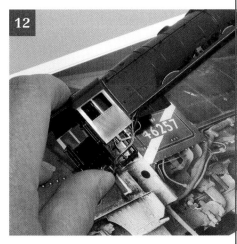

11 Reference to prototype source material is essential, especially for plotting pipework-runs, etc. Here, the model sits on top of a shot in Keith Pirt's latest volume featuring Scottish steam.

12 Irwell's 'Coronation' book was a constant source of prototype information. However, don't expect to replicate all such pipework if you want your model to negotiate tight bends.

13 Rear frame extensions fitted and the 'Delta' truck made up. I made a new pivot point for the pony (Hornby's long screw just didn't work). Comet's speedo was also substituted. That way you don't have to disconnect it to take the body off.

14. I had to take a bit off the top of the truck's springs to clear the back end. The pipework below the cab is a mish-mash of wire and plastic, though it's effective enough and the disparate nature of the bits will disappear under paint.

15. Comet give you a complete tender pack in the conversion kit, of a type only towed by the last pair, so none of Hornby's tenders will suit. As usual, a sub-frame ensured accurate running.

16. The tender body construction followed Comet's usual practice of an accurate sub-structure with etched overlays. Unless one's particularly clumsy, it's hard to get it out of square.

17. Checking the relationship between the loco and its tender is essential during all stages of construction. Here, the nearside tender side is just resting on the chassis to check ride height, etc

18. The curved design of the LMS Stanier/Ivatt tender dictated that one side would have to be soldered on from the outside. The fit of parts was, as usual from Comet, superb.

19. My one criticism of all Comet's tenders is the too-thin brass they use for the sides. I know half-etch relief means a half-thick finish, but why not use thicker brass at source, like DJH do? When soldering at the base, it buckled horribly, and, though prototypical, 'ripples' on brass sheet just look like bad building.

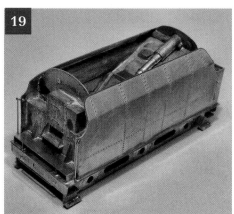

20. Despite some 'fighting' needed to eradicate too many buckles, the finished tender came out reasonably well. Sprat & Winkle couplings dictate a 'goal post' be provided on the rear bufferbeam.

21. No cylinder drain cocks are provided by either Hornby or Comet, so I made my own from scrap etch and 15A fusewire. Just drilling holes to fix (as I first thought) is no good - you'll just gum up the piston rods.

22. My method of coupling loco to tender was to use a nickel silver 'hook' on the loco's drag box engaging onto a 'goalpost' on the front of the tender, discreetly hidden beneath the fallplate.

23. Complete and ready for Ian to paint her (him?) in BR maroon. I've yet to plug the hole in the firebox where the original AWS battery box was attached. Bogie wheels (and tender wheels) on this model are from Alan Gibson (Hornby's are a bit crude). Even in the 'raw' as it were, it looks every inch an Ivatt 'Duchess'. One thing not attempted was to open up the spectacle windows to the larger size seen latterly on the ex-streamlined locos (and all the non-streamlined ones). Really, Hornby's model should have the large ones at source for a maroon 'Semi'.

LINESIDE LOOK REVISITED - 2: Fences and Crossings

Don't sit on the fence! Even in these standardised and privatised times old company or BR regional identities can still be distinguished by the type of lineside fencing. Most is readily available as etched frets or plastic mouldings. Concrete panel fencing is easily made from sheet plastic.

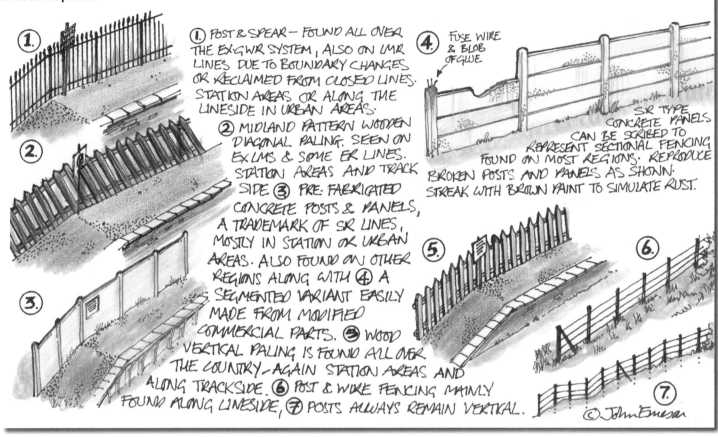

① POST & SPEAR - FOUND ALL OVER THE EX-GWR SYSTEM, ALSO ON LMR LINES DUE TO BOUNDARY CHANGES OR RECLAIMED FROM CLOSED LINES. STATION AREAS OR ALONG THE LINESIDE IN URBAN AREAS. ② MIDLAND PATTERN WOODEN DIAGONAL PALING. SEEN ON EX LMS & SOME ER LINES. STATION AREAS AND TRACK SIDE ③ PRE-FABRICATED CONCRETE POSTS & PANELS, A TRADEMARK OF SR LINES, MOSTLY IN STATION OR URBAN AREAS. ALSO FOUND ON OTHER REGIONS ALONG WITH ④ A SEGMENTED VARIANT EASILY MADE FROM MODIFIED COMMERCIAL PARTS. ⑤ WOOD VERTICAL PALING IS FOUND ALL OVER THE COUNTRY - AGAIN STATION AREAS AND ALONG TRACKSIDE. ⑥ POST & WIRE FENCING MAINLY FOUND ALONG LINESIDE, ⑦ POSTS ALWAYS REMAIN VERTICAL.

FUSE WIRE & BLOB OF GLUE

SR TYPE CONCRETE PANELS CAN BE SCRIBED TO REPRESENT SECTIONAL FENCING FOUND ON MOST REGIONS. REPRODUCE BROKEN POSTS AND PANELS AS SHOWN. STREAK WITH BROWN PAINT TO SIMULATE RUST.

© John Emerson

Farm tracks and minor roads often have to cross the railway in the form of occupation crossings or ungated crossings. Tracks in dockyards, industrial areas or Trading Estates, where speeds are lower, still need clear signage to indicate their presence to drivers. A little bit of thought and some time spent on detailing can make all the difference. Don't forget signage for road and rail users.

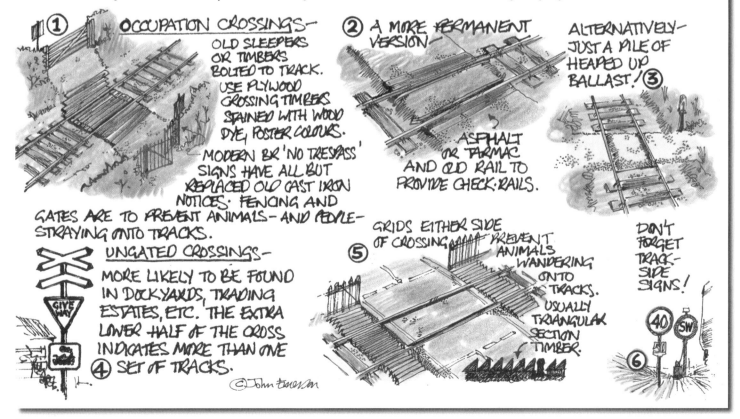

① OCCUPATION CROSSINGS - OLD SLEEPERS OR TIMBERS BOLTED TO TRACK. USE PLYWOOD CROSSING TIMBERS STAINED WITH WOOD DYE, POSTER COLOURS.

MODERN BR 'NO TRESPASS' SIGNS HAVE ALL BUT REPLACED OLD CAST IRON NOTICES. FENCING AND GATES ARE TO PREVENT ANIMALS - AND PEOPLE - STRAYING ONTO TRACKS.

UNGATED CROSSINGS - MORE LIKELY TO BE FOUND IN DOCKYARDS, TRADING ESTATES, ETC. THE EXTRA LOWER HALF OF THE CROSS INDICATES MORE THAN ONE ④ SET OF TRACKS.

② A MORE PERMANENT VERSION -

ASPHALT OR TARMAC AND OLD RAIL TO PROVIDE CHECK-RAILS.

⑤ GRIDS EITHER SIDE OF CROSSING PREVENT ANIMALS WANDERING ONTO TRACKS. USUALLY TRIANGULAR SECTION TIMBER.

ALTERNATIVELY - JUST A PILE OF HEAPED UP BALLAST! ③

DON'T FORGET TRACKSIDE SIGNS!

GIVE WAY

40 SW
50
⑥

© John Emerson

Young women paint the detail parts on 'Midland' 4-4-0s in the Bassett-Lowke factory.

The Bassett-Lowke story

Michael C Shaw delves into the history of this famous company.

Photographs from the author's collection.

For very many years of my childhood, my most treasured model railway book was the May 1934 reprint of *The Model Railway Handbook* by WJ Bassett-Lowke MI Loco E (1940 Tenth Edition). This encompassed 15" gauge to 16.5mm gauge and a lot more besides. It proved to be my key to the works of GP Keen, Ivo Peters, the Rev Edward Beal, JEP Howey, Victor Harrison and many others including Henry Greenley and WJ Bassett-Lowke himself. It was read with care, but handled so many times, it is now a frail relic of the torchlight reading and midnight feasts of long ago. I so much wanted to own and run those wonderful model trains it contained. I once put the externally fired O gauge steam Mogul, together with the GWR 2-6-2 suburban tank and the LMS 'Coronation' on my

Christmas list only to be told, sincerely, by my father 'You may as well ask for the moon'.

Although I was able to purchase a few simple items as a child, I never dreamt of my future involvement with the models, history, world or indeed the people to which they belonged, but life turned out to be stranger and more fantastic than fiction.

I enjoyed visits to Gamages and the Bassett-Lowke shop, which my father introduced me to, as he was both a sea-going engineer and modeller. It had a delightful Victorian flavour, which I thought quite as grand as Buckingham Palace, and of equal importance and permanence to the Science Museum at South Kensington, at which I was adept at getting most of its showcase Bassett-Lowke locomotive's wheels revolving at any one time - quite an athletic feat!

Origins

Bassett-Lowke, the model engineering company, was started between 1895 and 1896, issuing its first catalogue in December 1898. Wenmann Joseph, known as Mr WJ (born December 27, 1877) formed a partnership with Harold Fonda Robert Franklin, using the premises of Joseph Tom Lowke, known as Tom Lowke, their father, at Kingswell Street, Northampton. This premises was handed down to their father by his step-father Absalom Bassett, and both WJ and Harold were given the middle name of Bassett in recognition of this. As well as a training in his father's business, producing machinery and small boilers for the local shoemaking industry and agriculture, WJ Bassett-Lowke did a student apprenticeship at Crompton Parkinson Electrical Engineers at

Chelmsford. He had originally wanted to be an architect and maintained an interest in this, graphic design and advertising throughout his life. He was a businessman, publicist and opportunist first, and a model engineer by trade. He was a Fabian Socialist, an active Town Councillor for Northampton, a keen amateur dramatic society member and very early into the mail order business, advertising in the *Model Engineer*, soon after its founding in 1898, together with the Strand Magazine and the boys journal of the era, *The Chieftain*.

WJ met Stefan Bing, a German Jew, and George Carette, a German of French extraction, at the Paris Exhibition of 1900. Both were Nuremberg-based toy manufacturers, and eventually suffered banishment from the Fatherland. A large proportion of Bassett-Lowke's production in smaller scale model railway equipment, below 2½" gauge, was German produced until 1914, when greater use was made of British out-workers for specialist order work. After the Great War, Carette production ceased, however, despite the understandable Teutonic phobia inspired post-war by the popular press, Bing continued to supply Northampton until the rise of Nazi power in the 1930s.

The Bassett-Lowke company was officially founded in 1899, being incorporated into a limited liability company during 1910. It was never

George Bernard Shaw was a Fabian Socialist like Bassett-Lowke and had introduced him to Rennie Mackintosh. Bernard Shaw visited the Bassett-Lowke's at 78 Derngate, whilst supporting the Labour candidate for Northampton, Margaret Bondfield, in 1922. He is seen here discussing Waterline models with Bassett-Lowke.

a large organisation and did not employ more than 200 people at any time throughout its whole existence, although its influence was great. It opened its first retail shop in London in 1909, and published the well known *Model Railway Handbook* spasmodically, from 1906 until the death of its founder in 1953, by which time it had been overtaken by the development of the modelling press, and the weight of model railway specialists publications. WJ was a consummate communicator, writer, traveller and early radio and television broadcaster, taking his slides and films on lecture tours throughout the UK - he projected Bassett-Lowke. The organisation was divided into independent sections, which supplied their complete production through the Bassett-Lowke company. George Winteringham Precision Models originally supplied the standard 'Lowko' permanent way for railways throughout the companies existence, and eventually the ship models also. Ernest W Twining was employed from 1910 to produce architectural, industrial and historic models until the end of Bassett-Lowke in 1965,

The Bassett-Lowke factory, with the track production line in the foreground, and that of the locomotive chassis behind.

Left: W J Bassett-Lowke in 1902, aged 25. As a young man, he was a constant contributor to the engineering press and was a pioneer of the specialist modelling publication. Right: A post-war image taken of W J Bassett-Lowke in 1947, aged 70, in the last few years of his long career

Lowke's pacifist beliefs, he subsisted during the Great War by producing master gauges and calibration scales for standardised munitions and other productions, as industrial demand outstripped traditional supplies. He also provided many ship models to the Admiralty throughout this period, and encouraged his staff to stay in his employ on essential war work rather than go to the front. He actively supported interned German friends and company representatives, imprisoned on the Isle of Man, by regular visits during this period.

Company premises
Although originally a catalogue based mail order company, in addition to the London premises eventually situated at 112 High Holborn, shops in Edinburgh and Manchester were opened. The Edinburgh shop was sold back to its original proprietor who thereafter acted as a Bassett-Lowke agent at its new location.

Greenley and Howey
At sometime between the Paris Exhibition of 1900, that so influenced WJ, and 1902, Greenley and WJ met. Henry Greenley, trained by the Metropolitan Railway, had a good knowledge of both steam and electric traction and, being a professional engineer, had an eye for scale and realism. After working on miniature passenger carrying lines, Greenley turned his attention to the smaller

although Ernest left to work for the Bristol Aircraft Corporation to pursue wartime work in 1940. Twining was the artistic wing of the company and co-ordinated the exhibition work, with which the company became so associated.

During the First World War Carette and Bing were unable to supply the company from German manufacturing facilities. George Carette and his son, Theophile,

were of French descent and had to leave for France unexpectedly *via* the Swiss border, having given assistance to compatriots caught the wrong side of the opposing armies. However they managed to ship the 1914 Christmas order, whereas Stefan Bing didn't manage to ship theirs, but saved the day post war by despatching it in 1918, at the agreed 1914 price, after several years of gross inflation. Despite WJ Bassett-

Early quality control. Locomotives and station buildings being checked prior to despatch from the Bassett-Lowke factory.

Metal parts being stamped-out by machine on the Bassett-Lowke production line. Note the different jigs to produce various shaped parts.

gauges, as the pre-First World War efforts at Anglicising imported Bing and Carette products had not been entirely successful and the market was getting more sophisticated. WJ and Greenley set about drawing up a set of locomotive and rolling stock designs for the German manufacturers to produce, solely for the Bassett-Lowke marque and with the input of Ernest W Twining, previously employed in pioneer model aeroplane manufacture, and George Winteringham, a skilled draughtsman and engineer, who had developed his own miniature keyed bullhead rail and chair system, also taken into the Bassett-Lowke fold. This track remained its standard system throughout the companies existence, together with the sheet metal 'Lowko' metal-chaired track, secured to wooden sleepers of an intermediate quality. Immediately after the First World War, Greenley set to work with Bing's production team, to build a table top system based on half O (HO), as a direct result of pioneering British O gauge from 1911, many years after the gauge had started being used by scratch-builders. Bassett-Lowke was determined not to be caught out again. Thus between 1922 and 1925 the range developed from clockwork

to electric with over 30 items of stock, a complete, if crude and ill-proportioned system to the modern eye, it had a great deal of charm. Sadly for Bassett-Lowke it was under-priced and under-developed and thus foundered, although it did encourage other British manufacturers to take up the slack, eventually causing Bassett-Lowke to return to the market late in the day, in 1935, with the (originally)

German manufactured British Trix Twin system, which became a British company when Stephan Bing and family moved to the UK to avoid Nazi persecution in the late 1930s.

Miniature railways

During the early years, prior to 1914, Bassett-Lowke also concerned itself with the construction of various estate and seaside passenger carrying

The factory on the left-hand side and the offices on the right, of Winteringham Ltd, Engineers, Northampton, the model boat and exhibition division of Bassett-Lowke.

Correspondence between GP Keen and Bassett-Lowke. The document on the left is a receipt for the purchase of a locomotive, costing £8-15-5, on the right is a letter to GP Keen from the BL factory concerning the purchase of SR 'Boxpok' wheels, and that in the middle is a personal letter from WJ Bassett-Lowke to GP Keen, wishing him a happy birthday!

railways throughout Europe and the world. In addition to its exhibition lines, it also took over and ran the 15" gauge Ravenglass & Eskdale Railway, from 1914 until its sale to Sir Audrey Brocklebank in 1925, purchasing back Captain Howey's Bassett-Lowke Pacific *Colossus* during the first world war, to help power the converted narrow gauge line, with the 'Little Giant' type provided by the company to Greenley's design. This collaboration really began in 1904 when Henry Greenley and R Proctor Mitchell met at the Regent Street Polytechnic due to the Mitchell's close association with it. Greenley had just designed and built a 10¼" gauge 0-4-4T *Nipper* in partnership with Snooks & Smithies (of water tube boiler frame). Under the guidance of Bassett-Lowke and company secretary Charles H Battle, later a guiding light in the Northampton

General Hospital, they formed Miniature Railways of Great Britain Limited producing first the 'Nipper' then the 'Little Giant' 4-4-2s, the enlarged *Sans Pareil* and finally the 'Colossus' Class 'Pacifics'. Although the company was sold by the 1920s, the last large scale (10¼") 'Royal Scot' was not outshopped until 1939.

Due to changed circumstances after the Great War, when many of the country-house set and military class were sadly depleted, and the great technical advances of the era caused both the growth of the automotive industry and the interest and knowledge in it, estate railways were effectively dead. Those built after this date more often than not used ex-War Department materials. Bassett-Lowke continued to build larger scale models to special order for some time and supplied parts, assisted by the loan of Henry Greenley's services as engineer, for the construction of Captain John Edward Pressgrave Howey's 15" gauge line from Hythe to Dungeness across Romney Marsh, which was to become the Romney, Hythe & Dymchurch Railway.

Charles Rennie Mackintosh
WJ had many interests during his lifetime - swimming, cycling, photography and film making, modelling, architecture, drama,

'Lowko' wooden sleepered and metal chaired sectional track being assembled in the Bassett-Lowke factory.

politics (he was a member of the Fabian Society) and travel. He was in fact articled to an architect after a year or so of helping his father, Joseph Tom Lowke, in his engineering works. However, then as now, large projects rarely came the way of small provincial architectural practices, and it was, as the young writer Thomas Hardy found a little earlier, a profession in which who one knew was far more important than talent, ability or knowledge. So he left to form his own business, but his love and interests in the arts and architecture never left him.

In the summer of 1914, in preparation for his marriage, in 1917, to Miss Florence Jane Jones, an heiress to the Crocket & Jones shoe empire, WJ purchased a small red brick terraced house in central Northampton at 78 Derngate. During 1915, Charles Rennie Mackintosh, the well known Glasgow Art Nouveau artist and architect, and his wife Margaret MacDonald (who together with Frances MacDonald and Herbert MacNair were known as the Spook School), moved to Chelsea in London having suffered several of the career set-backs common to the profession after several triumphs abroad. Rennie Mackintosh had taken to drinking a little more than advised, in the true Glasgow School tradition, and was somewhat depressed. WJ, an early member of the Design & Industries Association, already knew people like Walter Gropius of the Deutscher Werkbund, Le Corbusier and Peter Behrens, later to design his second house, and was introduced to Rennie Mackintosh by the playwright George Bernard Shaw, well known in the Chelsea art set (and also a member of the Fabian Society) who had been a great friend of WJ for many years. Thus began one of the more unusual collaborations of art history and sadly Rennie Mackintosh's last major work. He re-designed the interior and parts of the exterior of the Derngate house in the most extraordinary and advanced manner. The Guest room and staircase of this all-electric house are of particular note. I have a classical art training and am a professional designer and thus was ideally placed to discover that, whilst working on Bassett Lowke's house, Rennie Mackintosh designed many items such as clocks, furniture and fabrics. I'm sure he also influenced the Bassett-Lowke 'corporate identity'.

WJ was proud of his modern house, but failed to mention the Rennie Mackintosh connection in *Ideal*

Home magazine, or to anyone else for that matter, a strange personality trait of his. Frustrated, and sadly disappointed at the lack of follow-on commissions from this, and other projects from the Chelsea and the Fabian set, Rennie Mackintosh and his wife left for the Mediterranean port of Vendres on the Franco-Spanish border to concentrate on water colour painting until he returned to London to die on December 19, 1928. By the early to mid 1920s Derngate proved far too small for the entertaining and gregarious Bassett-Lowkes and in 1923/4 WJ tried to contact Rennie Mackintosh, but he and his wife Margaret had already left the country.

WJ appointed Peter Behrens, a pioneer of the modern movement and famous for his AEG turbine factory built between 1910-1913, to design his next house. Although Behrens never visited the UK, he was known to WJ via Stefan and Franz Bing who he had also worked for in Germany. The site, chosen in order not to be overlooked,

was on high ground, adjacent to the Wellingborough Road, overlooking Abington Park in the fashionable and moneyed area of Northampton. It was called 'New Ways' and became Britain's first Modern Movement building, at least 20 years ahead of its time, although it included a maid's room and servants' quarters. The interior was plain and functional and included many Charles Rennie Mackintosh ideas, which the artistic WJ adapted for the new location. It was a stunning white building, unusual at the time and still 'modern' today, for the Bassett-Lowke name was associated with modern buildings through its architectural models, such as the Boots factory at Nottingham. WJ is known to have influenced as many inter-war architects as influenced him.

The devil's decade

In 1933 Hitler came to power and it became impossible for WJ to trade with his old friends Stefan Kahn and Franz Bing as they were Jewish. Although to his credit, WJ did

The Bassett-Lowke's first home at 78 Derngate, Northampton, remodelled by the famous Glaswegian architect, artist and designer, Charles Rennie Mackintosh.

Left: Bassett-Lowke, though they cannot produce models, maintain contact by offering catalogues and booklets - a good way of clearing 'dead stock'. Right: The cover of the pre-war catalogue for the new 'Twin Train Table Railway' - later Trix Twin.

manage to get them from Germany to England and continued production of their Trix Twin System in the United Kingdom. Thus he turned to Märklin, who produced an O gauge SR 'Schools' Class, an LMS 4-6-0 and 2-6-4T, together with GWR 'King' Class, *King George V*. Bassett-Lowke later provided their own mechanism, the whole model being badged as produced by Bassett-Lowke. During the 1920s and 1930s, a large stock of components built up in both retail premises and the factory and was only cleared as wartime shortages and lack of production bit during the 1940s. This, together with the sale of second-hand goods (officially at

least) at pre-war prices, kept the retail business going during the war years. Winteringhams and Ships Models were separate companies, providing their entire output to Bassett-Lowke, however during the 1930s they had to co-operate when Winteringhams' woodwork shop was closed down as an economy. They produced a Travelling Post Office model for the GPO for the 1934 Radiolympia Exhibition, together with a huge O gauge model railway for the Joint Railway Companies pavilion at the 1938 British Empire Exhibition in Glasgow, created by Bindon Blood, and another for the British Mining Federation pavilion. Another huge

contract was for Cunard White Star Line, an exhibition stand including a ¼" scale model of the new *Queen Elizabeth* with graphics and model cabins for the New York World Fair of 1939-1940. When war broke out in 1939, this stood W J Bassett-Lowke in good stead, as the company expanded previous war department contacts and began the busiest and most profitable period of its existence.

World War II

WJ was a Fabian socialist and a pacifist, but his horror of what he and many of his establishment friends knew from first-hand accounts to be happening first in Germany, Austria and later occupied lands of Western Europe, left him with no doubts, or indeed choice. He threw the company's entire efforts into the patriotic duty of the Nation, made some money, kept the company going for the future, and his people employed. In 1943 he became the first President of META (the Model Engineers Trade Association). The company had never been busier. Trix production ceased, Winteringhams became effectively part of the War Department's development wing and Ship Models and Checker Waterline Models were combined, and worked with the Admiralty. Bassett-Lowke was licensed to build hundreds of models, in kit form, of the famous Bailey bridge, to train the forces with. They also built many models of the famous Mulberry harbour units, floating pontoon roads, hundreds of model warships and aircraft, bomb aiming simulators, anti-aircraft gun simulators and much more. I have tracked down several of the models at the Royal Engineers' Museum at Chatham and the Imperial War Museum, London. The Mulberry harbour models are exhibited at Arromanche, Normandy. A large number of models of vehicles and equipment were also constructed for the Allies. Bassett-Lowke also provided the S45 cameras used by the RAF and RNAS, and many special orders for Combined Operations Command. The London shop suffered blast damage on numerous occasions, although the Manchester shop and Northampton factories escaped. As the war in Europe scaled down, Bassett-Lowke continued with Government work and looked forward to the future. WJ appeared in a couple of television programmes and also became a 'chat' feature on one of Richard Dimbleby's radio programmes. Bassett-Lowke continued with Bailey bridge models and the heavier 'Heavy Girder bridge'

The spray booth and drying area of the Bassett-Lowke factory circa 1928/30 - there appears to be no extraction equipment visible!

for the European replacement scheme and benefited greatly from the ship builders trying to replace their lost Merchant fleet. In 1948 Cunard ordered a companion quarter-scale model of the pre-war *Queen Mary*. The *Queen Elizabeth* celebrated her conversion from troop ship back to passenger service. It was a struggle against material shortages and staffing problems in a changed world, and the cracks were hidden for a while behind the post war boom, until after WJ Bassett-Lowke's death.

The dream fades

WJ Bassett-Lowke died on October 21, 1953. However, from 1951 it was his directors and secretary, Miss Molly Hardy, who were in control of matters, which certainly shows in the letters signed by WJ during this time. Initially things carried on as usual - in fact they seemed even more hectic. However, Trix Twin was gradually eclipsed by the 'Hornby-Dublo' and Tri-ang ranges during this period, which also caused O and larger scales to decline during the 1950s and 1960s. Gradually the old order of Directors, Managers and suppliers retired or died. Trix Twin was transferred via Dufag Limited to Courtaulds, who belatedly transformed it into a two rail 12 volt system. In 1964 the retail businesses of Bassett-Lowke were closed down, and the two shops sold to Beatties. In July 1968, a new company called Bassett-Lowke Railways Limited was formed, but, although several models were produced, it came to nothing despite the valiant efforts of Roland

Fuller. The industrialist model making side continued well into the 1980s but that too eventually failed. The name was revived, and several diecast steam traction engines and lorries produced, but that ended in tears too! Finally, the name was snapped up by Corgi as part of their portfolio.

During the 1950s the industrial and ship modelling not only continued but expanded, whereas the model railway, ship component and finished products were hard hit by the television boom - until the novelty wore off. The Bassett-Lowke company died by a thousand cuts, well intentioned takeovers, whizz kid managers and people dabbling in an industry they knew little about. But by far the most grievous harm was caused by the changed mass market, cheaper products and smaller scales in all things. The company had been under-capitalised for years and the retail business, which had produced cash flow for the longer term ship models and exhibition/architectural projects, was no longer available. Without the quick minded visionary at the helm, the ship was doomed and the dream faded. Bassett-Lowke had been a dream - a collection of companies, small workshops and out workers, expertly marketed as an institution, represented by its founder in person - an act no one could follow. Even the name was his invention, although it breaks my heart to write it this way. This was the work of a propagandist, a writer who unravelled the technicalities and a charming salesman, in whose web everyone became wondrously and fascinatingly ensnared. The magic worked!

Some of the clientele of Bassett-Lowke's London showroom in Holborn.

Cecil J Allen
Earl of Anglesey
Lord (Albert Stanley) Ashfield LPTB
Prince Albert (King George VI)
Vincent Astor
J Logie Baird (inventor of the television)
Prince Birabongse (Prince Bira of Siam, racing driver)
Lord Brabazon (Chairman, Bristol Aircraft Company)
Sir Malcolm Campbell (World land speed record holder)
John Clements CBE, KBE (actor and producer)
Jackie Coogan (American actor)
Lord Cowdray (S. Pearson & Son, construction company) Terence Cuneo (artist)
Walter Disney (animator)
Grand Duke Dmitri (murderer of Rasputin)
Douglas Aircraft Company
Prince Edward (King Edward VII)
John Galsworthy (Writer)
Dr Gerbels
Lord Glenconner
Lord Glentworth
Sir Alec Guinness (actor)
Admiral Halsey
Lord Harewood
Colonel Ronnie J Hoare (racing car team) RJH
Richard Hearne (Mr Pastry)
Prince Hopkins
Capt J E P Howey (RH&DR)
Jack & Claude Hulbert
Sir Alec Issigonis (designer of the Morris 1000 & Mini)
Maharajah Jodhpur
G P Keen (President MRC)
Capt W F P Kelly
Rudyard Kipling (writer)
Lord Lascelles
Lord Latham
Sir Leyland Barrett
Lord Leverhulme
Stanley Lupins
Sir Edwin Lutyens (architect)
Maharajah Mayerbangh
Earl of Moray
Stirling Moss (world racing champion)
Earl Louis Mountbatten (admiral of the fleet)
Sir Edward Nichol
Lord Northesk
Maharajah Patiala
Ivo Peters
King Peter of Yugoslavia
Air Marshall Salmond
Sir Gilbert Scott (architect)
Sir Henry Seagrave (world speed record holder)
Sultan of Selanger
Frank Sinatra (singer)
Sir George Bernard Shaw (playwright)
Sir Berkeley Sheffield
Neville Shute
Count Sikorski
Lord Howard de Walden
Sir Robert Walker
Edgar Wallace
Duke of Westminster
Duke of Zaragoza
Count Louis Zborowski

Wartime and Mr Wynn Bassett-Lowke inspects a Bailey bridge construction kit, this one being of a size suitable to cross the Rhine. It is contained within the big sister of the Nissen hut, called the 'Romney' hut.

Contact Details

■ **Bassett-Lowke Society Membership Secretary**
Tracy Brookes, Dept BL, c/o Anglo Holt, 150 Birmingham Road, West Bromwich, West Midlands B70 6QT.
Tel: 0121 6021209.
email: tracyhw@blueyonder.co.uk
www.bassettlowkesociety.org.uk

Woodhead

Gary Atkinson describes his N gauge layout based on this much lamented lost route across the Pennines. Photography **Ray Lightfoot**.

Woodhead is my third N gauge layout built for exhibitions, and is my first attempt at modelling an actual location. My other two layouts were Inkaston Moor (December 1999 *BRM*) and Somewhere in England (March 2001 *Railway Modeller*).

Woodhead station closed in 1964 and was midway between Manchester and Sheffield/Wath on the ex-GC/LNER line, electrified with 1500v DC overhead in 1954. The line closed in 1981 and now forms part of the Trans Pennine Trail. It was the sole preserve of the EM1 (Class 76) and EM2 (Class 77) electric locos. I chose this location to model as it is probably the most distinctive part of the line and gave its name to the entire route. It is also a very small station, so the layout could be built relatively quickly, construction time being six months, and serves as a

showcase to run my small fleet of EM1 and EM2 locos which took two and a half years to acquire, modify and complete.

Baseboards

Baseboards were constructed with ¼" ply braced with 2¾" x ¾" timber around the edges. The main baseboard is 6' 6" long with a separate, non-scenic, board measuring 18" x 3' 0" to enable the

EM1 26020 (preserved at the National Railway Museum in York) approaches Woodhead with a Sheffield train.

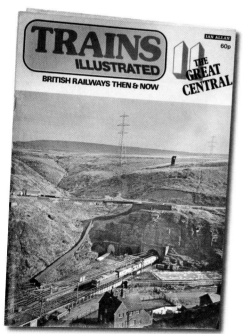

Trains Illustrated No.11 featured the Woodhead Route - the cover price was just 60p..!

tracks to curve round the back of the layout to the six storage roads located beneath the roadway, the whole layout measuring just 8' 0" x 3' 0". The ply was covered in 3mm thick cork tiles as a base for the track to be pinned onto.

Track

The trackwork on the front of the layout is Peco finescale code 55. The storage roads at the rear are code 80 with insulated frog 'Setrack' points. The ballast is a mixture of four shades of Peco scatter material. This is mixed with wallpaper paste and spread over the track with a small knife or screwdriver, pushing it into the spaces between the sleepers. The ballast should be laid level with the top of the sleepers as this hides their overscale depth. When dry, excess ballast can be removed with an old toothbrush. The sides of the rails were painted with Humbrol track colour (170). Time and care should be taken with ballasting as many N gauge layouts I have seen have been spoilt by using ballast that is too coarse or has been poorly laid.

Scenery

The hillsides were made from expanded polystyrene packaging and ceiling tiles. This was cut to shape piece by piece and glued down with PVA wood glue. When the glue has dried, the polystyrene can be further shaped with a knife and rough glasspaper to achieve the desired contours. This method is extremely messy, but provides a strong and light basis for the scenery itself. I covered the polystyrene with newspaper soaked in wallpaper paste and when dried, I painted it all with green undercoat. Finally Woodland Scenics material was again mixed with wallpaper paste and spread over the contours of the layout. While it was still wet, different shades and textures were added, either just scattering over the top or pressed into the mixture and left to dry.

The rock face that surrounds the tunnel mouth is another Woodland Scenics product. I purchased a rock face kit containing a rubber rock strata mould, a quantity of powder and some paint. After taking approximately eight castings, I cut up six of them into narrow strips using a bandsaw and glued them in place at a slight angle as per the prototype, this was backed with a plywood support at the rear. Painting with water colours finished the job. Having done some

12 exhibitions with the layout, the paint is showing signs of flaking off so I would suggest you try a different method of painting as it requires regular touching up.

To construct the river, the ply base was cut to the river's shape and then re-fitted about an inch below the baseboard level. This was lined with 'Modroc plaster bandage type material. When this had dried I painted the river bed with acrylic paint. Numerous coats of varnish were applied and the rocks in the river are pieces of concrete that I smashed with a hammer to gain the various sizes and grades. These were dropped into the wet varnish.

The backscenes were hand painted in oils by railway artist Alan Maynard.

Buildings and structures

Buildings on the layout are, of course, all scratch-built using photos from various Woodhead route books as a reference. The station building and signal box are constructed with Peco stone walling sections. The building next to the tunnel mouth is made from Slater's 'Plastikard'. This building still exists and is a pumphouse for the cable ducting cooling water system. There are three tunnel mouths on the layout. The double-track tunnel that the trains on the layout use is adapted from the SD Mouldings product. The two single-track tunnel mouths hidden behind the pumphouse and which now carry National Grid cables are scratch-built. I started with a card former which I covered with a thin layer of Polyfilla. After it had dried I smoothed it down with glasspaper and then scribed the stone effect into the Polyfilla using a mini-drill with a pointed grinding tool. It was finished with Humbrol grey paint. The pointing on the section of wall between the two old tunnels may appear a little crude, but this is true to the prototype as this section was rebuilt when the castellations were removed prior to building the pumphouse.

The most dominating structure on the layout is the large electricity pylon (or 'Tower' to give it its correct name). This is built entirely from brass 'L'-section of three different sizes. After many, many hours of soldering and clearing out the stock of several model shops and traders the structure was spray painted light grey and fitted into position. I estimate the cost of the tower was between £70 and £80 plus a couple of burnt finger tips! The

76 025 and 76 022 burst out of Woodhead tunnel and over the River Etherow with a coal train for Fiddlers Ferry power station.

remaining scenic feature is the stone walling that winds its way up from rail level to the road above and provided a boundary wall for the cottages that used to stand by the roadside and look down on the station. With the layout's first show rapidly approaching I needed a quick solution. During a visit to a model shop I spotted a roll of ballast sheet made by Javis. This is basically a roll of thin card with granite chippings stuck to it. I cut the roll into strips and

folded it over on itself applying glue at the same time. Cutting a groove in the polystyrene that forms the hillside I slotted the walling in place and glued it down with PVA. When the glue had dried the walls were painted with varying shades of Humbrol grey and brown paint, thinned down so as not to obliterate the stone effect of the granite chippings. I think the result is very convincing and it is certainly quick to do.

Catenary

The overhead catenary on the layout is another first for me. The wiring system on the Woodhead route consists of a catenary wire, an auxiliary catenary wire and a contact wire. All three wires had to be represented and not knowing of any commercially available product suitable it has all been scratch-built using brass wire at 0.3mm diameter. I have found that when modelling catenary in N gauge you have to make a compromise between having the wire a reasonable thickness and allowing the pantograph to rub along the wires without pushing it out of the way, or having a very thin wire and the pantograph not touching at all. I decided to have the contact wire about 1mm above the fully extended pantograph but as the loco approaches the tunnel I was able to get enough tension on the wires to enable the pantograph to depress slightly without deflecting the wire too much. The wiring support gantries are also made of brass. The box section gantries nearest the tunnel are an N Brass Locomotives product supported on scratch-built brass section legs.

Locomotives

The electric locos that traversed the route were unique to this particular line. They first entered regular service in 1952 and were known as EM1s. The EM2s entered service in 1954 and were primarily for passenger

Steel empties returning to Sheffield with 76 053 in charge.

Rail enthusiasts look on as another coal train heads for Manchester.

work. Only seven of these were built compared to 58 of the EM1s. The prototype EM1 was trialled in Holland from 1947-1952 and was nicknamed 'Tommy' by the Dutch railwaymen, a name it officially took on its return to this country. Under the TOPS classification system the EM1s were designated Class 76 and the EM2s Class 77, although the EM2s were withdrawn in 1968 before receiving the 77 TOPS numbering. All the EM2s were sold to the Netherlands railway where they worked on until 1986.

The model form of the locos are all modified from one-piece resin body kits made by Cenpro. To the best of my knowledge they stopped producing them around 1999. I made a phone call to Cenpro in December 2000 and was lucky to get, what I think, were the last eight kits they had left. They were stored in the back of a cupboard and almost forgotten about. In their original form the EM1 bodies are about 10mm too long. They were designed to fit on a Graham Farish Class 20 chassis but with Class 31 bogies attached. The centre wheel of each bogie is removed, as the EM1s were a Bo-Bo wheel arrangement. I decided that the bodies had to be shortened as the extra 10mm was

A Harwich Parkeston Quay to Manchester 'Boat Train' hauled by an English Electric Type 3 races through Woodhead station.

'Electric Blue' E26050 *Stentor* with a Sheffield-Manchester service enters Woodhead station. Road traffic trundles by on the A628 Woodhead Pass above.

not a compromise I was prepared to accept. The body sides of the EM1 are in five sections with a window in the middle of each section on one side. To reduce the length of the body and keep the window central the only way I could think of was to cut out each section of the bodyside and reduce each piece by 1mm each side. This would keep the window central and when glued back together would reduce the overall length by the required 10mm. The roof sections were slightly easier and just required cutting into three pieces

Just like the real thing! Compare this dull day image of a Class 76 leaving the tunnel with the model picture above. The old twin-bores are long bricked-up, visible just above the loco. Tony Wright presents some further prototype images of the Woodhead route in the following pages.

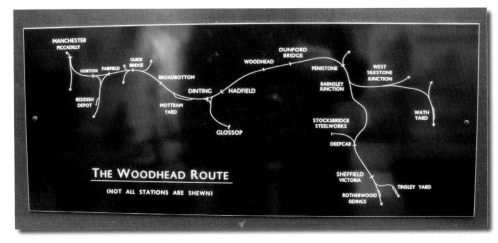

This route map is attached to the end of the layout for people at exhibitions who don't know where Woodhead is.

A view here from above the tunnel mouth looking down the Longdendale Valley.

wheels despite constant cleaning and there were too many derailments, as I had no time to test run the stock before the show so the service was a bit erratic. I was also operating the layout alone so that did not help either, as when I was fettling the layout it meant trains were not running which is never a good thing at an exhibition. I was paying the price for not giving myself enough construction time. After three shows the trackwork seemed to develop a 'polished' effect and wheel cleaning and track cleaning is now only occasionally necessary.

Woodhead was always meant to be a 'quickie' layout to run my loco fleet on. I will be building an extension to the layout in 2008 to give the scale length trains a more realistic setting to run in. I expect the layout will finish up about 14' 0" in length.

It is also nice to talk to people at exhibitions who have travelled or worked on the line. I'm happy to say I have brought back fond memories of this much-loved railway, and let's hope one of the schemes to re-open the line will come to fruition one day.

■ *See Woodhead at the Keighley model railway show, March 15/16, 2008.*

into the central bodyside window to make it look like two windows, as per the real thing. Brass wire is used for the handrails and the cables that run along the roof. Buffers, airhorns and dummy front couplings are from BH Enterprises. The pantographs are from Sommerfelt and are actually on the small side as the EM1 pantographs had a very high reach. I was not prepared to scratch-build these, I am not that insane (or perhaps not that clever). The chassis I used for the locos are the Minitrix Class 27. Only minor filing is required to fit the body over the chassis block and the bogie side frames need to be cut off to fit the EM1 side frames. These also need to be reduced in length to suit the body. The Class 27s are quite readily available on the second hand market for around £30 and although very old they are a good, sturdy design with good pulling abilities.

The EM2 body is constructed in a similar way to the EM1. Using two EM1 bodies and cutting out the panels again. The EM2 is longer than the EM1 so the body was lengthened instead of shortened. The chassis I have used for this Co-Co wheel arrangement loco is a Lifelike PA donated from an American loco.

and reducing to match the new body length. Now if I were reading this I would be questioning the sanity of someone who buys a one-piece body moulding and then proceeds to cut it into 15 separate pieces only to glue them all back together again after removing small amounts from each piece! Well, I can't disagree with you really, but it does make the locos look a lot better. Further modifications to the now correct length body include filing the cab roof down to give a lower profile, filing out the front windows to make them slightly larger and inserting a piece of 'Micro strip'

And finally
Why model the Woodhead Route in the first place? Well, I do like to model something unusual (the layout I am currently also exhibiting, Somewhere in England, is set during World War Two) and the Woodhead Line is unique in its motive power and as it should never have been closed in the first place, I like to think I am keeping it alive in my own small way.

I first showed the layout at the Retford exhibition organised by the Bassetlaw (North Notts.) Railway Society in November 2003. I did have problems with dirty track and

Woodhead in N - current stock list

EM1 (later Class 76)

26020	Lined black. Pulled inaugural service through Woodhead tunnel. Preserved at NRM, York.
E26000	Lined green. Model of prototype *Tommy*. Differences to production EM1s include rounded cab front corners, smaller front windows, different side window/vent arrangement and roof ventilators. No cab quarter light window and larger cab doors.
E26050	'Electric' blue, named *Stentor*.
76 053	BR corporate blue, named *Perseus*.
76 022 76 025	Coupled together for MGR trains, 76 022 being famous in Woodhead circles as it carried the old BR totem until withdrawal when the line closed in 1981.
E26031	Lined green but with full yellow ends.

EM2 (later Class 77)

27003	Light 'Electric Blue' named *Diana*.

Class 506

EMU	Early DMU green, Bill Bedford brass sides, 'Plastikard' ends and various coach parts for the rest. Runs on a Green Max chassis.

Easter, 1981 and a light-engine Class 76 heads past Huddersfield Junction box and is about to pass through Penistone station heading westwards. Just look at the extension on those pantographs. The route behind the loco and that heading towards the camera still survive I believe, though in a greatly rationalised state.

Wandering around Woodhead

Tony Wright presents a selection of shots taken during the final years of this 'modern' trans-Pennine route.

I suppose it was inevitable that I should have an affinity with the ex-MS&LR/GC/LNER/BR ER route across the Pennines. It was, after all, the first main line I travelled on, though I have no recollection of the journey. You see, I was a mere babe-in-arms at the time, taken over to my grandparents' home near Sheffield during the cruel winter of 1947 when my parents, in Chester, were running out of coal. My grandfather, being a miner at Dinnington, had plenty, so the infant Wright survived frostbite and returned home as the temperature increased.

Up to 1953, when my father bought a car, several more steam-hauled journeys were made through the old twin bores (my earliest memory is of a bright green B1 fairly storming up to the summit, with me in the front vestibule). We'd travel from Chester Northgate *via* the CLC to Manchester Central, walk thence to London Road and catch the train to Sheffield Vic' where we changed trains for the service to Kiveton Park and then go by bus to Anston. What an interesting railway journey? Beginning D11-hauled (or even a D10?); the middle bit by B1/A3/V2 and finishing D11-hauled again. It was many years later that I travelled the route once more, but by then it was diesel/electric/diesel.

Down the years, though, through the mid/late-'50s/early-'60s, the Pennine route was observed many, many times, but this time from the road. My father always used the Woodhead pass between Manchester and Sheffield, never the 'Snake, so we followed the route of the line from the other side of the valley. With luck, where the road and railway came closer, numbers of the EM1s and EM2s could be noted, especially in their black days when the numbers were large. Green livery, and the application of the diesel/electric numeral-style rendered detection impossible - no matter, for most had been seen by then. Many of the Woodhead electrics were 'copped' at Guide Bridge, during days' out spotting in Manchester. Also, a pair of EM1s was almost invariably parked at the end of the electrified section at Woodhouse, just east of Sheffield, where the A57 (we'd picked it up again by then) dropped down from the tram stop to pass under the line to Leicester/Lincoln, so electric 'cops' could be achieved there.

I must admit I paid scant attention to Sheffield Vic' itself. As mentioned, the electric-hauled expresses had been seen elsewhere and the ex-GC service to Marylebone was too infrequent to excite the number collectors of the day, especially when the ECML was so near. After all, a day out from Kiveton Park was much more exciting if you went east!

So, it was only during the final rites of the 1500V DC cross-Pennine system's life that I gave it the attention I should have done much earlier. I only made two photographic 'safaris', both at Easter, in 1979 and 1981 respectively. By then, of course, the bigger EM2s had gone across the channel and it was only the EM1s (Class 76s) that I could photograph, working exclusively on freight. Both

Judging by the rusty rails, the track on the Worsborough incline has seen little recent use in this Eater, 1979 shot, taken at Kendal Green crossing. Evidence of the line's pre-1923 ownership has been painted out and the sign is probably in a collection by now. Note the semaphore - unusual on overhead electrification systems, but worthy of modelling.

In typical Pennine weather, a light-engine Class 76 heads towards the tunnel in 1981. This loco is one of the few left not fitted for multiple working - many of the trains over the route were double-headed by this time. With typical lack of forethought, I took no notes of the loco numbers - the total opposite to what I used to do!

Two more 76s pause at Penistone, two years before the picture above, when the weather was a little kinder. I couldn't tell whether the station's running-in board was ER blue or MR maroon (visible above the wall), such was its state of weathering. Despite this side having been closed for several years, the platforms were still in excellent order.

A pair of Class 76s approaches Penistone during the Easter, '81 visit heading a delightfully mixed train. A lone semaphore signal is 'on' in the background, though colour lights predominate. None of the semaphore signals in the area had safety mesh around them in those pre-Health & Safety days!

days started at Torside, thence to Woodhead itself, across the 'spine' to Dunford Bridge and then down the valley to Penistone., Thurgoland and Sheffield. The Worsborough Incline, Wath and Tinsley were also visited, but nowhere near enough pictures were taken - the story of my life!

So, please enjoy my brief personal glimpse of one of BR's most 'modern' lines, right at the end of its existence. I hope these shots complement Garry Atkinsons beautiful model railway, for he's captured Woodhead absolutely. Though I'm sure it's still possible to travel by train from Manchester (now Piccadilly) to Guide Bridge, it won't be hauled by a Goddess (EM2s were female in gender - the named EM1s were male), and it certainly won't carry on to pass through the newest tunnel on the system and on to the steel city. Absurd isn't it? Can you believe that when the new Woodhead tunnel was bored in the early '50s, in less than 30 years it would be abandoned? The designers, engineers and labourers must be whirling in their graves!

Not only have I managed to photograph the prototype, it's also been my pleasure to take pictures of models depicting the Manchester-Sheffield electrified system. Here we have a scene on Steve and Christopher Saxby's delightful OO gauge Tinsley South, a father and son creation, popular on the exhibition circuit. The layout featured in full in the Spring, 2005 issue of *Modern Railway Modelling.*

ABOVE: Two Class 76s head towards Sheffield in the fair weather of Easter, 1981. They're crossing over the line to Huddersfield as it leaves the 'main line' just east of Penistone station. Note the two different sides of these locos.

BELOW: More rain at Woodhead as a single Class 76 is about to plunge into the new bore. It's observed by one of my colleagues on days out like these, the late Pete Lander. More into military vehicle preservation than railways, though a fabulous companion and frequent driver on expeditions in his souped-up Escorts. I miss his humour greatly.

ABOVE: Torside was our starting point for the two expeditions to Woodhead. If the signalman's Cortina survives after more than a quarter of a century then it'll definitely be a classic today. Block coal trains such as this were the life-blood of the Woodhead route at the end. Even with fewer of them, complete closure must rank as an act of total folly.

BELOW: At one end of Wath yard, this line-up of five 76s was observed during 1979. The weather has deteriorated a bit from that earlier, when the shots at Penistone were taken. No matter, for these locos weren't going anywhere, at any speed. Which they are, I haven't a clue, since none of us on the day took notes.

Cementing a new relationship

Plastic kit guru **Steve Knight** takes a sharp knife and teases
apart the complex history of Airfix plastic kits.
Photography as credited.

It is hard to make money from running a plastic kit business it would seem. Since the very first injection moulded kits were introduced into the UK in 1936, many companies have come and gone. On paper the business model does not look attractive - invest heavily in expensive steel tools, with strong marketing and promotion, to sell a low-cost product with unattractive margins, to a public that at best is nit-picking and can even be downright hostile. If you can sell 8-10,000 of each model you will recoup your tooling costs.

Airfix, Kitmaster, Revell GB, Merit, Kleeware, Comet, Lindbergh, Faller, Lincoln, Aurora, KielKraft, Gowland, and FROG have all come and, in most cases, gone again over the past 50 years. Some have changed ownership, some have merged with competitors whilst others have simply disappeared; all of them tried to develop their own range of injection-moulded plastic kits. So it seems slightly ironic that Hornby Hobbies, one-time owner of Tri-ang Model Land and FROG kits should now be the proprietor of perhaps the most famous kit line of all – Airfix Products. Both companies had dabbled in each other's markets with Airfix introducing model racing cars as early as 1961 and ready-to-run model railways in 1977. These competed directly with Hornby Hobbies' mighty Scalextric and Hornby Railways brands, whilst Airfix kits took on Hornby's FROG construction kits up to 1976.

Don't try this at home kids

The history of the two organizations is inextricably interwoven, as tools were bartered, sold, swapped, exchanged and even lost between the two protagonists. To try to unravel the story, let's go back to the early 1950s.

Airfix Products was founded by Hungarian refugee, Nicolas Kove, to make cheap plastic combs by the revolutionary new method of plastic injection moulding. He chose the

Later colourful header cards from the Airfix 'Trackside Accessories' range.
The Water Tower kit cost 3/- (15p), the others 2/- (10p) each! John Emerson Collection

name 'Airfix' as he believed successful companies should have names that put them at the beginning of trade directories. By 1948, Airfix was the country's largest producer of combs

and was approached by Harry Ferguson, the tractor manufacturer, to see if Airfix could produce a cheap plastic model of one of his tractors for use by Ferguson salesmen. The

LEFT: The very first Airfix kit of them all - the 'Fergy' tractor. ABOVE: The Shaw Savill MV Southern Cross from 1955. Box images Steve Knight, models courtesy Matt Irvine

limitations of the early low pressure and rather small injection moulding machines, most of which were hand-operated, meant that the Ferguson tractor had to be moulded as a series of smaller parts which were then assembled by a team of skilled workers into finished models. Ferguson pronounced himself very pleased with the model tractors and allowed Airfix to market them as a new toy under their own brand name 'Airfix – Products in Plastics'.

Soon it became obvious that more tractors could be sold if the price were lower, and the best way to achieve this was not to assemble them, but to supply them as a kit of parts with a set of assembly instructions. Samples were made up in presentation boxes and approved by the Airfix board. However, when the boxed samples were shown to buyers at High Street retailer Woolworths, they were

thought to be too expensive and a suggestion was made that the kit be supplied in a simple polyethylene bag with a printed paper 'Header Card' which would double as an instruction sheet. Thus was born the very first bagged Airfix kit. It was an instant success and Woolworths buyers began to ask for different subjects to be modelled in the same way. Tooling began for a small sailing ship, the *Santa Maria*, and a model of the 4.5 Litre Bentley in 1:32 scale. However, before these could be issued, another special commission was received, this time from the Shaw Savill shipping line. To promote their two new luxury cruise ships, the *Northern Star* and the *Southern Cross*, they wanted a plastic scale model to be available in the on-board shop. Airfix rose to the occasion with a respectable, if somewhat simplistic, 1:600 scale model of the liner *Southern Cross*, issued in 1955.

The range of poly-bagged kits now

included eight galleons, four cars and numerous aircraft, the earliest of which was the Spitfire (coded BT-K), an Me109G, Gloster 'Gladiator' and Westland 'Lysander'. In 1956 a rather good model of the Westland S55 in full BEA markings joined the range, the first of many helicopters. That year also saw the introduction of an entirely new series of Trackside Accessories 'for use with OO/HO scale model railways', although in fact they were all 4mm:1' scale. The first six kits featured a Detached House, Country Inn, Thatched Cottage, Service Station, Bungalow and a Signal Box. The latter was an accurate external model of the Midland Railway box controlling Oakham Level Crossing in Rutland. Although there was no interior the Signal Box was heralded by the model railway press of the time as a revolution in structure modelling. Several kits were re-packaged for the US and Canadian markets, the Booking Hall becoming 'Railroad Station', the Shop and Flat became 'Store and Apartment', Signal Box became 'Signal Tower', whilst Telegraph Poles became 'Telephone Poles'. The Trackside series eventually ran to more than 20 different models and remained in production with Airfix until their demise in 1980. From 1982, the range became part of the Dapol stable and is still in production today, some 50 years later!

Meanwhile, Airfix diversified into more and more subjects. In the late 1950s, Armoured Fighting Vehicles joined the kit line and polythene ready-made versions of the same joined the Toy Division (always kept separate by Airfix managers). 1960 saw the famous 1:12 scale figures introduced such as Napoleon, Joan of Arc and Henry VIII. Later still came life-size birds, a range of dinosaurs and science fiction

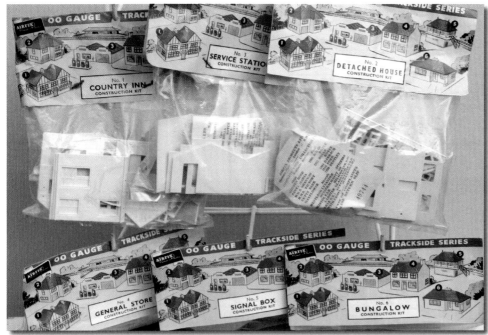

Original packaging for the OO gauge 'Trackside Series' models from 1956. Steve Knight

Another Airfix favourite - the Vickers-Armstrong Wellington or 'Wimpey' as it was affectionately known. Steve Knight

The first aircraft in the Airfix range was the Supermarine Spitfire. Steve Knight

subjects. By 1980 there were over 800 tools in the factory although not all of them were in use at once, as subjects came and went from the brightly-illustrated annual catalogues. Indeed some models such as the excellent Scammel Scarab, introduced to the Trackside Series in 1960, exited the catalogue by 1963 never to return, whilst stablemates such as the Mineral Wagon and Brake Van remained in near-continuous production from 1959-1980. The model trains section was boosted enormously by the acquisition during 1963 of the Rosebud Kitmaster range of locomotives and coaches. Eventually nine locomotives from the original 34 issued by Kitmaster entered the Airfix range. The ex-Kitmaster tooling also gave Airfix their first motorcycle kit, the Ariel Arrow Super Sports in 1:16, forerunner of an entire series in this scale.

Modellers licence

Airfix began to produce licenced products in the 1960s. The earliest was the Fireball XL5 model for Lyons Maid in 1963, although this was only a promotion and you could not buy the kit in the shops. It was followed by another Lyons Maid kit for Stingray in 1964. The 1965 introduction of the Angel Interceptor, Monkeemobile, James Bond and Odd Job figures and Bond's Aston Martin DB6 showed that Airfix could successfully licence and market film and TV related product. In today's TV obsessed world licenced products will be a key part of Airfix' sales strategy with subjects such as Wallace & Grommett already proving popular.

With interests in plastic shoes, storage containers and children's toys, Airfix was a diverse group. When Meccano and Dinky Toys were purchased from the Receiver of Dunbee Combex Marx (owner of Tri-ang Hornby Railways) in the early 1970s, the group was at its most diverse.

It was also financially at its most stretched. The 1977 introduction of an entirely new ready-to-run model train system, Airfix Model Railways (Later 'GMR'), was a severe financial burden on the company, with enormous tooling and launch marketing costs. The choice of a Class 31 diesel as the launch locomotive was unfortunate. The model was little better than that already marketed by Hornby and the Mk.2 coaches, whilst well received, were limited in the liveries they could carry. In addition, equal numbers of each type of coach were ordered from

the Chinese factory, leading to massive overstocks which persisted long after the demise of Airfix Products Ltd. Indeed, when Palitoy pulled out of the European market in 1982, pallet loads of Mk.2 brake coaches, which they had inherited together with the Airfix Railways business, were literally bulldozed into a large pit outside the Coalville factory!

The financial pressure on Airfix led to its first collapse in 1981. Tooling for a ready-to-run 'Schools' class loco and a range of Bulleid coaches was in preparation at Haldane Place and a

Some of the popular kits from the FROG range, originally owned by Lines Brothers, but sold off to Russian interests. Steve Knight

very nice OO scale assembly kit of a London taxi and Leyland Titan bus had been drawn up. They were not to see the light of day. The assets of Airfix were then bought by Palitoy, owned by US conglomerate General Mills. Kit production was moved to the Heller factory at Trun in France, whilst model trains were consolidated at the Mainline plant in Coalville. Unfortunately, General Mills decided to abandon toy production in Europe in 1984, resulting in Airfix coming back onto the market. This time it was bought by the group which owned Humbrol and Heller, Bordon International. Kit production remained with Heller, but design management moved from Coalville in Leicestershire to Humbrol's HQ at Marfleet, Hull, the trade name Humbrol being an acronym for 'HUMBeR OiL company'.

It was very tempting for the new owners of Airfix to work through the tool store rather than try to develop new models and there was certainly a lack of good new tools until very recently. Only in the last ten years has Airfix been able to once again develop modern tooling to extend the range. A whole series of superb 1:48 scale models heralded the new era including a Blackburn Buccaneer and a de Haviland Mosquito. These were very well received and the future for Airfix as they passed their 50th Anniversary looked bright.

However, Bordon had financially split the group into separate operating companies. Whilst Airfix appeared healthy and was launching fast-selling new products such as

the ill-fated, but highly regarded, British Aircraft Corproration TSR-2 in 1:72 scale, Heller was moribund. As Heller were still producing the mouldings for Airfix, this caused a major headache when in July 2006, Heller suddenly called in the French Receiver. Production was immediately halted at Trun and try as they might, Airfix could not get hold of kits made from their own tools! Unfortunately, with no end in sight to this dispute, Airfix lost the confidence of their own bankers, who called in their overdraft. This forced the UK company into liquidation as well. Two new moulds, the 1:48 scale Nimrod and a 1:72 scale Lifeboat were in advanced stages of development, but not actually in the country or under Airfix control.

Hornby

This was the situation that Hornby Hobbies found towards the close of 2006, from which they have now successfully extricated the Humbrol and Airfix businesses. Hornby are well placed to run these as their Chief Executive, Frank Martin, is a former CEO of Humbrol. In addition, Hornby have always had an association with plastic kits ever since 1936. In that year, Lines Brothers, owner of Tri-ang, took an interest in a small company called IMA, International Model Aircraft. Earlier, they had developed a flying scale model aeroplane powered by a patented geared elastic band system with a novel winding handle. The name of this new product was 'Flies Right Off the Ground', or FROG for short.

The idea caught on rapidly in the

UK and overseas and every boy wanted a FROG for Christmas. Cheaper versions were produced as well as different models attempting to portray other prototypes. In 1936 FROG decided to introduce smaller, more accurate, but static scale model aircraft. They had been experimenting with a machine for making propellers for the flying models by injection moulding in cellulose acetate. It was suggested that this same, rather primitive, moulding machine could be used to produce the new smaller aircraft models. To distinguish them from the flying models these would be known as FROG Penguins (a non-flying bird). Production was halted by the war, but at that time there were roughly 20 designs in production ranging from a Percival Mew Gull to a large Short Singapore flying boat. Numbers were limited and the cost was still very high by later standards, but post-war improvements in production techniques and polymers meant that by 1950, FROG was a leading manufacturer of injection-moulded polystyrene kits.

Throughout the 1950s and 1960s FROG kits sold well, eventually counting some 200 subjects in the catalogue including the R100 Airship (pictured) airliners such as the Jersey Airlines Dart Herald and Quantas 707, together with the latest military planes such as the V Bombers represented here by the Handley Page Victor. The company was fully a part of Rovex Ltd and as such production moved to Margate in 1962. The parent company was Dunbee-Combex-Marx, a wide ranging but poorly managed combine with interests in several sectors of the toy market. When Dunbee Combex Marx was approached by a Russian trade delegation to discuss licensing its old tools, it was FROG kits which made the biggest impression on the men from Moscow. From 1972 until

The ill-fated BAC TSR-2 was also a subject of the Airfix range. Steve Knight

1976 more and more FROG tools were sent to Russia until eventually there were none left in the UK. The idea was that the Russians would pay for the tools by sending back completed mouldings that could be marketed as cheaper kits in the West. Unfortunately the appalling quality of the polystyrene in use, the over-pressure running of the tools and unfeasibly long delivery times from the inefficient Russian factories all conspired to produce a wholly unsaleable product. Thus ended major kit production at Margate. But not every plastic kit tool had gone to Russia.

Tri-ang

Tri-ang Railways had themselves developed a range of plastic assembly kits during 1960 called Real Estate. These were made by IMA at Merton for Tri-ang Railways and depicted a very nice range of buildings for OO and TT model railways (according to the catalogue). As the range grew and more buildings were added, production was transferred to Margate in 1964. This was the height of the range, which was re-launched as Tri-ang Model-Land and now ran to more than 20 different models. The self-coloured plastic kits were easy to assemble and combined

traditional dwellings such as thatched cottages and country inns with ultra-modern offices and shops. A church was included in the range and a fine model of an electricity pylon (based on one outside the Margate factory) was introduced. These two kits were to become the last items of Model-Land to stay in production, with both marketed by Hornby Hobbies up until the late 1990s.

In 1972 Hornby had licensed a series of trackside structures from Germany kit company Pola. These included an operating lifting bridge and a coaling stage – both to Continental scale and pattern. Several of the subjects chosen to join the Hornby range had previously been licenced to both Jouef and Playcraft Railways, so had

really done the rounds! The rest of the Tri-ang Model-Land tools were shipped to Hong Kong at some point in the complicated history of DCM and got separated from the bulk of the Hornby Railways business when it underwent a management buy-out.

The tools eventually returned to the UK only to find their way to Dapol Model Railways in Winsford, Cheshire (later at Llangollen in Clywd and now in Chirk), who had also purchased from Palitoy the Airfix Trackside kits, together with Mainline and Airfix GMR trains. Dapol put the former Model-Land tools into production as Dapol-Land (imaginative!) although they did re-name some of the kits. When in 1998 Dapol was approached to sell the Airfix GMR and Mainline tools to Hornby, the circle was completed. However, the plastic kit tools remain with Dapol to this day.

So today we have Airfix construction kits being made by Hornby, together with Airfix GMR trains, but not the Airfix trackside kits, which are controlled by Dapol along with the original Tri-ang Model-Land tools. And what of FROG? Some of their tools were sold off to Revell and Matchbox as the Russians did not want models of 'fascist aircraft' whilst others are with Eastern Express and still in production.

After such a long and convoluted history, one wonders what the future holds now for the famous Airfix brand? At least today Hornby Hobbies is flying high with good financial results, sound management and a broad distribution network. Airfix fits well into their portfolio and Hornby may be just the right company to give it the stability it needs to develop and launch the products that will once again make it the most famous kit manufacturer of them all!

Airfix also entered the ready-to-run model railway and slot car racing markets. Steve Knight

Two kits from Tri-ang's relaunched Model-Land range - forerunners of the Skaledale range? Steve Knight

LINESIDE LOOK REVISITED - 3: Some cutting remarks..!

Where tracks run below the ground level in urban locations, retaining walls are to be found. Expensive to construct (in materials and man-power) they can pre-date your layout by more than 100 years, but often show evidence of later additions – usually where new roads cross the formation. As always, a little observation of the prototype will pay dividends

More on cuttings – in rural areas where the price of land was not at a premium, the railway companies could avoid the great expense of constructing retaining walls and leave shallow sloped sides to cuttings. Retaining walls were only used where the danger of earth slip existed, for example on the approach to tunnels. Tunnels hold their own pitfalls for the unwary modeller - details such as ventilation shafts help create (and disperse!) atmosphere...

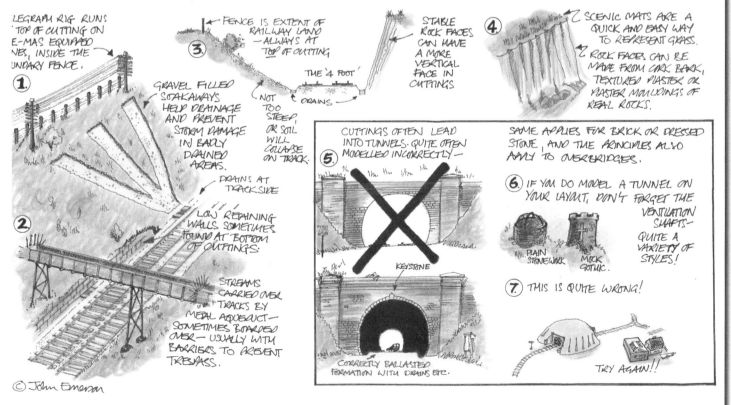

Shepherds Bush in 3mm scale

This scale has experienced something of a renaissance recently - **Colin Cook** introduces us to his compact Great Western terminus, built in this 'ideal' scale.

The layout of Shepherds Bush was inspired by a reference to the Ealing & Shepherds Bush branch in the book *Great Western Suburban Services* by Thomas B Peacock, published by the Oakwood Press. The proposal for the Ealing & Shepherds Bush branch was authorised by the Company's New Railways Act of 1905. The branch was to be just over four miles long from Ealing Broadway to a point 1.5 chains east of Providence Place,

Shepherds Bush. The site of the terminal station was to be located between the Uxbridge Road, Caxton Road, and Sterne Street.

The original purpose of the branch was the provision of a subsidiary terminus for suburban trains. Suburban trains at this time were handled at the Bishops Road station, adjacent to the Paddington main line terminus. A subway would have been provided linking the stations of the GWR and the Central London

Railway at Shepherds Bush.

The project was in abeyance for six years, the time for completion being extended by the Company's General Powers Act of 1909. Eventually the plan for the terminus was abandoned. Instead, the CLR was authorised by their Act of 1911 to extend their line to a Junction with the GWR at Wood Lane.

The fact that the branch would have been double-tracked, with a fairly busy service of suburban passenger

A rail-level view of Shepherds Bush. The Main Line & City stock, headed by a Class 61XX 2-6-2T, awaits departure time.

trains would make a very different GWR branch line terminus from the type usually modelled. On this basis, the layout was planned assuming that the GWR terminus had been built as originally intended. The track plan of Minories, designed by C J Freezer, was used as a basis for this layout, which was constructed to a scale of 3mm to the foot with a track gauge of 12 mm. The period of the layout is supposed to be from 1925 to 1935, to allow a wide range of stock to demonstrate the changes that took place on the GWR in this period.

Baseboards
These were constructed in 3'0" long units to enable them to be loaded across the width of my car. The two scenic boards have an overall width of 16". The fiddle yard board is slightly wider to accommodate the swing of the sector plate. The sector plate also extends from the end of the fiddle yard board. The general construction of all three boards follows general practice, and needs no special comment.

Trackwork
All trackwork was hand-built using code 60 bullhead rail. The rail was soldered to PCB sleepers, and the completed sections of track glued to an underlay of 1/16" cork. The cork underlay was glued to the baseboard prior to fixing the track.

At this stage a fault in the planning appeared. It had been intended that the exit to the fiddle yard should be double track. However, limiting the length of the baseboards, together with using pointwork having a 1:5 crossing angle (causing the points to be longer than anticipated) did not leave sufficient room for a double track exit to the fiddle yard. After a long ponder, it was decided to make do with a single track exit rather than lift the track, and start again.

Couplings
B&B couplings are fitted to the stock to be used on this layout, and electromagnets are used to activate the couplings. The magnets are fixed below the baseboards with the pole pieces between the rails and just above the surface of the track ballast.

Buildings
The station is in a brick-lined cutting, which is represented by the brick paper covering of the walls. The buildings, which line the backscene, are the Georgian house backs from the Bilteezi range in 3mm scale. The buildings screening the layout from the fiddle yard are also from the Bilteezi range.

To produce a station building bearing some resemblance to those of the GWR, a design was produced using elements of the building at Langley on the GWR main line. This was built with a plastic card carcass, and was clad with embossed brick styrene sheet. The platform canopies were constructed in a similar manner. The platforms are provided with station nameboards produced to order in etched brass by the Worsley Works. The lettering on these boards is of the same form as the GWR boards.

The signal box was built from a drawing of the one at Cwmgors, and is of a 'standard' signal box of the 1900–1923 period in brick. It was chosen because the staircase to the operating floor of the box was internal, thus avoiding the complication of building an outside staircase. Construction of the signal box followed the same method as that for the station.

The goods depot is located adjacent to the station building, and again the Bilteezi sheets came in useful. This section of the depot houses the staff

Rail-level view of the tunnel mouth. A Class 57XX 0-6-0T, on station pilot duties, pauses. Just in view is a gas tank wagon - this is used to supply gas to the older coaches for their lighting systems.

A view of Shepherds Bush station from the signal box to the station building. The goods depot is to the left of the station building. The stand-in clerestory stock headed by a Class 39XX 2-6-2T is awaiting the signal to depart.

A steam railmotor arriving at Shepherds Bush with a trailer car in tow. This unit operates between Westbourne Park and Shepherds Bush, via Greenford and West Ealing.

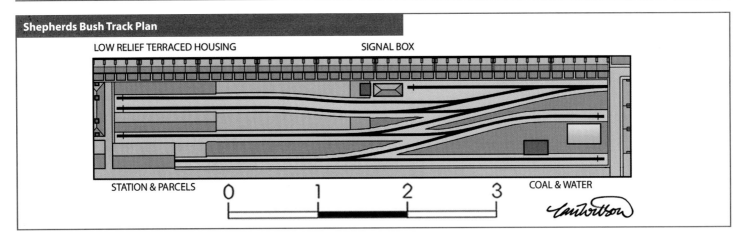

Shepherds Bush Track Plan

LOW RELIEF TERRACED HOUSING   SIGNAL BOX

STATION & PARCELS   0   1   2   3   COAL & WATER

offices, together with a hoist to lift the goods items up to road level. Behind this section of the Goods depot is the loading and unloading shed. The frame for the shed was originally the roof for a Tri-ang TT loco shed. Styrene sheet was

result that the aspect of the signal would be the same as that for the signals having semaphore arms.

At present the signals do not operate, because the method of operation has not been decided on. It is felt that this is will need a few

problems to be overcome. Various suggestions have been made, but for practical reasons it has been found that they do not provide solutions to the problem.

Locomotives
The passenger locomotives in use on the layout are representative of the classes used on the inner London suburban services. They comprise:
Class 2221 4-4-2T 'County' tank
Class 61xx 2-6-2T Prairie tank
Class 36xx 2-4-2T
Class 3901 2-6-2T
Class 2-4-0T large 'Metro'

The goods locomotives belong totally to the latter part of the period being represented and represent the new locomotives introduced for goods working. These are:
Class 57xx 0-6-0PT and the 97xx sub-class 0-6-0PT condensing engines
Class 8750 0-6-0PT

The locomotives were either built from scratch, using tinplate, or from kits. The kits were either etched-brass or white metal.

Coaches
Three sets of coaches are operated on the layout. In the period that the layout represents, suburban stock

A rail-level view of the platforms, showing the parcels train. This train comprises a parcels van sandwiched between two passenger full brakes. All vehicles in this set are mounted on bogies.

used for the ends and one wall, and finally corrugated styrene sheet was used to cover the roof, ends and wall to simulate corrugated asbestos.

At the opposite end of the layout to the goods shed is a loco servicing area. This is equipped with a water tank, two water cranes, and a coaling stage. The siding beside the signal box is used for stabling the station pilot.

Signals
The signals installed on the layout represent the GWR approach to colour light signalling. This system differed to the usual pattern in using a coloured glass screen to be lifted in front of the light source, with the

The station pilot awaits coaling at the stage.

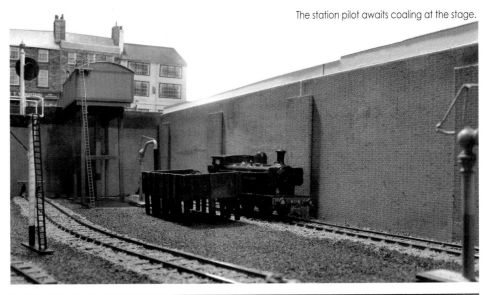

Above: A further view of the parcels train and railmotor. The locomotive is a large 'Metro' 2-4-0T
Below: A view looking towards the tunnel exit from the station. The locomotive service siding, with water tank and coaling stage, is to the right of the tunnel mouth.

was non-corridor compartment vehicles. The first set is a four-coach bow-ended set. This has a formation of brake third, composite, composite, brake third. The two composite coaches were scratch-built in tinplate. Because of the time it took to produce the sides, it was decided to build the two brake thirds from Worsley Works components.

The second set is a six-coach Main Line & City set, with the following formation - brake third, third, composite, composite, third, brake third. Unfortunately, this set is longer than any of the platforms and has to be run without one of the composite coaches. This rake of coaches was built using Worsley Works components

The final set is a stand-in for a five-coach clerestory set being built. The stand-in set comprises a rake of four 38' coaches in the formation of brake third, third, third, brake third. The two thirds in this set are clerestory coaches. All the vehicles in this set would have been downgraded from suburban work to operation in rural trains from about 1910/11. The etched-brass kits for these vehicles were produced by Blacksmith for the 3mm Society.

A fourth passenger unit on this layout is a steam railmotor with an autocoach as a trailer car. These items were built from etched-brass kits produced for the 3mm Society.

Goods stock

Because of the location of Shepherds Bush relative to Paddington, it is thought that the traffic involved would have been light. For this reason most of the goods traffic was to be in vans or sheeted wagons. Other railway vehicles carrying specialised loads would also appear. This traffic is considered to be trip workings from other goods depots in the London area, usually hauled by a Class 97xx condensing tank.

A parcels train also operates between Reading and Shepherds Bush.

Goods stock was produced mainly from the products of Parkside, Cambrian Models, and Finney & Smith, the last mentioned particularly for the earlier vans and wagons. Some Tri-ang stock has been used with a new chassis under the original body. Etched-brass kits have been used for the production of the parcels stock, but the names of the producers of these kits have been lost in the mists of time.

Operation

The passenger trains from Shepherds Bush are considered to be operating in the inner suburban area of the London district. The terminals would be Uxbridge, Slough, (or Slough Estate for workmen's trains), Windsor, and High Wycombe *via* Maidenhead.

The steam railmotor would operate on a circular route *via* North Acton, Greenford, West Ealing, Ealing Broadway to terminate at Westbourne Park, returning in the reverse order.

The sequence of trains is dictated by a series of flip-over cards, which specify the train and its movement.

The Three Millimetre Society

I started railway modelling in the early 1960s, with Tri-ang TT equipment. When I became aware of the Three Millimetre Society, I joined it in 1968/9, and I would say that it has had a most profound effect on my modelling.

With the incentive that I received from being a member of the Society, I was encouraged to try scratch and kit-building. Now the result is that I model in 3mm scale.

This I could not have done without the Society 'shop', with the various items it supplies. I also make use of the independent producers, who fill in around the Society product range.

Further Information

Membership Secretary 3mm Society, 9 Podington Meadows, Chickerell, WEYMOUTH, Dorset DT3 4NX
www. 3mmsociety.org.uk

In this shot, the steam railmotor and trailer are evident, and also the stand-in clerestory set. The 39xx Class 2-6-2T is being coupled to the clerestory set.

Workhorses of the BR regions

Eric Sawford presents a selection of his photographs of hard working classic freight locomotives. Photographs by courtesy of **The Transport Treasury**.

Among the many once familiar features of our rail system that have long since become part of history were the loose coupled freight trains conveying both general merchandise and mineral traffic. Preparation of these trains was all important and many goods yards even during the night echoed to the sounds of shunting locomotives marshalling trains with the distinctive noise of wagons buffering up.

Such was the volume of this traffic that all six regions of British Railways,

the 'Big Four' and pre-Grouping companies before them, required very considerable numbers of heavy goods locomotives. It is these during the 1950/60s that are the subject of this feature.

If I was asked to choose my favourite class from these everyday workhorses it would have to be the wonderful ex-LNWR 0-8-0s frequently referred to as 'Super Ds'. Those I was particularly familiar with were the Bletchley depot's engines, no doubt the time spent at the nearby

RAF station had much to do with this. These locomotives produced very unusual asthmatic sounds, this and their sharp exhaust made them easily identifiable - even if you could not see them.

Long and varied history

Among the stud of ex-LNW 0-8-0s at Bletchley was No.48898, a particularly interesting example. It was built in 1903 as a B Class four-cylinder compound 0-8-0, three years later it was converted to an F Class four

The climb over the bleak windswept Shap fells was a challenge to heavy goods trains, these requiring a banker from Tebay. Carlisle based 8F No.48612 battles its way to the summit in September 1963 with Fairburn 2-6-4T No.42110 assisting at the rear. Several tank locomotives were allocated to the small shed at Tebay for banking duties.

cylinder compound 2-8-0. It remained in this condition until September 1923 when it became a G1 0-8-0, its final change was in March 1942 when rebuilt as a G2A. It was also distinctive in being one of the few to run with a tender cab. Withdrawal was in 1962 having completed 59 years service in its various forms.

The Bletchley engines worked both up and down the West Coast Main Line, and one of their duties was the Leighton Buzzard sand trains. In addition they worked to Cambridge over the Bedford-Sandy line and in the opposite direction to Oxford. In the 1950s these very useful engines were to be found at a large number of depots. They were commonplace in the north west and were familiar in central Wales. In spite of more modern goods locomotives being widely available the last of these engines was not withdrawn until early

1964. Without doubt a very successful locomotive and one which justifiably deserved to be among those under the heading a 'classic design'.

Well proven
Another locomotive design that unquestionably also well deserves the 'classic' heading is the ex-Great Central 2-8-0, first introduced by J G Robinson in 1911, a true workhorse for both this railway and later the LNER and BR. In addition this was the design chosen for military purposes in the First World War with a large number constructed for the Government. Many of these were to see service overseas in the Second World War, some eventually finding themselves after the end of hostilities in such distant locations as Australia and China.

There was considerable variation to be found in the class which became 04 in LNER days. Although many continued throughout their working life very much in original form until withdrawn in the 1960s. From 1924 the LNER purchased a considerable number of the engines originally built for the Railway Operating Division, these had steam brake only and no water scoop.

The final change to some members of the class was in 1944 when a number of engines were rebuilt with 100A boilers (already well proven on the B1 4-6-0s) becoming 04/8, at the same time retaining their original cylinders. In that same year Edward Thompson also introduced a rebuild with the 100A boiler, Walschaerts valve gear and new cylinders, these engines were classified 01.

The 04s were widely used by the Eastern Region to handle coal traffic from the Midlands and Yorkshire coal fields, they were frequent visitors to New England and March. Only on a few occasions did they work south of Peterborough on the east coast main line. When they did it was usually on the Barford power station supplies which was normally worked by a New England WD 2-8-0.

In 1918 an experimental 2-8-0 was built by the Great Northern Railway at Doncaster and introduced by H

N Gresley, later to become Chief Mechanical Engineer of the LNER. It was to be a further three years before any more examples were built with ten being constructed by the North British Locomotive company and delivered in May 1921. Following the grouping construction started at Doncaster, the class being designated 02, in all a further 56 were built between 1923-43. The early engines were not fitted with side window cabs although a considerable number were later to receive them. In due course a number of the class were fitted with 100A Diagram boilers, these became Class 02/4. The prototype engine was withdrawn in May 1948 having been fitted with a side window cab in March 1940. It still carried its 1946 number 3921 and never received a BR one. Withdrawals commenced in 1960 with the last members of the class being condemned at the end of 1963.

The North East
With huge quantities of mineral traffic this area required a considerable amount of heavy goods engines to handle the coal, iron ore and limestone traffic. The Q5 0-8-0s introduced in 1901 did not last long into BR days. It was the Q6 class which made their debut in 1913 that provided the backbone of the motive power together with 0-6-0s. The Q6s were steam brake engines.

In total 120 Q6s were built between 1913-21, all surviving to be taken into British Railways stock. While there was little variation on the locomotives themselves, this was not the case with the tenders as five different types were in use. These very useful popular engines all survived into the 1960s, heavy inroads were made into the class in 1963/4 with a fair number surviving into the penultimate year of steam finishing on British Railways.

In spite of having a very successful heavy goods locomotive design in 1919 Vincent Raven introduced a three-cylinder locomotive, later in LNER days to become Class Q7. Why these engines were introduced at this time is somewhat shrouded in mystery as the Q6s were quite capable of handling trains of the day. The 15 Q7s were all built at Darlington in two batches, five appearing in 1919 and a further ten in 1924. At this time Darlington was engaged in reconditioning ex-ROD 2-8-0s (04) that had been purchased following the end of the First World War.

The work for which the class is best

depots. In 1938 Collett introduced a further series which had side window cabs and various detail alterations. Eventually the class totalled 167 locomotives. The first was withdrawn in 1958 and the last in 1965.

As with other railways the Great Western took advantage of the ex-ROD Robinson 2-8-0s offered for sale following the First World War, initially purchasing 20. Another 84 were hired over the period 1919-22. In 1925 all of the locomotives on hire were returned and a decision was made to purchase a further 80, some

Several of the LNWR 0-8-0s had a long and varied history. No.48898, seen at Bletchley on April 29, 1956, was one of them being rebuilt on several occasions, even running as a 2-8-0 at one period. It was complete with tender cab, only fitted to a small number of the 'Super Ds' as they were commonly known. Several of these locomotives were at Bletchley in the 1950s.

remembered was on the Tyne Dock to Consett iron ore trains. In 1951 new large capacity bogie hopper wagons were introduced, these had bottom opening doors worked by compressed air. This required several of the Q7s to be fitted with twin Westinghouse air pumps. In 1952 several 01 Class 2-8-0s were allocated to Tyne Dock shed, they were also fitted with this equipment. In due course the Q7s lost their pumps which passed to BR Standard 9F 2-10-0s. In December 1962 the entire class of 15 engines was withdrawn.

On Western metals

The heavy goods locomotive of the Great Western Railway and later the BR Western Region was unquestionably the large 2800 Class 2-8-0s, a Churchward design of 1903 and to be found allocated to many

O4 Class No.63717 was built by R Stephenson & Company for the Railway Operating Division and completed there after the First World War ended. Purchased by the LNER, it entered traffic in 1924 and is seen nearing Peterborough with a typical coal train on September 24 1955, shortly after receiving a general overhaul. In March 1958 it was rebuilt as an O4/8, remaining in service until April 1965.

Judging by the pile of scrap gas fittings work to replace them with electric lighting had been taking place at Consett shed on July 7, 1956. Q6 No.63377 was typical of many classmates in the area and completed almost 59 years service. These engines had steam brake only.

of which had previously been on hire. After overhaul these became simply known as the ROD class. The first was withdrawn in 1927, 45 passing into British Railways ownership in 1948. They were mostly allocated to South Wales depots often working in the Midlands. The last of the class was withdrawn in 1958. Despite the GW fittings, chimney, top feed, dome, safety valve cover and cabside number plates the unmistakeable outline of a Robinson 2-8-0 remained.

In 1919 Churchward introduced a mixed traffic 2-8-0 design principally for fast goods workings. Only nine were built over the period 1919-23, all passed over to BR ownership. The 47XX 2-8-0s were to a degree one of the less well known GW classes, many of their duties being during the

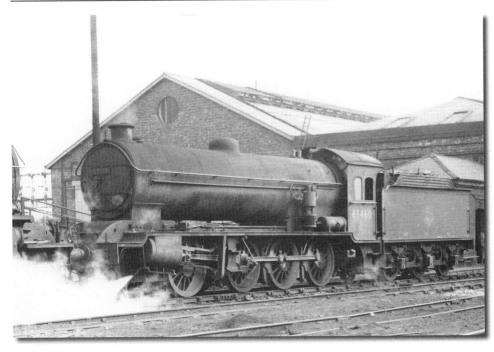

The Tyne Dock-Consett iron ore trains required locomotives fitted with Westinghouse air pumps to operate the doors of the hopper wagons. Q7 No.63460 awaits is next duty at Tyne Dock on July 7, 1956. The Westinghouse equipment was later removed from the Q7s and fitted on BR Standard 9F 2-10-0s. All fifteen Q7s were withdrawn in 1962.

Massive proportions

In 1921 Urie introduced two classes of large tank locomotives. The first to appear from Eastleigh works was the G16 4-8-0Ts, these were huge engines intended for hump shunting at Feltham marshalling yards. Four were built, apart from their shunting duties they were also used on short distance goods workings in the London area.

Later that same year the first of the H16 Class 4-6-2Ts emerged from Eastleigh. Only five were built, in this case principally for

night. In the '50s several could usually be seen on Old Oak Common shed. During the summer they were often used on excursions and specials, their 5'8" driving wheels giving them a fair turn of speed.

The Southern Region was more concerned with general freight traffic as it did not have heavy industry or much in the way of mineral traffic originating in the region. Coal was of course still widely used in the '50s for domestic purposes, steam locomotives and other uses. On the South Western and Central sections goods traffic was usually in the hands of the S15 Class 4-6-0s.

Five Class O1 2-8-0s were also allocated to Tyne Dock shed to work the Consett iron ore trains. No.63856 is at Tyne Dock with a train of hoppers on July 7, 1956. Note the very impressive array of signals and the signal box.

interchange workings to Willesden and Brent, although they often were seen in other areas. Another class of large tank locomotives handled interchange traffic, this time to the LNER and later Eastern Region. This was the W Class 2-6-4Ts introduced by Maunsell in 1931, a development of the N1 Class 2-6-0s. Hither Green shed had a number of these engines in its allocation.

The Southern Railway was not the only one to use large tank locomotives although the Great Western Railway had a sizeable stud of 2-8-0 heavy

Western Region 28xx Class No.3841 stands outside St Phillips Marsh shed on August 31, 1955. This engine was one of the later batch introduced in 1938 with side window cab and other detail alterations, and had not long previously received a general overhaul judging from its condition.

In the mid-fifties seven of these ROD 2-8-0s were allocated to Pontypool Road depot, including No.3012 seen at Oxford on October 31, 1954. The engine had failed - note the 'not to be moved' signs on both sides of the buffer beam. Despite receiving Great Western fittings, the unmistakable outline of a Robinson 2-8-0 is easily recognisable.

Class, these having extended bunkers and trailing wheels. In total 54 were rebuilt and classified the 7200 Class. Here again the majority were at South Wales depots, and were often visitors to the Midlands.

LMS days

In 1925 Fowler became Chief Mechanical Engineer of the LMS, a position he held until 1931. In 1929 he introduced an 0-8-0 design developed from the well known LNWR Class G2 0-8-0s. During the 1950s the remaining engines were to be found in the north west.

Working in conjunction with Beyer-Peacock, Fowler introduced a Beyer-Garratt 2-6-6-2 in 1927, three were completed that year. It was to be 1930 before production started in full, with the remainder of the class

goods locomotives. As far back as 1910 G J Churchwood introduced a 2-8-0T design principally for working heavy mineral trains, these were known as the 4200 Class. In 1923 a development made its debut with enlarged cylinders and other detail differences, these became the 5205 Class, in BR days they received the classification 8F. Weighing just over 80 tons they were sizeable powerful locomotives. The vast majority of these 2-8-0Ts were allocated to South Wales sheds. In 1934 Collett commenced rebuilding of the 4200

The nine examples of the powerful 47xx Class were introduced by the Great Western Railway in 1919 to a Churchward design. Built for fast goods workings they were sometimes used for excursion and special trains. No.4701 was photographed at Banbury shed on March 27, 1955.

of 33 delivered during the year. I can well recall seeing these massive engines hauling heavy coal trains on the Midland main line. Withdrawals commenced in 1955, the majority were condemned in 1956/7 leaving just one to make it into 1958, their duties largely taken over by BR Standard 9F 2-10-0s.

The year 1935 was to see one of the finest heavy goods locomotive designs introduced, Stanier's famous 8F 2-8-0 or 'Eight Freights' as they

Goods traffic on the Southern Region, South Western and Central sections was mostly in the hands of S15 Class 4-6-0s. No.30499 at Feltham on July 12, 1954, was one of a batch built by the LSWR being completed at Eastleigh in May 1920. These engines were a development of the 'King Arthurs'. No.30499 received a U1 chimney in 1941. It was the last of the first batch built to be withdrawn, being condemned in January 1964.

The massive G16 4-8-0Ts were designed for hump shunting at Feltham marshalling yards. They were also used on short distance goods workings locally. No.30495 is seen at Feltham depot on July 12, 1954. Classified 7F, these engines had a tractive effort of 33,990lb.

engines were to become well known in several Middle Eastern countries and in Turkey.

One of the best places to see an 8F in full cry was on the climb over Shap. I can recall standing at the lineside in the quiet solitude of the Fells and hearing the distant whistles of an 8F and its banker leaving Tebay for the long climb north. When the summit was reached the banker (a 2-6-4T) would drop back, cross over and run back to Tebay ready for the next freight requiring assistance. At several quieter periods it was not unknown for a number of goods trains to follow one another.

One locomotive design that received little attention from enthusiasts in the 1950/60s was the WD 2-8-0. With a huge number in service they were an everyday sight in most parts of Britain

were commonly known. These engines soon proved to be powerful and reliable and were well liked by enginemen. The design was chosen by the War Department for quantity production for World War 2 as had the G C Robinson 2-8-0 years previously for World War 1. Initially Crewe works was responsible for building 8Fs. Examples were later also constructed by Horwich, Swindon, Darlington, Doncaster, Eastleigh, Brighton and Ashford, also the North British Locomotive Company and Vulcan Foundry. These very useful

Feltham shed was a good place to visit in the 1950s being home to four G16 Class 4-8-0Ts and the five H16 4-6-2Ts. Both classes were designed by Urie for the LSWR in 1921. H16 No.30517 is about to be coaled at Feltham on July 12, 1954. The H16 Class weighed in at just over 96 tons.

excluding the Southern (although some had previously spent time there) with examples north of the border and in Wales. The Ministry of Supply 'Austerity' 2-8-0s were introduced in 1943 to a Riddles MoS design. Over 900 of these engines were sent to North-West Europe in 1944/45. After they were surplus to requirements many returned to England, others were to see further service on the Continent and even as far away as Hong Kong and Syria.

The Southern Railway's W Class 2-6-4Ts were introduced by Maunsell in 1931 and totalled 15 locomotives. Several were to be found at Hither Green where No.31923 was photographed on May 24, 1956. Among their duties were inter-regional transfer freights to and from the Eastern Region. The W Class was a development of the N Class 2-6-0 design.

5205 Class 2-8-0T No.5264 prepares to take water near St Phillips Marsh shed on August 31, 1955, on its way back to Newport via the Severn tunnel with a long train of coal empties. No.5264 was the last of the class to be built. These engines were a development of the 42xx design with enlarged cylinders and detail alterations.

outlived by the more numerous eight coupled locomotives by five years.

End of the line

Over the years a great many locomotive designs were produced to handle the increasing traffic. It was the Standard 9F 2-10-0 which was the last of a long line. The first of the class made its debut in 1954, these were without doubt one of the most successful BR designs, eventually totalling 251. Among these was the last steam locomotive constructed for British Railways, No.92220 *Evening Star*, this was built at Swindon Works complete with double copper capped chimney and painted in BR green fully lined livery. It left the works in March 1960 completing just five years service before it was withdrawn from Cardiff East Dock shed in March 1965. Fortunately it was

An excellent purchase

In 1946 the LNER purchased 200 of the surplus locomotives with British Railways taking 533 of the 2-8-0s in 1948 together with 25 of the 2-10-0 design. The WDs or 'Dub Dees' as they were commonly known proved to be invaluable and a very worthwhile addition. The last of the 2-8-0s was not withdrawn from service until 1967.

Only brief mention has been made of the 2-10-0s which in the 1950s were mostly to be found at work north of the border. The 25 purchased entered traffic in 1949/50. The 2-10-0s were

Fifty four members of the 42xx Class 2-8-0Ts were rebuilt with extended bunkers and trailing wheels, becoming known as the 5205 Class. No.7246 seen at Oxford on April 29, 1956, was a Severn Tunnel Junction engine. These massive tank engines had the power classification 8F.

scheduled from new for preservation as part of the National Collection.

Construction of the 9Fs was at Crewe and Swindon. When they first appeared it was immediately apparent that these were very different to existing heavy goods engines with their massive proportions, ten coupled driving wheels, smoke deflectors and 9F power rating.

It was not uncommon for new designs to experience some teething troubles, this was the case with the 9Fs,

The Beyer-Garratt 2-6-6-2Ts were still a familiar sight at Wellingborough shed up to the mid-'50s. No.47978 is ready to work north with a train of coal empties on February 5, 1956. These engines were introduced in 1927, eventually their duties were taken over by the increasing numbers of 9F 2-10-0s, one of which can be seen in the background.

During slack periods goods trains heading north could be given the main line at Huntingdon. WD 2-8-0 No.90730 gets to grips with the long 1 in 200 climb to Abbots Ripton at the head of a long train of coal empties on March 10, 1954. Note the TPO lineside apparatus on the Up line. Just one set existed here with the Down line having four to dispatch, the first also having a net to receive pouches.

built at Crewe Works with the latest type of Franco-Crosti boilers, the idea being to achieve worthwhile savings on coal consumption. These engines were allocated to Wellingborough and were easily recognisable by their very different appearance.

Within three years most were in store due to high maintenance requirements and corrosion, in addition having failed to produce the expected coal savings. Rebuilding commenced in 1959, still retaining the smaller boiler and firebox but with

notably the brakes. Among the first depots to be allocated these engines was New England where their duties included the heavy coal trains to Ferme Park London. It was arranged that braking trials would take place at two places en-route, the first location after the long descent of 1 in 200 to Huntingdon. The regulators of these locomotives also had a tendency to stick at slow speeds. The problems were soon resolved and the engines proved themselves to be capable of handling the heaviest trains.

Living in close proximity to the East Coast main line the Standard 9Fs became very familiar to me. Just how powerful they were was very evident if heading a long train of empties they were given the main line north from Huntingdon.

In 1955 ten members of the class were

The ten Franco-Crosti 9Fs (actually rated at 8F) were designed to achieve substantial savings on coal consumption, although this failed to materialise. Within a short period they were mostly in store due to high maintenance costs and corrosion problems, and all were eventually rebuilt. No.92026 was at Wellingborough on July 27, 1956.

normal draughting arrangements.

While never attracting the attention given to express locomotives heavy goods engines were certainly as important to the rail system. It is unfortunate that the 9Fs in particular had such short working lives as they were capable of giving a great many years service. Such is the passage of time that the diesels that replaced them are also part of our rail history. Indeed the movement of freight on our railways is also very different to what it was in steam days.

New England Standard 9F 2-10-0 No.92040 is seen with a train of 'Presflo' wagons on September 21, 1961. During the mid-late 1950s, New England had 25 members of the class on its allocation. The train is about to leave the Up slow north of Huntingdon. This had been put in between Abbots Ripton and Huntingdon, but was later taken out.

Springbank North signal box, showing to advantage the all-wood construction. In summer 1958, No.46409 was at 53C Springhead from May-September of that year. **Mike Lake**

Springbank North signal box, Hull & Barnsley Railway

Mick Nicholson recounts the history of this busy Hull signal box. Photographs from the author's collection unless otherwise stated.

When Springbank North signal box opened with the line on July 20, 1885, it controlled what was then the only three-way junction on the railway. As can be seen from the enclosed plan, and reading from top to bottom, the three lines concerned were: Main Lines to Locomotive Junction, Goods Lines to Springbank West Junction, and Goods Branch to Springbank South Junction. Although not shown on the plan, Springbank West and Springbank South Junctions, as their names suggest, formed the respective tips of a triangular junction, or as it was always referred to locally 'The Angle'. The Down Goods Independent was a later addition, and was not brought into use until 1904, when an existing siding or shunting neck at Springbank West became a through road. Originally the box had a frame of 26 levers, but this was increased by one lever when the Down Goods Independent was brought in to use. The box was situated on the Down side, approximately midway between No.2 signal and No.24 points on the present plan. As part of the Joint

Dock Agreement, the Hull & Barnsley Railway was granted running powers into the North Eastern Railway's Hull, Paragon station. Before these could be exercised, it was necessary to build about 800 yards of new railway, lay-in two double junctions, and provide two replacement signal boxes and associated signalling. The new railway would leave the H&B 342 yards east of the existing Springbank North junctions and join up with the NER's Scarborough line, a few yards north of Walton Street level crossing. Despite the fact that a good part of it would be carried out by the NER, all of the new works would have to be paid for by the H&B Railway. This was beyond their financial means and as a result the intentions were never achieved during the independent life of either company. The premature amalgamation of the two railways, on April 1, 1922, no doubt made the necessary funds available, but a further two years and three months were to elapse before the LNER actually implemented the scheme. More than 80 years on, it's

interesting to reflect on the contract price for the new signalling works, and the relevant LNER minute states: 'January 3, 1924, Westinghouse Brake and Saxby Signal Company contract of £3804-8-0 for signalling work to construct a new loop from the H&B section to the NER Hull to Scarbrough line'. In terms of real hardware, this amounted to two locking frames totalling 72 levers, plus two gate wheels, three bracket signals, four ordinary signals complete with 14 signal arms and several ground discs, plus all the ancillary equipment such as point rodding and cranks, etc. A quick calculation shows that at Springbank North and Walton Street at this date almost three miles of point rodding was required. On top of this can be added the cost of the new earthworks, Permanent Way and replacement signal boxes at both Springbank North and Walton Street.

With the new spur calling for an additional junction and signalling, the original 1885 signal box, owing to its size and location, was inadequate.

A good view of the 1957 plate and angle Up Starting bracket, taken from an RCTS excursion on October 10, 1964. The signalman stands in the 'four-foot' of the Up Main, ready to give driver the Block Conversion Ticket for the goods lines. **J Foreman**

No.34 Bridge, looking along Springbank West, from the Walton Street direction.

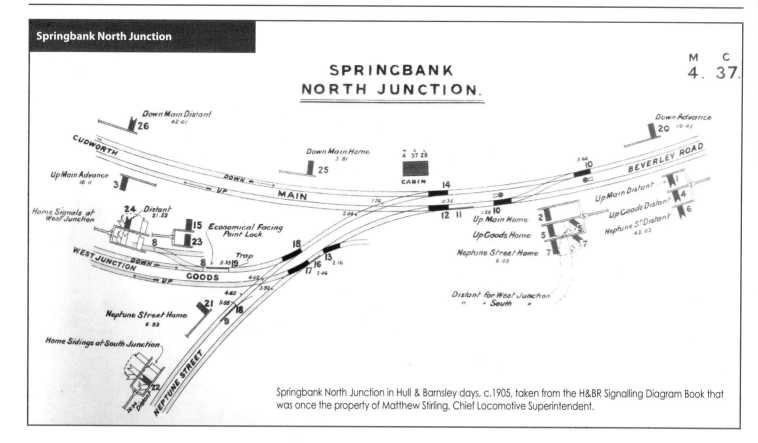

Springbank North Junction

SPRINGBANK
NORTH JUNCTION.

Springbank North Junction in Hull & Barnsley days, c.1905, taken from the H&BR Signalling Diagram Book that was once the property of Matthew Stirling, Chief Locomotive Superintendent.

A new box, situated approximately midway between the new and existing junctions was necessary. This was to the long established NER 'S4' design, and being on the edge of the embankment, it was, apart from the usual slate roof, constructed of timber throughout. The replacement box contained a locking frame of 45 levers and of these, on opening day, Sunday June 22, 1924, six were spare. Three weeks then elapsed before the new spur was brought in to regular use, on Monday July 14, when all HB Section passenger trains were diverted to Hull, Paragon. The new signals also followed standard NER practice, and as one would expect these were the usual slotted post lower quadrants. As an aside, it was 1927/8 before the LNER adopted upper quadrant signals as standard, even so, and for many years after, lower quadrant signals continued to be installed. This was especially so on secondary lines, where redundant but serviceable equipment, recovered from main line resignalling schemes, was cascaded down for further use.

My drawing is copied from the 1962 S&T department plan, which presumably was redrawn that year, owing to the commissioning of the then new Hessle Road power box. Obviously, during its 44 year existence, Springbank North saw more than a few changes and alterations, and these, where known, are set out in the following paragraphs:

■ Track circuit provided at No.39 Up Main Advance Starting signal, this work carried out by December 23, 1925.

■ Following the conversion of the goods lines to Permissive Block working, No.5 Down Goods Advance Starting signal, which was only 267 yards in advance of No.4 Down Goods Starting signal, ceased to serve any real purpose and was abolished. Although the exact date is unknown this work was almost certainly carried out during 1925. Prior to this date all lines at Springbank North apart from the Down Goods Independent were worked by the Absolute Block Regulations. Unusually the H&B was one of only a handful of railways north of the Thames to employ Sykes Lock and Block in lieu of the more usual needle instruments. Following the grouping, and no doubt owing to the strong ex-NER influence, the Sykes Lock & Block was considered non-standard and soon removed. Even so, and to be compatible with the existing boxes, the new Springbank North box did almost certainly have, for a short time, some Sykes instruments.

■ **Tuesday October 5, 1937**. Ella Street signal box closed at 10.00am, and replaced by a ground frame electrically released from Springbank North. Lever No.11 Ella Street GF Release brought in to use. Key for ground frame kept in signal box and

must be given to guard.

■ The installation of track circuits made it possible to combine the working of certain Trap Points or Facing Point Locks on to the same lever(s) and rearrange the interlocking accordingly. The exact date this was carried out is unknown, but either October 10, 1937 or June 29, 1941 seem likely. This assumption is based on contemporary operating notices which respectively state 'All Junction lines relaid' and 'Alterations to interlocking'. As no recorded changes were made to the outside equipment, the later date seems the most probable. This partial relocking caused the following levers to be taken out of use:
No.15 Facing Trap on Up Branch
No.16 Facing Trap on Down Independent
No.18 Facing Point Lock to No.19 Trap
No.22 Facing Point Lock to No.21 Points

■ **Tuesday June 20, 1939**. No.40 Up Main Starting signal renewed. This comprised the main post/right-hand doll of the existing H&B bracket signal of 1885, the renewal was carried out using recovered ex-NER lower quadrant slotted post fittings. Some years later, and on the same bracket, No.37 Starting to Up Branch and No.38 Starting to Up Goods signals were renewed with upper quadrant

Above and below: No.34 Bridge, looking along Springbank West, towards Walton Street. The clour light signal was the, then modern, equivalent of Nos. 3,4 and 5 bracket as shown on the plan.

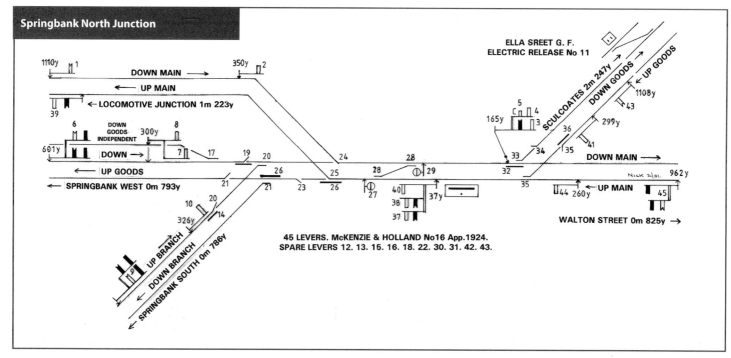

Springbank North Junction

1110y 1
DOWN MAIN →
350y 2
← UP MAIN
← LOCOMOTIVE JUNCTION 1m 223y
39
6   DOWN GOODS INDEPENDENT   8   300y
601y   DOWN →   7   17   19   20   24   28
← UP GOODS
← SPRINGBANK WEST 0m 793y   21   26   25   28   29   32   35
21   23   26   27   40   37y   44 260y ← UP MAIN   45
10   20   38
326y   14   37
↙ UP BRANCH
↙ DOWN BRANCH
9   SPRINGBANK SOUTH 0m 786y ↙
↙ SPRINGBANK SOUTH 0m 786y

ELLA SREET G. F.
ELECTRIC RELEASE No 11
SCULCOATES 2m 247y   DOWN GOODS   UP GOODS
5   4   165y   3   36   299y   43
34   35   41   1108y
33   DOWN MAIN →
32   35   962y
WALTON STREET 0m 825y →

45 LEVERS. McKENZIE & HOLLAND No16 App.1924.
SPARE LEVERS 12. 13. 15. 16. 18. 22. 30. 31. 42. 43.

arms. The lower distants retained their original lower quadrant arms, and thereafter this bracket until renewed carried a mixture of H&B, NE and upper quadrant arms.

■ **Sunday 21 April 1940.** No.35 Bridge filled in. This was a cattle creep, serving allotment gardens on both sides of the railway. It had a span of about 25' and was situated approximately 30 yards on the signal box side of the mains cross-over.

■ **At an unknown date**, but probably during 1944, the goods line distants Nos. 6, 9 and 43 were disconnected, and effectively became fixed. These

read on to the Main Lines only and in practice will have seen very little use. Although long disconnected, the respective levers, almost to the end, were not deemed spare and remained painted yellow.

■ **Late December 1944 or early January 1945.** No.39 Up Main Advance Starting signal reduced in height.

■ **Sunday October 15, 1950,** No.7 Down Goods Home, No.8 Down Independent Home bracket signal renewed by steam crane, as a standard NE Region 12' right-hand plate and angle bracket.

■ **Saturday January 6, 1951.** Boothferry Park platform opened at Springbank South for Football specials from Hull Paragon. When these trains ran, block converted from Permissive to Absolute working, by means of special instructions and block conversion ticket.

■ **October 1951.** No.21 Up Goods Trap Points installed. These were necessary for the protection of loaded passenger trains from Springbank South on the Up Branch.

■ **Saturday April 23, 1955.** No.9 Down Branch Distant, Springbank South's Up Home signals with lower distants already renewed as a standard NE Region 6' right-hand plate and angle bracket, dated photo.

■ **Thursday March 24, 1955.** No.2 Down Main Home renewed, 85 yards further from signal box.

■ **Thursday April 7, 1955.** No.44 Up Main Home Signal already renewed as upper quadrant, dated photo.

■ **Saturday July 30, 1955.** Passenger service from Hull Paragon to South Howden withdrawn. Apart from seasonal football trains between Hull Paragon and Boothferry Park, for the first time in 70 years no part of the HB carries booked passenger traffic.

■ **July 1956.** No.10 Branch Home signal renewed at reduced height and two yards further from signal box.

■ **Late January early February 1957.** No.6 Down Goods Distant

Above: Looking towards Goods-Mains Junction from the decking of No.34 Bridge over Springbank West. 1957 bracket on left. **Courtesy Challenger Publications**

Right: An LNER/BR official photograph of the Hull & Barnsley Railway three-doll bracket signal, installed for the opening of the railway. None of the arms are original. The four H&B arms shown are of the Company's final design and were eventually used throughout the system. Details of the right-hand doll and arm are in the text.

A typical H&B plate girder bridge, seen on September 19, 1965. This example was actually at Loco Junction, but two almost identical bridges were used at Springbank North, No.35 Bridge as mentioned in the text and No.36 over the NER's Newington branch. The later bridge was between Nos. 24, 25 and 28 point ends

renewed. Springbank West's Down Goods Starting signals renewed as a standard NE Region 6' right-hand plate and angle bracket.

■ **February 1957.** No.37/38/40 Up Starting signals and lower Distants bracket renewed, as a standard NE Region 12' right-hand plate and angle bracket.

■ **February/March 1957.** No.3/4 Down Starting signals and lower Distant bracket renewed as a standard NE Region 6' right-hand plate and angle bracket.

■ **1957/58.** No.41 Up Goods Home signal renewed. This signal was moved further out in 1962.

■ **Wednesday September 3, 1958,** New signal, No.5 Down Goods Calling On, fitted below existing No.4 Down Goods Starting signal. Despite permissive block working having been in force for 33 years, this was the first and only application of a Calling On arm at Springbank North.

■ **Sunday March 4, 1962.** In connection with the stage-work for the new Hessle Road signal box the lines to and from Springbank South signal box are redesignated. The former Down line is now the Up line and *vice versa*. To save confusion, the 1962 nomenclature has been used throughout these notes.

■ **Sunday October 7, 1962.** New Hessle Road power box commissioned and all lines between Springbank North-Springbank South-Hessle Road fully track circuited. Track Circuit Block (Goods) Regulations now apply to Springbank South or Hessle Road.

■ **Sunday March 7, 1964.** No.45 Up Main Distant renewed as four aspect colour light signal.

■ **Monday June 29, 1964,** Nos. 24 and 25 points spiked out of use, pending removal. Up and Down Mains to Locomotive Junction and associated signalling abolished.

■ **Thursday November 12, 1964,** Nos. 14, 17, 19, 20 21 and 23 points spiked out of use pending removal. Up and Down Goods Lines and Down Independent to Springbank West and associated signalling abolished.

In reality, this was already dead line, because Springbank West box was closed the previous Saturday.

■ **Sunday May 16, 1965.** Nos. 20,21 and 23 points recovered and replaced by plain line.

■ **Tuesday December 21, 1965.** Alterations to interlocking. No.45 Up Main Distant now altered to clear to Springbank South. This was now the only available route and it is therefore likely that, apart from tests, this signal was last cleared in 1955.

■ **Monday January 29, 1968.** No.28 Trailing Mains Cross-Over spiked out of use pending removal and associated signalling abolished.

■ **Saturday March 16, 1968.** No.37 Up Starter with Springbank South's fixed Distant below, bracket recovered for use in Normanton area. A straight post fixed Distant for Springbank South erected on same site.

■ **Saturday May 4, 1968,** at about noon, signal box closed. Junction to Walton Street and new colour light signals worked by Hessle Road signal box from Monday, May 6, 1968.

LINESIDE LOOK REVISITED - 4: Buffer stops

Have another look at the many different ways that sidings and other tracks end. Several buffer stop kits are available and can be easily modified, or 'distressed' to represent the result of a heavy shunt. Not all buffer stops are painted red - in some areas white is the colour most often used. A sleeper (with red stop lamp) across the rails provides a temporary stop block, and don't forget end loading bays where a hefty timber baulk provides protection for the platform. Why not incorporate some of them on your layout?

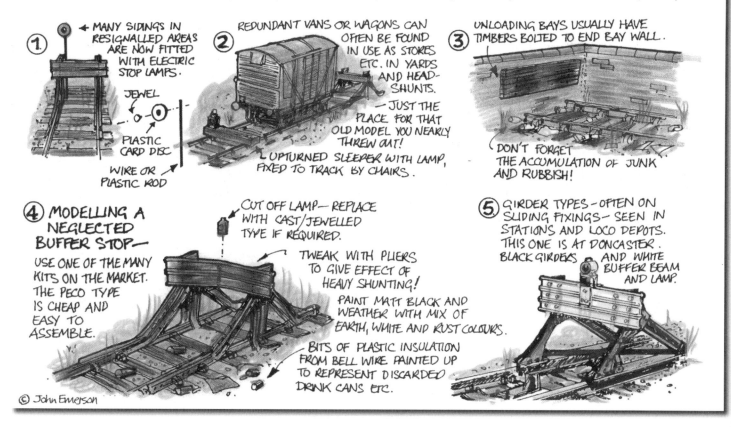

① ← MANY SIDINGS IN RESIGNALLED AREAS ARE NOW FITTED WITH ELECTRIC STOP LAMPS.

JEWEL

PLASTIC CARD DISC

WIRE OR PLASTIC ROD

② REDUNDANT VANS OR WAGONS CAN OFTEN BE FOUND IN USE AS STORES ETC. IN YARDS AND HEAD-SHUNTS.
- JUST THE PLACE FOR THAT OLD MODEL YOU NEARLY THREW OUT!
└ UPTURNED SLEEPER WITH LAMP, FIXED TO TRACK BY CHAIRS.

③ UNLOADING BAYS USUALLY HAVE TIMBERS BOLTED TO END BAY WALL.
└ DON'T FORGET THE ACCUMULATION OF JUNK AND RUBBISH!

④ MODELLING A NEGLECTED BUFFER STOP—
USE ONE OF THE MANY KITS ON THE MARKET. THE PECO TYPE IS CHEAP AND EASY TO ASSEMBLE.

CUT OFF LAMP— REPLACE WITH CAST/JEWELLED TYPE IF REQUIRED.

TWEAK WITH PLIERS TO GIVE EFFECT OF HEAVY SHUNTING!

PAINT MATT BLACK AND WEATHER WITH MIX OF EARTH, WHITE AND RUST COLOURS.

BITS OF PLASTIC INSULATION FROM BELL WIRE PAINTED UP TO REPRESENT DISCARDED DRINK CANS ETC.

⑤ GIRDER TYPES - OFTEN ON SLIDING FIXINGS - SEEN IN STATIONS AND LOCO DEPOTS. THIS ONE IS AT DONCASTER. BLACK GIRDERS AND WHITE BUFFER BEAM AND LAMP.

© John Emerson

LINESIDE LOOK REVISITED - 5: Ballast bins

Bin and gone – who writes this stuff? Commonly referred to as 'ballast bins', these lineside bins are in fact used for a variety of purposes. Their use has declined with the univesal spread of automatic track machines and the use of continuous welded rail, but are still to be seen, often in a derelict state of repair. Again, there are kits and ready-to-use models on the market but they are one of the most simple structures to build on your layout - I prefer plastic sheet, assembling with a suitable solvent, but you can use card and an adhesive such as UHU. Some bins were positioned on concrete 'stilts' if the land fell away sharply from the tracks. Finally, don't forget to put some sand or ballast in your completed bins for your PW gang to use...

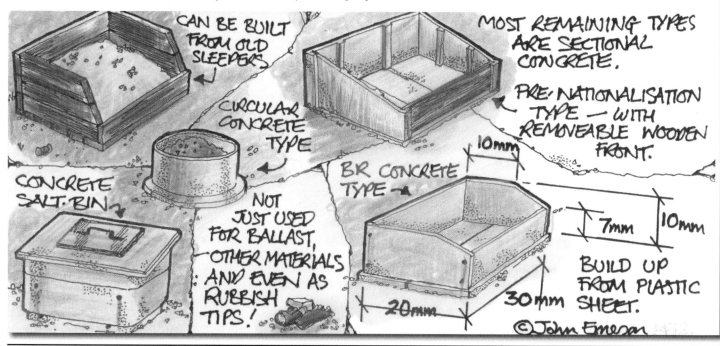

CAN BE BUILT FROM OLD SLEEPERS

CIRCULAR CONCRETE TYPE

CONCRETE SALT BIN

NOT JUST USED FOR BALLAST, OTHER MATERIALS AND EVEN AS RUBBISH TIPS!

MOST REMAINING TYPES ARE SECTIONAL CONCRETE.

PRE-NATIONALISATION TYPE — WITH REMOVEABLE WOODEN FRONT.

BR CONCRETE TYPE

10mm

7mm 10mm

20mm 30mm

BUILD UP FROM PLASTIC SHEET.

© John Emerson

air of Chicago Great Western SW1200s rounds the curved bridge over the Harvey river. This is a small area of green in the otherwise concrete covered City of Ansell.

Ansell Ferry

A fictional HO gauge layout set in the midst of Chicago's industrial heartland, built and described by **Steve Adcock**. Photography by **Ray Lightfoot**.

When I was a casual uninformed observer of the freight railways of North America, they appeared to me very romantic - huge freight trains being hauled thousands of miles across large open plains, or over the Rocky Mountains. Ask anyone for a railroad name and most would come up with the Union Pacific, Santa Fe, or maybe one of the other six large railroad companies that operate the bulk of long distance intermodal freight.

However, when it came to my first foray into American modelling, I decided my layout would be based on the lower end of US railways - the shortline. These are the small railroad companies, of which there are about 350 in North America, which feed traffic to and from the larger trunk businesses. Personally I find this carload traffic fascinating, the boxcars, hoppers and gondolas, being moved between industries in the US offered endless possibilities, a Pandora's box of modelling delights! This interest in carload traffic led me to design my layout to incorporate various industries and a yard to switch and interchange the freight cars, and to add extra spice I decided to create my own shortline railroad company to handle these trains.

When I first started building my railroad, the shortline company was called Transrail, nothing to do with the former British Rail company of the same name, it sounded American and I had a lot of Fox transfers left from my British modelling days. This company, I decided, was an amalgamation of a number of transfer railroads based in the Chicago suburbs. It handles

Not quite a cab unit, not quite a road switcher! A Chicago
Great Western EMD-built BL2 waits beside an Indiana Harbor
Belt SW1500 for their next switching duties in Ansell Yard.

freight from the big class one companies - CSX, Norfolk Southern, Union Pacific and BNSF - as well as the small Illinois Central and Iowa Interstate. Trains also arrive from fellow shortlines in the area - Indiana Harbor Belt and Belt Railway of Chicago. Using its own track and access rights on a number of the local railroads, it delivers to over 100 industries. Most are situated along the South Branch Chicago Channel between Canalport, on former BNSF trackage, just south west of downtown Chicago and Argo near the EMD plant at La Grange.

However, as my thoughts and ideas developed over the years I grew a little tired of the Transrail name and livery. If I was honest, when I first devised my scenario I was still a little naive about American railways. It was at the same time that my like-minded band of railroad friends and Ansell Ferry operators startewd to suggest that the Transrail name be dropped and we rebranded the layout. It was Grahame Robinson that I have to thank for the idea of using the Chicago Great Western (CGW) name and for coming up with the new livery. He had done a large amount of research into the CGW and we

set about adapting the history of one of America's 'fallen flag' railroads to suit my layout.

The CGW hauled its first train in 1885 and in the next 80 years built up a large network of track west from Chicago to Kansas, Omaha and the twin cities of Minneapolis and St Paul. Unfortunately, in the mid 1960s, they had a number of financial problems and were swallowed up by the Chicago North-Western Railroad. But for our purposes on Ansell Ferry we assumed they managed to hang onto much of their track within the state of Illinois. This fictitious move by management, concentrating on operating transfer freights in the Chicago suburbs allowed a period of stability and then by the mid 1980s through a series of other mergers the CGW was on the up again. Finally we see a take over of Transrail by CGW and the railroad you see before you.

When I looked into the types of locomotives that CGW might still operate we found a gold mine of modelling potential. They had a large fleet of first generation US diesels, 'F units', that on some of the largest trains would be grouped into lash-

ups of ten locomotives. Add this to the striking red livery and there was no going back, Transrail was history.

The yard at Ansell Ferry is one of Transrail's main interchange facilities, not as large as the Global West and East yards in downtown, but located to the south west of the city centre, where numerous freights are switched and dispatched to customers in areas such as Willow Springs, Glenn and Bridgeport. Transrail also operate Ansell Ferry transfer runs to yards at Blue Island, Corwith, Ashland Avenue, Cicero and the Belt Railway's Clearing Yard, in addition to several longer haul freights across Chicago land.

The historic significance of the area should not be overlooked, as it operated one of the last few railcar barge ferries in the US. Indeed the yard owes its existence to the nearby waterway, originally being placed here to handle freight cars moved along the Southern Branch of Chicago's navigable waterway. The service was finally withdrawn in 1991 but many of the architectural and industry related features remain.

My layout represents a mile long section of track in an urban area of West Chicago. The name of Ansell

also try to have a good idea of why the railway is where it is located and its purpose. You also need to be sympathetic to how the railway fits into the surrounding environment. In model form you can rarely afford the actual space given to buildings and industrial sites in the real world, but you also need to allow for open spaces, this is especially so for North American layouts. On Ansell Ferry I deliberately tried to stick to this last one, but I still get told at exhibitions that there are too many structures on my layout. Never mind - I always blame Walthers for coming up with a steady stream of excellent structures to build.

A guided tour

Close your eyes and imagine you are on a 'Metra' train taking a guided tour of the city of Ansell, with points of interest listed along the way. Let us start at the eastern or right-hand end of my layout as you view it from the front. At this location the two tracks from Cicero and Corwith converge and then run parallel after emerging from a short tunnel under Commercial Street. A number of sidings can be found here serving a Caterpillar manufacturing facility. The large red brick building was formally one of Chicago's 1920 power stations, now converted into an assembly plant for an assortment of component parts used on medium sized earth moving equipment. Boxcars can usually be seen on one of the tracks being loaded by forklift trucks, the palletised assemblies being despatched to several final assembly plants around the US.

Ferry is purely fictitious, and all of the ideas and features of the layout are also straight from my imagination; however, the location I have chosen, beside the Chicago Southern Branch channel, does exist. If you consult your *SPV Rail Atlas of Great Lakes West* (page 11, map reference C3), you will find railroad lines currently owned by Illinois Central and BNSF run down each side of the waterway in the Glenn area - this is where I have placed the city of Ansell.

Another authentic and well-researched aspect of the layout is the train destinations that CGW (formerly Transrail) connects with. From the former Chicago North-Western yard at Proviso in the north of the city to the Belt Railway's Clearing Yard are real places, as is the location on which Ansell Ferry is based, but a little modeller's licence has been used. I do not pretend all the following scenario was written before the layout was built, but in order to create a believable model railway, it is important to know in your own mind the final result that you want. There are a number of rules I try to keep to: always work from a scaled track plan is the first,

Metra Rapid Transit Authority operate an extensive passenger network right across the Chicagoland conurbation. A Budd Railcar is pictured passing under the disused coaling tower leaving Ansell depot heading for Aurora.

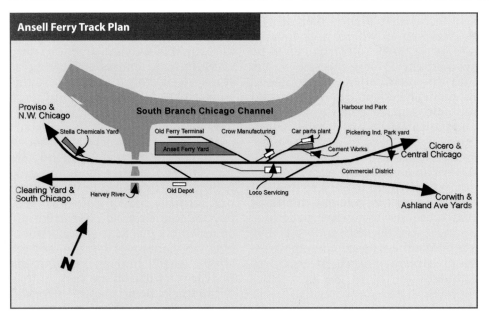

Ansell Ferry Track Plan

Proviso &
N.W. Chicago

South Branch Chicago Channel

Harbour Ind Park

Stella Chemicals Yard

Old Ferry Terminal   Crow Manufacturing   Car parts plant   Pickering Ind. Park yard

Ansell Ferry Yard

Cement Works

Cicero &
Central Chicago

Commercial District

Clearing Yard &
South Chicago

Harvey River

Old Depot

Loco Servicing

Corwith &
Ashland Ave Yards

N

Cars are trip worked from Ansell yard to the facility on request of the customer. To the south of the track space is at a premium and industries crowd in. Train speeds are reduced to a maximum of 15mph at this point, as the engineer (driver) prepares to enter the street running section. Situated between the two tracks is the old tower; although not controlling the movement of trains, the tower is manned to protect road transport from the railroad.

The severe speed restrictions at this point are a major hindrance to trains in the Ansell area. On the line from Corwith and Ashland Avenue is the 50 yard run along Rayner Avenue where locomotive crews pass three local stores, a barbershop, fashion store and antiques emporium plus one of

Chicago's premier hobby shops. The operation is made more hazardous by the sharp curve taking the track through almost 90° to meet the line from Cicero and the central Chicago area. The Cicero line runs to the rear of the commercial building before it meets the main line. At the northern extremity of the layout, a rather run down, almost derelict, apartment building can be seen next to the local Fire Houses, one of several serving this district of Chicago. A large rail-served scrap yard can also be seen here, often with gondolas being filled by a mechanical excavator.

Continuing along the right of way, after a train has completed its journey over the on-street running section of Rayner Avenue, the tracks dive under the Freeway 155 flyover.

The road traffic is always heavy here, where a bottleneck is caused by the toll-booths. The next landmarks, on the north of the layout, are the Red X Cement works and Ford car parts warehouse, both rail served, receiving regular shipments delivered by Transrail. Also passing between the two structures is the entrance track to the harbour industrial estate. In the foreground, the CF freight storage and Red X Cement loading facilities can be seen, either side of a storm drain.

At this point, just before the sidings of Ansell Ferry yard start to fan out, there is some emergency track repair work being carried by Transrail permanent way staff. Several sections of old track are being replaced. As well as good old-fashioned brute force, the team are using a Burrow crane and a Permaquip tie (sleeper) remover to speed the repairs and get the track back into service. It is here that Transrail's locomotive and freight car maintenance facility is located in the middle of the tracks. This modern structure was only recently erected on part of the old yard area.

Adjacent is the Transrail Train Control Center, where dispatchers control train movements throughout the network. The building itself is a modern prefabricated structure that personnel have only recently moved into, previously the attached brick-built yard tower was used to monitor traffic flow. This building still retains its use though, as it is

Canadian Pacific maintain a small fleet of cabooses to use on local trains where a number of backing-up moves maybe required. One such example is in front of the chemical plant, west of Ansell. When the train needs to reverse for any distance the switchman will ride on the back of the caboose, keeping the driver informed by radio of progress and any hazards.

from here that the Train Master controls the switches (points) for Ansell Ferry Yard. The switches were automated in 1995 around the same time as Indiana Harbor Belt's Gibson Yard. Ansell is one of the most efficient flat yards in Chicago land for car handling; the use of automated switches also makes life a lot easier for train crews.

Behind the railroad, we can see the Crow Manufacturing plant, a sprawling site with a mixture of modern and old buildings. A large trailer loading dock is the busiest location on the site with vehicles coming and going all day. On the south side of the track, more industries reside in a natural bowl at the foot of the cut, and here are two more factory units, busy trying to claw back some of the US trade gap.

At Ansell Ferry, freight cars were loaded onto barges and shipped south to Joliet. The imposing, classically styled structure is the old harbour building. Originally, boxcars entered through the central door at the front and merchandise would be transhipped, sorted and moved out through the side doors onto barges. The main body of the building is now only used for storage, the first floor at the front being used as office space for Transrail's Operations Control department.

More sidings continue westward past the Walker Plating Inc. building, a former Redmire mill. On a 'heavy traffic' day, you can see two or three switchers working hard to sort the sidings, full with freight cars, before despatching them to their destination.

Travelling further west, and back

to the south side of the right of way, a new McDonald's Restaurant helps to cater for Ansell residents' culinary needs. Next to this is the new depot building, as in recent years, Metra have reopened Ansell as a commuter station, using this new prefabricated waiting room and office building. The idea is to encourage the long-suffering commuter out of the car and onto the rails. Metra has leased a number of older Budd cars to operate this passenger service into downtown Chicago; trains terminate at Ansell and run into the city *via* the Cicero line. The success of this recently introduced local service has led Metra to divert a number of their fast trains from Joliet to call at Ansell station. Keep an eye out for these trains, as they make a pleasant change from the continuous stream of freight through Ansell.

Next to the very modern Metra station building, we find a rather run down, disused depot. It is over 20 years since Burlington Northern operated their commuter service through Ansell into their Chicago Union station, and this classic wooden structure is under threat from vandals and also the need for more car parking for new Metra customers keen to let the train take the strain.

Just after the depot building, the tracks of the main yard are truncated; overhead a box girder bridge once carried the Illinois Central Railroad line from Tuxedo Park

When Conrail was split between CSX and Norfolk Southern, their small fleet of 5,000hp SD80MACs where divided up between the two 'mega' railroads. Here a CSX owned locomotive glides under the disused coaling tower on the point of an east-bound train.

Businesses in Rayner Avenue have learned to live with trains disrupting trade. Here a CGW sand train edges its way round the curve. All six locomotives are powered so you would guess there is a fair amount of vibration felt inside Totally Train's model shop!

to Midway. Continuing the rather run down theme, an old coal tower sits astride the main two tracks. This structure became obsolete over 40 years ago, but due to the difficult nature of demolition, it has remained in position. It has witnessed the diesel

revolution take hold on American Railroads, and stands there as if to remind the modern day engineer how hard their predecessor's job was in steam days.

In this part of town, a mixture of industrial and old residential is the

theme. In the foreground, the rails are again squeezed by the factories, while on the north side, we find a block of old tenement buildings still occupied by many of Ansell's less well-off residents.

We now enter a semi-rural area, the three main lines cross the Harvey River by means of a simple concrete bridge. The description of river is applied very loosely, as it is more a neglected muddy stream running into the berthing basin of the canal. Continuing round, a couple of pieces of old stock are abandoned on the spur track. An old Illinois Central 50' open hopper car will never move again, as there is a tree growing through the unloading doors and an old Sheerness box car can be seen, left rotting in the basin of the river, after a switching accident many years ago. Fifty yards north of the track there are a number of empty classic-style residences that local vandals have taken over.

The tracks then pass under the Harlem Avenue Highway Bridge - packed with traffic as usual - after which the Ansell West Yard fans out from the Proviso line. This area was originally a small quarry facility, but Stella Chemicals now use the area to store and process various hazardous liquids. Transrail moves tank cars regularly to the sorting yard; from

A close up portrait of a Union Pacific GP40 seen here on the point of a mixed freight.

here the cars move onto many different Stella Chemicals customers across the United States.

At Ansell City limits, we pass though a short rock cut and then under three rail overbridges. The first carried the former Transrail line to McCook, this has recently had its rails removed and is obviously disused. The other two are the ex-Chicago Belt Railroad cut-off line between Summit and La Grange Park - you will be exceptionally lucky to see a train on this track, especially since the Belt Railroad now uses Indiana Harbor Belt trackage rights to reach Franklin Park. After clearing these bridges, the double track to the Clearing Yard and South Chicago starts curving southwards. The Proviso and northwest Chicago track starts to rise in preparation to cross the channel.

This is the end of my imaginary cross section of industrial Chicago; I hope you have enjoyed the trip. Many people comment how ugly and run down much of North American inner urban areas are. In amongst the man-made decay, I can find strange beauty, and modelling inspiration, especially when there is railroad present. For me, in a strange way, it is similar to that received from mother nature in the Arizona desert, or the majestic Rocky Mountains. So next time you watch that video, or are lucky enough to visit the United States, enjoy those huge girder bridges, massive power

Once a day, the Norfolk Southern 'Triple Crown' roadrailer train can be seen at Ansell heading for Calumet Park. Here an SD70 in their famous black livery passes the chemical plant on Ansell West Yard.

stations or chemical works, and have a go at modelling them. Happy rail-fanning, but please do not trespass on Railroad property.

Construction details

The 20 baseboards are made from a 9mm plywood framework, with 6mm plywood top, and were constructed on a jig to ensure correct alignment. This prevents mismatching when they are built up together in an oval. Plywood was chosen to reduce weight, as some of the boards were

to be 30" wide, and also to prevent the instability that I found with chipboard on my previous layout. Both Russell Bridge and Ansell Ferry were constructed and stored in a less than perfect garage, making exposure to dampness a problem.

The layout has been built in three phases and because of this, there are three different types of track. On the front scenic section of the layout, I have used Walthers' code 83 track to try and achieve that American look, on reflection though, I may regret this in

CSX train Q539, a transfer freight from Barr Yard to CBR Clearing Yard is headed by an SD40 in CSX 'stealth' livery with yellow ends, under the disused Illinois Central girder bridge.

A superb close-up roster shot of Belt Railway GP7 No.470, part of a four-unit lash-up crossing the Martin Luther Avenue crossing.

the future as the track and points look superb, but are nowhere near as robust as Peco; after only two exhibitions there were signs of damage at the board joints. The rail is attached to the track base by scale spikes rather than chairs; this looks very good, but for a layout that has to be moved regularly, it seems impractical. In 2005 I decided to extend the railway from 30' 0" to 35' 0" by adding one more scenic section. This project was started just as the new Peco Code 83 track came out, so for this one section, as it was readily available, I decided to mix and match the scenic trackwork. There is a slight difference in width on the top of the track between Walthers and Peco - nobody has noticed this yet! The two end scenic boards were phase two of the railway, and I used Peco code 75, really just for ease of availability. Finally the fiddle yard has code 75 Peco track and points - originally mainly for cost reasons, but also because I did not need the variety in lengths of point that Walthers offered.

When it came to ballasting the trackwork, I settled on the N scale buff coloured Woodland Scenics material. On a number of SPV videos of Chicago land, this seemed to be representative of the area. For foliage and general scenic materials, I have used a mixture of Woodland Scenics and Greenscene flocks.

Buildings

There are 20 main structures around the layout - a mixture of kit-built, modified kits and scratch-built. I have tried to use these to create that urban feel. Comments have been made that there are too many for the area I have at my disposal, and I will admit that prototypically there would be more space between buildings. However, I was keen to achieve that built-up city feeling on the railway, and in order to keep public interest in a display, it is important to pack in small dioramas within your layout. Here is a quick *resumé* of the main features and how I built them.

At the east end of the layout, two tracks leave the fiddle yard under a scratch-built concrete tunnel mouth, with DPM frontages on top. We then find a heavily modified DPM power station kit, used at the back of the baseboard in low-relief, with the siding tracks disappearing under a modified Walthers storage building. The lower low-relief buildings in the foreground are made up of parts of Rix Products industrial buildings. Rounding the corner we pass a Cornerstone interlocking tower, then past the small business district, a mixture of Smalltown USA and Walthers red brick buildings have been used. To the rear is a tall iron fronted building produced by City Classics, which stands next to a Walthers Fire House. Under the scratch-built I55 overbridge, and on past two more Cornerstone buildings; the cement works and the Ford car parts storage unit, developed from a modified blast furnace building. In the far distance, before the large

A BNSF lettered GP40 waits with a mixed freight in front of the imposing Caterpillar plant. This locomotive originally belonged to the Burlington Northern Railroad and is in their famous forest green livery. When they and Santa Fe decided to merge in 1995 a large number of engines were left in their previous owners livery but had the initials BNSF added.

factory, a loaded boxcar sits under one of the new Cornerstone low-relief mill buildings. At the front, I have scratch-built a cement loader, using parts from the Heljan silo kit. A Rix building has been used for a CF freight warehouse.

Still in the foreground, the next couple of industrial buildings are kit-built, with a modified Volmer Burger King kit converted to a McDonald's restaurant, and finally a Walthers Cornerstone depot.

Along the back of the layout Crow Manufacturing takes up much of the real estate, utilising a heavily modified Modern Structures/Rix Products building. Just for good measure, and to represent the older part of Crow Manufacturing, I have used a Kibri factory building kit in low relief. Still working westwards from, and in front of the main Ansell yard, I have modified the Cornerstone pier terminal, and part of the papermill factory for the low relief building. An old Redmire feed mill, produced by Walthers, is used for

the Walker Plating Company.

Continuing round the layout, to the left we find the rail bridge over the end of the yard. This is the classic Walther rail over box-girder bridge. The next 4' of scenery is what I call 'Phase Three' of the railroad, and the most recent to be built. The new modern Walthers' coaling tower sits astride the main two tracks, while at the back, in low relief, is another recently released Walthers' Cornerstone building, the tenement block. I have combined three kits to make the structure you see here. After this Transrail crosses the Harvey River on a scratch-built structure. I have used another Rix overbridge to carry Harlem Avenue, and now we are onto the final scenic board. At the back the tank farm is a mixture of several model products, again Walthers feature heavily, using the unloading gantry and piping kits. The rock faces are plaster cast using Woodland Scenics moulds and much of the orange scattered rock is from

our local builder's merchants. Finally the main lines pass under three further bridges, before entering the fiddle yard proper. These are mainly scratch-built, but I have used the Peco girder work.

Train Movements

The volume of traffic at Ansell Ferry yard can vary greatly from one day to the next. While the trains operated by the shortline Chicago Great Western (CGW) remain constant, there are normally a large number of run-through freights. CGW's network of tracks in this part of the 'Windy City' help relieve track capacity problems on a number of the class one main lines that cross this huge Chicago conurbation. Add to this the occasional light engine movement, with power belonging to any of the area's companies, and Ansell Ferry can truly be classed as a railroad hotspot.

On an average day at Ansell, you could expect to see as many as 60

A Belt Railway Alco is dwarfed by the huge Faulkner-Aston paper mill in the background.

freight and ten passenger trains. At least 60% are run-through traffic from any of the big four Chicago land companies, with Indiana Harbor belt, Illinois Central and Grand Trunk all making appearances. Mixed trains are most common, but almost anything goes here.

BNSF and United Parcels operate a large intermodal yard at Willow Springs, this is only five miles west of Ansell, so 'trailer on flat car' (TOFC) trains are common. They could be either making their way to Cicero, to be added to another train heading west, or possibly for interchange at Corwith or Barr Yard, for trailers going east.

During daylight hours, Norfolk Southern 'Triplecrown' Roadrailers can often be sighted in the Ansell area. A nightly service from Calumet to Fort Wayne is marshalled from various points around Chicago land; keep an eye out as NS uses some of their older power to collect trailers. Occasionally ex-Conrail GP15s or GP30s are used, more often than not SW1200 switchers can be seen, heading for Calumet Yard *via* Belt

Railway trackage.

Continuing the Intermodal theme, and arguably the most impressive trains Ansell has to offer, are the 'double stack' container freights. Heading west, the BNSF trains from Cicero are starting their hot-foot journey, in the Joliet or Galesburg direction, to south west Illinois and then onto Kansas City. BNSF power is the norm for these services, but occasionally leased foreign power can be seen.

Norfolk-Southern and CSX also operate some big 'Container on Flat Car' (COFC) trains *via* the Ansell cut-off line. NS Freights, from Ashland and Corwith Yards, head out from downtown towards the tracks to southern Illinois, while the CSX run trains up to Cicero Yard to interchange with BNSF.

The CSX Corporation 'entertains' the Ansell railfan with a number of trains heading from Barr Yard to interchange with Union Pacific or Canadian Pacific. The block working of Pennsylvanian coal in Bethgons is not to be missed. It can be seen at Ansell several times a week, heading for the Illinois State power plant at Dubuque on the Mississippi. CSX power works the train to Bensenville Yard, before handing over to Canadian Pacific to finish the journey on former Soo tracks.

From Ansell Ferry Yard itself, CGW make many short moves to various industries, not only within the immediate City limits, but also further afield. The Caterpillar parts operation in the east of Ansell

A BNSF C44 locomotive waits for the right of way. Behind, a number of freight cars can be seen waiting for delivery to local industries.

has daily deliveries, while Crow Manufacturing and Ford Car parts also accept boxcars into their facility, adjacent to the yard, on most days. Still at the east end of the layout, Red X Cement has seen a marked upturn in cement output since the start of the Chicago I290 Tri-State freeway extension. At the west end, the Stella Chemicals plant also sees switching action most days.

One of Transrail's most impressive long haul trains is the daily (except Monday), sand service. This through working consist usually has a mixture of old ore cars and other open hoppers. Starting at Waukegan, about 20 miles up the Lake Michigan shoreline, sand dredged from the floor of the lake, is brought ashore and shipped to Joliet for use in the construction industry. Union Pacific power handles the train from Waukegan, through Ansell, to Transrail's yard at Landers. A locomotive change is made to CGW power, and the train continues to Joliet. On the returning empties, CGW power is kept on the head end until the Global West yard and up to six old GP or even F unit locomotives are sometimes used.

The most unusual trains seen at Ansell have to be the molten steel 'torpedo' wagons that run from Brighton Park to Lawndale Avenue. This short run, of about ten miles, was made necessary when Bethlehem Steel closed its blast furnace at Lawndale. Normally two of CGW's older switching locomotives are employed from furnace to slab mill; train speeds are down to below 10mph for the entire journey. As far as I can tell this is one of only two such operations in the Chicago land area. Norfolk Southern still runs a similar train for US Steel in the harbour front area of northwest Indiana. The heat haze and smoke rising from the 400°C molten steel in the full wagons can be seen before the trains comes into view.

When it comes to passenger trains, Chicago is not a typical North American city. The concept of mass movement of people from the suburbs into Downtown is not at all common. You could count on your fingers the number of cities that offer a commuter railway system. Many are at the moment planning and installing modern tram systems, but it is fair to say that Chicago is unusual to offer such an extensive all day passenger service.

It is also fair comment that when we find a commuter railroad sharing the right of way with freight trains, more often than not the passenger will play second fiddle. This is certainly the case with Ansell Ferry Train Masters. Metra, the Chicago Rapid Transit Authority, offers a number of good inter-urban services from downtown stations at Randolph, La Salle and Madison Streets, as well as the former Pennsylvania Railroad's now combined Metra/Amtrak Union Station. Several tracks head west, like spokes on a wheel, to points all around Chicago; as far as Milwaukee on Lake Michigan in the north, Madison and Rockford in the east and Aurora and Joliet in the south. Ansell City is situated on the corridor out to Joliet, Metra run fast trains on an hourly service, while still leasing a fleet of Budd cars to run the slow, stopping at all stations, service.

Conclusion
As a final chapter to my story, I wish to say thank you to a number of people that have made it all worthwhile. As with most hobbies, I believe it to be a fact that the more you put into model railways, the more you receive back, this is certainly true in my case. Apart from the fun and excitement of creating the layout, and all that goes with this over the years, I have been lucky enough along the way to meet and befriend many excellent people, so to all of these, a sincere thank you, for their help and encouragement. Sorry, you are all too numerous to mention but Harvey, Tony, Steve C, Chris, Graham, and Nigel, thanks for all your efforts.

I hope you have enjoyed this in-depth article, giving an insight into my world of model railroading. The conception, planning and construction of Ansell Ferry have taken over ten years and now in order to start a new project I have sold the layout - my next project is American O scale and I very much look forward to meeting you at a future exhibition with it.

An impressive line up of first generation diesels is captured in front of Crow Manufacturing. A GP20, B unit and two SW1200 in Chicago Great Western livery plus an SD9 and SW1200 belonging to Elgin, Joilet & Eastern.

Great 'Grids'

As the *BRM Annual* was about to go to press, Hornby released their new Class 56.
Brian Daniels photographed the class on his travels.

56 115 was the last Doncaster-built Class 56, the final 20 being built at BREL Crewe. Nos.56 056-135 were built with detail differences including larger horn grille, protruding marker lights and steps above the buffers. Named *Bassetlaw* from June to December 2001, 56 115 *Barry Needham* is seen at Didcot in the later version of EWS livery.

One of the Crewe-built batch, 56 123 was named *Drax Power Station* on May 11, 1988. It is seen at Immingham on September 4, 1990. Note the prominent steam-age coaling tower in the background.

In LoadHaul livery, Romanian-built 56 027 heads another loaded MGR train through Knottingley on June 17, 1997.

The first version of English, Welsh & Scottish Railways livery is seen on 56 114 on a Freightliner working at Eastleigh.

ABOVE: The Western Region had a small fleet of 'Grids' to handle aggregate traffic and the heavily loaded Port Talbot-Llanwern iron ore trains. On October 12, 1988, Nos.56 052 and 56 034 *Castell Ogwr/Ogmore Castle* power the train through Newport. On May 1, 1997, 56 052 was named *The Cardiff Rod Mill*, the plates being removed in 2000.

LEFT: Transrail-liveried 56 092 waits at the head of a train of 'Avtur' (aviation fuel) tank wagons at Colnbrook on September 1, 1998.

BELOW: Wearing Railfreight large logo livery, 56 063 *Bardon Hill* rests at Toton on October 2, 1988. The locomotive was named on October 6, 1986, and makes an interesting comparison with its Romanian-built counterpart pictured opposite.

ABOVE: More action at Knottingley with 56 111 at the head of yet another 'merry-go-round' train of power station coal on March 3, 1994.

RIGHT: Loadhaul liveried 56 090 earns its keep on a well-loaded MGR working at Melton Ross on August 6, 1997.

BELOW: Nos.56 001-083 were outshopped in the standard BR livery of 'rail' blue with full yellow ends, while 56 084-135 were given a 'revised' livery with wrap-round yellow ends and black window surrounds, grey roof, and large numbers and logos. On July 18, 1979, Romanian-built 56 028 eases its MGR train through Worksop station. The Romanian built batch were assembled by Electroputere (a subsidiary of Brush) and differed from the later BREL-built locos having small horn grilles, lipped buffer beam, recessed marker lights, and cab side windows with a prominent rubber seal. Serious problems were identified with these locos when they arrived in Britain and they were not finally released to traffic until after the first British-built examples were in service. 56 028 was named *West Burton Power Station* on September 10, 1988, the name lasting until February 1993.

A matter of scale

Nigel Burkin takes a brief look at the popular scales and gauges. Photography by the author.

Scale and gauge can be confusing issues for a newcomer to model railways. With so many people joining the growing ranks of railway modellers around Christmas, a recap of the commercial scales and gauges may help the undecided!

The overall size of our models and their compatibility with each other is the result of two key parameters: scale, and its close relative, gauge. Scale is expressed in several ways, whilst gauge is fairly specific, being measured (usually) in millimetres as the distance between the running rails of the track. Everything would be quite straightforward if it were not for the finescale modeller and the huge variety of narrow gauge modelling gauges. In 4mm scale alone, there are several closer-to-scale gauges, which have done much to cause confusion. Chuck in a healthy dose of 'OO gauge is obsolete!' by the British HO gauge fraternity and one soon comes to realise that scale, together with gauge, is a hot topic as well as an important technical issue in the hobby. This need not spoil your enjoyment of the hobby and to provide some clarification, here's a simple explanation – without the intra-scale (and gauge) politics!

Z gauge

The smallest practical scale for mainstream modelling is called Z gauge. In terms of scale, it is modelled to a ratio of 1:220 and runs on a track gauge of 6.5mm. In other words, it is tiny and the number of commercial products for the British modeller is very limited. Continental and US-outline modellers are enjoying growth in this smallest of scales, including quality ready-to-use track now available off-the-shelf and models straight from the box.

N gauge and 2mm finescale

A scale that is growing in popularity because it offers the chance to run

US N scale and British N gauge are not the same. The EMD SD60M model in the centre is modelled to 1:160 scale but is still taller than the Dapol models on either side which are to 1:148 scale. This means that some products are not interchangeable between these scales. A 45' intermodal container from US manufacturers such as Deluxe Innovations or Walthers are too small for British N gauge. Some buildings might not work either, being taller to suit the larger prototype and consequently, larger models.

long trains in a relatively small area. It is possible to really make the pips squeak with space, because N gauge models will perform around very tight radius curves. Commercial N gauge is modelled to a ratio of 1:148 and runs on 9mm gauge track (it is not true 2mm/1ft scale). There are several mainstream manufacturers producing products for British outline N gauge, including Peco, Bachmann, Hornby and Dapol. British N gauge should not be confused with N scale from America. N scale is modelled to 1:160, even though it runs on the same 9mm gauge track. In truth, 9mm gauge track for 1:148 scale is not strictly correct and 2mm finescale modellers work to the slightly smaller 1:152 scale and their trains run on 9.42mm gauge track.

3mm

Originally popularised by the now obsolete Tri-ang TT3 range, with a track gauge of 12mm, 3mm modelling has undergone a rennaisance in recent years with the 3mm Society developing finer modelling standards (14.2mm gauge) and encouraging independent traders to support the scale. The society also produces a wide range of parts and kits.

OO gauge

OO gauge is based on 4mm/1ft scale models running on 3.5mm/1ft scale track, which came about through an historical anomaly when available motors were found to be too large to fit in British outline models when modelled to 3.5mm or HO scale. OO gauge is by far the most popular of all the commercial gauges and is modelled to a ratio of 1:76, running on HO gauge track at 16.5mm gauge. Two closer-to-scale groups exist to correct the track and wheel standards so they are exactly to or as close as possible to 4mm/1ft scale. EM gauge modellers work to 18.2mm gauge, with reasonably tight tolerances, which is regarded as close enough for many modellers. 'Scalefour' (S4) and 'Protofour' (P4) modellers go the whole way, with little or no compromise, working to 18.83mm gauge. Both P4 and S4, together with EM, are not considered as commercially viable, although most modellers use ready-to-run OO gauge models as a starting point and fill in with kits. OO gauge enjoys dramatic commercial support and continues to thrive, despite the gauge compromise and calls for British HO scale to replace OO gauge.

HO gauge

It is worth noting that HO gauge (Half O) is modelled to 1:87.1 scale and runs on HO gauge track gauged to 16.5mm. There have been attempts to make it mainstream with British outline modellers in recent years but without much success. In the US and continental Europe, it is very popular with huge commercial support. There has been some cross-over with UK OO gauge thanks to the shared track gauge, enabling some ferry wagon prototypes to be used to cover for the lack of 4mm scale models. The slight difference in physical size is generally ignored.

Mainstream commercial support for OO and N gauges is excellent as demonstrated by these models of the most up-to-date Class 66s. The OO gauge 1:76 scale model is from Bachmann whilst the smaller one is modelled in 1:148 scale for British N gauge by Dapol.

Class 37/4s are available in OO gauge and N gauge. The larger OO gauge model is by ViTrains, a new entrant to the hobby in 2007. The N gauge model is produced by Bachmann under the Graham Farish label. Bachmann also offers a quality OO gauge model of the Class 37/4 released in 2007.

S gauge

This is not a commercial gauge in the UK, requiring most of the rolling stock components to be scratchbuilt, although it enjoys much commercial support in the US, where its popularity is growing. It is modelled to 3/16" (1:64) scale with a gauge of 0.884".

O gauge and scale seven

Called the 'senior scale', O gauge is modelled extensively in the UK, even though commercial support was initially restricted to kits, until the recent introduction of finished off-the-shelf models from Danish manufacturer Heljan. Modelled to 1:43.5 scale (7mm/1ft), models run on 32mm gauge track. Like many scales and gauges, there is some compromise to make it work. However, Scale Seven modellers model to the true gauge of 33mm (1:43.5 scale) with prototypical crossings and other refined track features.

Class 73 electro-diesels are popular, with both Dapol and Hornby offering good models. The Dapol one is modelled in N gauge and is seen here sitting on the roof of the Hornby OO gauge model.

modelling in gauge 1 - 10mm/ft or 1:32 scale - both running on commercially available 45mm gauge track. Traditionally the preserve of (expensive!) 'live-steam' there is now a growing number of electrically powered locomotives available and a considerable amount of commercial support. Bachmann recently entered the gauge 1 market with 1:32 scale RTR brass locomotives, including a J94, 'Jinty' and Pannier tank. Also distributed by Bachmann, Aristocraft are currently offering garden railway models through Bachmann Europe that are modelled to 1:29 scale, running on 45mm gauge track, but rugged enough to survive in the garden.

G scale

The German firm of Lehmann introduced G scale (the 'G' stands for 'Garden') in the 1960s, with the trade name LGB (Lehmann Big Railway). The track gauge is 45mm (the same as gauge 1 but with a heavier rail profile), allowing the modelling of narrow gauge railways in various scales (1:20.3, 1:22.5, 1:24, 1:29 to 1:32). If it's big stuff that takes your fancy, it's more likely to be G gauge, which is very competitively priced.

Hopefully, our brief guide has cleared things a little! Whatever you chose to buy, have fun!

Gauge 1

The waters get a bit muddied here. As in the other scales/gauges, there are two UK standards for those

Little and large comparisons are fun but on a more serious note, they illustrate the differences in some scales when such photographs can be staged. N gauge offers more railway per square foot although OO gauge offers more detail. You choose!

Tebay Interlude

Derek Shore introduces some of his, so far unpublished, photographs of this classic Shipley MRS layout.

A Durham - Ulverston miner's special arrives at Tebay, having travelled via Stainmore and the North Eastern branch. BR Standard Class 3 2-6-2 tank No.82029, a Kemilway kit, will be replaced at Tebay by a Fowler 2-6-4 tank.

'Black 5' No.45481, a K's body with a Comet chassis and Wrenn tender, awaits the arrival of trains from Newcastle and Durham, which will be joined at Tebay, No.45481 will then take the combined train to Blackpool.

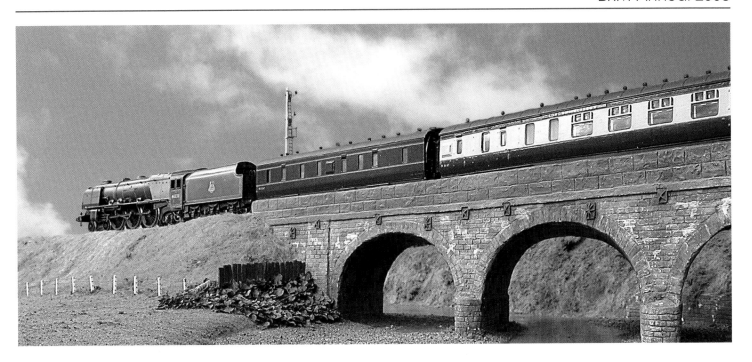

Above: Blue 'Duchess' No. 26220 *Coronation* crosses the viaduct over the River Lune at Tebay with the Down 'Royal Scot'.

Left: A Fowler 3F 0-6-0 stands in the shed yard at Tebay with the station building and footbridge in the background. To obtain a round boiler, two Tri-ang loco bodies were used and the tender was scratch-built.

Below: Still carrying its LMS number and insignia, dirty black streamlined 'Duchess' No. 6226 *Duchess of Norfolk* roars through Tebay with the Down 'Royal Scot'. The loco is a detailed Hornby model.

A Crewe - Carlisle goods, with a large number of containers, slows to take on a banking engine for the climb up Shap. The Stanier Mogul 2-6-0 No.42952 was built from a Milholme kit.

A ballast train with 4F 0-6-0 No.44469 in charge, heads for the main line from the engineer's sidings. The terraced houses behind the station can still be seen today, both from the train and the M6 motorway.

'Duchess' No. 46257 *City of Salford* starts the climb to Shap with the Down Special TPO. The loco is a DJH kit and the coaches a mix of Badger and Stevenson kits.

Pulling away from a stop at Tebay with the Euston - Carlisle and Windermere is un-rebuilt Royal Scot No.46137 *The Prince of Wales' Volunteers (South Lancashire)*. The loco is a detailed Mainline model, running on a Comet chassis.

A heavy Crewe - Carlisle parcels heads north behind two Stanier 'Black 5s'

Not long after its return to Swindon on October 7, No.6000 receives admiring looks from some of the Swindon workforce outside the main works offices, after being been turned on the works turntable and reunited with its Bulmers' Pullman coaches.

SWINDON STEAM

Former Swindon apprentice and employee **Garry Stroud** looks back at the final years of steam at Swindon. Photography by the author.

Swindon Works, a name which even today is forever linked with the likes of 'Kings', 'Castles', 'Granges' and 'Manors', still played host to steam right through to its final years. Although the works had seen both good and bad days in its long and chequered existence, 1985 was a bad year in the works history, marking what was to be the beginning of the end for this once proud bastion of the GWR. In what was a disaster of bad timing and publicity, British Rail Engineering Ltd (BREL) announced in May 1985 the complete closure of the works site. The month long exhibition at the works planned for August which, ironically, was to be the crowning glory in the 'GWR 150' celebrations that year, was inevitably cancelled, leaving the remaining staff employed there looking forward, not with pride and celebration, as many had hoped, but with anger, sadness and the looming prospect of unemployment.

Having seen better days, No.8466 (still with original smokebox number and brass cabside plate) with centre wheels removed and sporting a rather unusual stovepipe chimney, stands outside No.21 Wagon Repair Shops in October 1966.

Now, over 20 years on from this rather infamous period of the work's history, and with the Swindon 'Festival of Steam' which takes place in September at the STEAM Museum in the remaining part of the works, I'd like to look back to those final years and some of the steam locomotives that could still be found there.

How the mighty have fallen! Their days of BR main line working long gone, two Hawksworth 94XX 0-6-0PTs lingered on at Swindon, relegated to stationary heating boilers for the Carriage and Wagon shops. By October 1967, it was all over for these last two operating steam locomotives at Swindon, and with the workshops east of the Gloucester line being run down, the cutters torch awaited both locomotives. They were photographed again in October 1967, prior to cutting up and, as far as I know, were the last steam locomotives disposed of at Swindon works.

It was only a matter of months before steam would re-appear and make the headlines again at the works. Not long after the last of steam locomotive No.8497 was disposed of in May 1968, then it became the turn of more prestige motive power to grab the attention of the railway media. Housed for many years in the former stock shed at the rear of Swindon's steam MPD, and now acquired for preservation by H P Bulmers at Hereford, flagship of the GWR fleet, No.6000 *King George V* was, on August 9 1968, and with due ceremony, manually pulled by ropes out of the shed by volunteers, to be greeted by the then Chairman of Bulmers Cider and Mayor and Mayoress of Swindon. As the photo shows, the weather could have been better!

Making history, being purchased and preserved by the Dart Valley Railway in 1971, 2-6-2T No.4588 became the first steam locomotive to receive an overhaul at Swindon since the end of steam in the mid '60s. Returning to her birthplace No.4588 is seen on August 16 1971, making a welcome sight inside Swindon's famous 'A' shop.

King George V made history again when, on October 2 1971, No.6000 became the first steam locomotive to haul a passenger train on BR metals since the end of steam in August 1968. This 'Return to Steam' week long extravaganza of railtours culminated in the loco making a return visit to Swindon Works on October 7 1971, where it was exhibited outside the main works offices for two days, before its final tour back to its home base at Hereford on October 9 1971.

No.8466 stands in Swindon's infamous Con Yard. The roof of 'C' shop can be seen in the distance, a site where so many steam and later diesel locomotives were to meet their fate.

A side on view of No.8497 awaiting its final journey to 'C' shop and eventual cutting up. This locomotive lasted until May 1968, where upon arrival at 'C' shop it became the very last steam locomotive to be disposed of at Swindon works.

With its supply of coal in the wagon behind, No.8497 (again with cabside and smokebox plate) has steam in abundance in this view taken in January 1967 outside No.19 Carriage Repair Shop. The supply pipe to the workshops can be clearly seen in this view entering just above the workshop door. *(Can anyone tell us the meaning of 'SUBEX' as on the wagon?..Ed)*

After undergoing mechanical repairs, No.4588 nears the end of her restoration and undergoes final painting before being outshopped (in steam) on August 20, to the then waiting Dart Valley Railway Managing Director and its eventual diesel-hauled journey to Totnes.

The early '70s saw the start of more foreign steam motive power appearing at the works. Looking a little out of place amongst the hydraulics inside 'A' shop, the Bluebell Railway's 1884-built ex-LSWR 4-4-2 'Radial' tank No.488 made a surprise visit during the autumn of 1971. Even though it wasn't a Western locomotive, a full mechanical overhaul authorised by the Bluebell Railway for this veteran was testament to the steam skills still available from Swindon's workforce. No.488 is seen not long after arrival in October 1971.

A dark and wet August day greeted No.6000 as it appeared from the former stock shed. The author and many others were participants on this day and Bulmers generously provided free cider to those who participated - pulling a 'King' was thirsty work!

After being displayed at Butlins Holiday Camp, Minehead, since 1964, Stanier LMS Pacific No.6229 *Duchess of Hamilton* was dispatched to Swindon Works for cosmetic restoration, before becoming a static exhibit at York museum. Departing Taunton on March 17, 1975, No.6229 is seen on April 26 inside 'A' shop. With its tender almost complete in the foreground, the 'Duchess' awaits the attention of Swindon's painters before onward movement to its new home in Yorkshire.

An unusual view taken from near the turntable at the main works entrance, on another Open Day, with more steam on view. *En route* from Barry to the Swindon & Cricklade Railway, No.7903 *Foremarke Hall* paid a brief visit to the works on Saturday June 6 1981, and is seen on a road transporter. No.7903, with its number painted on the smokebox and in typical Barry condition, receives admiring looks and the hope of better days to come.

The Works Open Day was a major event in any railway enthusiasts diary, with something interesting to view almost guaranteed, and September 14 1975 was no exception. On loan from the Great Western Society, Didcot, former Wantage Tramway Co 0-4-0 No.5, with its cab open to visitors, looks in fine shape if not a little dwarfed by its more modern, main line, counterparts.

A scene more reminiscent of Eastleigh than of Swindon. A welcome visitor in the summer of 1984 was ex-Southern Region Pacific No.35028 *Clan Line*. After undergoing weight and balancing tests, No.35028 moves off from the works tender first, in preparation of a test run to Bristol and back, on the morning of Friday July 27, 1984. Although name and crest are in place, No.35028 is still to have its cabside number applied.

A steam age scene witnessed countless times in Swindon's past, except that it was taken during early morning preparations for the works Open Day on Sunday October 5, 1980. Ex-works and ready to go, with just a trace of smoke from its copper-capped chimney, No.7812 *Erlestoke Manor*, on loan from the Severn Valley Railway, stands outside the works weighbridge building.

The completed 21 Ton hopper wagon finished and weathered as described in the text.

21ton steel hopper

Charlie King built this 7mm scale model from the M&M Models (EMKDE) kit. Photography by the author.

These 21 Ton, all-steel hopper wagons were introduced on the LNER in 1936. Although built to the LNER's specification, the railway company did not build any of these wagons itself. Metro-Cammell and Head Wrightson were the main contractors for these initial wagons with others contributing to later batches. Construction and development continued under British Railways, many of these being built at the wagon works at Shildon in County Durham which was also the main repair centre for them too, until some 38,000 21 Ton steel hopper wagons in their various guises existed, many lasting in traffic to the mid-1970s and even later in NCB internal use.

Although all of these hopper wagons were built to the same basic design, observation of photographs will show up a range of variations; different axleboxes, buffer types, position of grab rails, etc, all of which

are easy to incorporate using the M&M kit as a base. On the prototype, the acidic content of wet coal meant that steel bodywork deteriorated and although these wagons did not seem to succumb to this as fast as the well known 16 Ton steel mineral wagons, replating and rebuilding the body on the original chassis was quite common. Similarly axleboxes were replaced by later versions and some even ran on roller bearing axleboxes, there are even instances of the later BR welded wagons being repaired with riveted panels

Although based on the original LNER riveted design which was perpetuated in the early British Railways period it is fair to say that the M&M kit does not represent any specific diagram of these wagons. What the kit does is build up into a good representation of this distinctive type of wagon that can form a base for further detailing to

accommodate the many variations, in detail and more substantial, that these wagons underwent during their working lives.

Apart from the 'W'-irons and axleboxes, cast buffers and couplings, the M&M kit is completely etched-brass. It is possible to get the kit with original RCH design split axlebox or the later LNER/BR flat-fronted version, either of which appeared on these wagons. Alternatively, ABS Models do a range of axleboxes including the roller bearing type, that are also appropriate to this wagon and which can be substituted to give further variation. I discarded the cast buffers and replaced these with self-contained sprung buffers, RCH four-rib pattern were the most common but heavy duty and Oleo buffers also appeared on these wagons during their lives. The cast couplings also went in the scrap box being substituted with Instanter couplings,

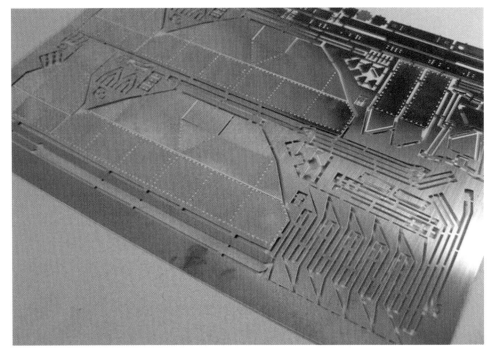
All of the parts on one etched sheet.

from the kit is the absence of the internal hopper chutes, they clearly did not fit on the etch, and a drawing is supplied for the modeller to mark and cut these out themselves from a piece of brass or indeed 'Plastikard' would do if left until after all of the soldering had been completed. As I have a number of these wagons to do, I got these parts profile milled for me.

Let construction commence. Before removing any parts from the fret, I pressed out the dozens of rivets. I have no idea if the number of rivets on the kit is accurate, life is too short to count them and there are not many of these wagons in preservation to go and check. Although I have a rivet press, for this job I used a drop hammer type rivet punch simply because it was quicker. As an aid to accuracy, the rivet markings on the kit are a bit inconsistent; I taped a

although it should be noted that in the LNER period three-link couplings were used. What is omitted are the 'clasp' brakes that these wagons were fitted with. ABS do a suitable set of white metal castings, but photos seem to indicate that later in life not all types were so equipped.

As mentioned, the kit is etched-brass and builds up into a robust model which is not too heavy for those who would want to run a rake of several of these. The etching is not as crisp as some kits and there is a bit of fettling to do on some parts but this is not a big problem. The castings clean up well under a wire brush and, as I have already said, I only used the axleboxes anyway. The instructions are a mixture of text and exploded drawings and are adequate enough although details of how the wagon looks from underneath are

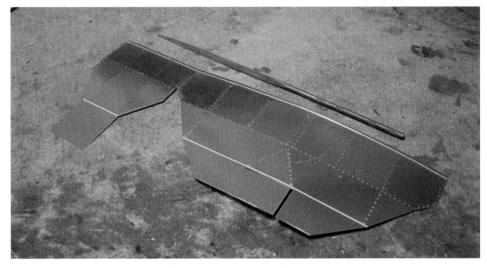
Using a triangular file to sharpen the half-etched lines prior to bending.

absent. A few photo's - as always - are a useful reference and also to aid working out where some of the parts are supposed to go. One omission

steel rule along the lines of rivets as a guide for the tip of the rivet punch. The second task is to go along all of the half-etched fold lines where a 90° fold is to be made with a triangular needle file. This sharpens the line and makes folding that much easier. This is especially important on the chassis side frames where there is not too much metal to get hold of in the folding bars. I find half a dozen strokes is adequate but you do need to take care not to over do it as it is possible to file right through the line.

I broke construction down into three main parts: the main body, the basic chassis and adding the details.

The body comes in two halves and the first thing to do on each one after removing it from the fret is to carefully fold the top edge over. A set of folding bars is needed for this but if you haven't got any of these,

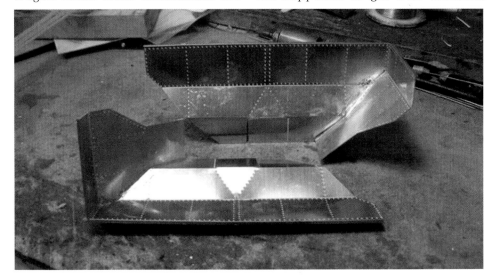
The half-body sides folded into shape and soldered.

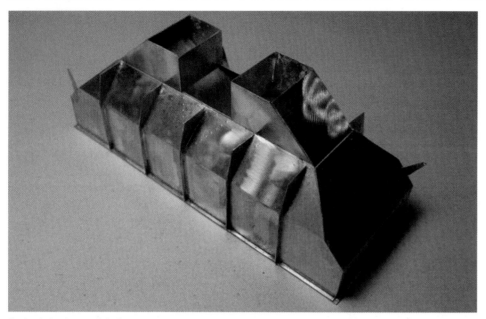

The basic body completed.

two lengths of timber and a couple of 'G' cramps will make an adequate substitute. An alternative is to fold the edge carefully in a vice but if you do this don't make a full 90° bend - go half way then move on to the next bit and fold that halfway and so on until the whole side is part done. When you have the whole side part folded, go back and make a final fold to the full 90°. By doing this you will reduce the risk of creasing the metal.

The next stage is to carefully bend up one of the body halves; the wagon end folds and fits inside the wagon side, and solder the seams together. I tack soldered at the very top, where the body side folds inwards and also at the bottom of the hopper and checked for true before soldering the seam completely. With both halves of the wagon body made up, the next step is to join them together. This is one of those jobs where you wish you had three hands. As I don't, I have a board which I work on that has a batten fixed along the top and down one side making a square corner. I found that I could hold the two parts of the body together upside down in that corner and tack solder the bottom of the hopper. This kept the top edge of the wagon aligned and the tack was sufficient to allow the body to be turned over so that I could tack solder the top and half way down the sloping side as before. I should point out that I did all of the soldering on the inside and I realise that I could have soldered on the outside of the wagon but then I would have had more cleaning up to do.

It is important to take your time and get the wagon body square and true. Tack soldering and checking and

finding any faults before soldering up the seam is time well spent. The etch is supposed to fold round at the bottom to make the inner ends of where the coal drops through when on the real thing the bottom doors were opened. I found to get these properly square, it was easier to break this part off, solder it back in position, and then fettle up the joints rather than persist with the folded joint. I then soldered in the internal hopper chutes. As previously mentioned, these are missing in the kit so I had some profile milled for me and if you ask him nicely and part with a few coins of the realm, John Taylor will do you some too. The hopper chutes need a little bit of fettling but once soldered in place finish off the wagon interior.

With the bodyshell assembled the next step is to solder all of the side and end stanchions in place. Cut these off the fret carefully and using the top edge as a datum point solder each one in place. Again I tacked the top, where the body side slopes under and right at the bottom of each one. Before fully soldering all of the stanchions in place, check that they all line up and adjust as necessary. At this stage mark out and drill holes at each end for the upper hand rail that fits across the wagon end (I drilled through the third or fourth rivet down from the top as there were slight variations in the position of this handrail) and to solder a lower handrail support in place, one at each end. It is easier to position these with the body off the chassis.

The wagon body can be set to one side while we turn our attention to the chassis. I made a simple jig to help hold the chassis parts while soldering them together. This jig is no more sophisticated than a piece of hardboard with a timber frame to make three sides of a rectangle to hold the main chassis square and true. The chassis construction replicates the real thing in that the main side frames are stiffened by cross members and an inner frame that supports the body. I made up the outer frames which comprise the main side frames, and buffer beams. The inner frames can be soldered together then placed in position in the chassis; marks on the inside of the mainframes indicate where this should go. This leaves the short frame sections that joint

The hopper interior showing the milled internal hopper shutes.

the inner and outer frames together along the sides to put in. They need a bit of fettling to get a good fit and it is important to line them up with the marks on the outer frame otherwise they will not line up with the body stanchions and the wagon will look wrong. The next job is to solder the end platforms in position but before doing so make sure that your basic chassis is square and true. Again before soldering a seam, tack the part in place and check that everything is still square. Finally, in this part of the build, fit the grab rails that are fitted to one side of each platform. I bent a piece of 0.7mm wire for these and gauged the correct height of the grab rail with a piece of card applying solder from underneath. Carefully clean off any surplus solder and bring the two parts of the wagon together. If all is well the two parts should come together with the side stanchions on the body lining up with the short cross frames on the chassis.

We can now join the two parts of the wagon together. To do this, position the wagon body in place in the chassis. I placed the chassis on two short lengths of timber so that it was supported, then, using hand pressure, held the body down into place. I tacked each of the side stanchions to the top edge of the chassis, the two pieces of timber that the work is resting on reduces the risk of introducing distortion into the chassis, having taken the time and trouble to get it square and true. With the sides secured to the chassis you can now solder the end supports in place. These need to be folded along the half-etch lines and again the filing with the tip of a triangular needle file will ease the process of bending as there is not much metal to get a hold of. For these bends I used a vice and a square ended pair of pliers. There are etched lines on the top of the end platforms to show where the end supports fit. They should tuck up against the end stanchions on the wagon body. For each end support, position it in place on the platform and tack solder in place. This is simply to hold it while you position it on the wagon body. By keeping the work on the pieces of wood you are keeping the chassis flat and if there is any slight distortion it will be pushed into the wagon body not the chassis.

With the end supports in place the next step is to add the grab rails that run the full width of the wagon ends from 0.7mm wire. Although the basic positions of these are the same

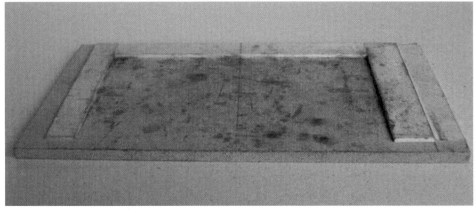

The simple chassis jig.

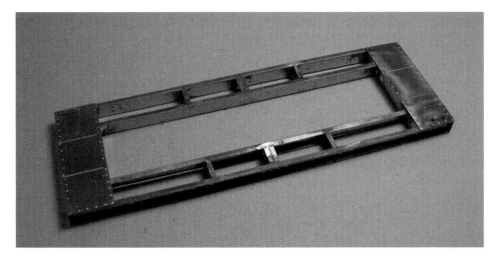

The basic chassis.

there is some variation between the different wagon builders and checking photographs is always worthwhile. The upper rail is straightforward enough, it simply solders into the holes drilled into the ends of the wagon as mentioned previously. The vertical rail requires a hole to be drilled in the top corner of the headstock with the other end butt jointed against the horizontal handrail or through a hole drilled in the body end. This is where referring to photographs helps as there were different ways of doing this. Try to set the vertical grab rail in line with the hole in the end of the mounting bracket which supports the lower horizontal grab rail. For reasons that will become apparent shortly, make the lower horizontal rail; thread the rail supports onto a length of 0.7 wire then solder one end of it into the hole in the support bracket that you should have soldered in place before marrying up the body and chassis. The free end of this wire needs to be carefully butt jointed to the vertical grab rail checking that it is horizontal. With the grab rail in position, it is quite easy to manoeuvre the support brackets that are fixed to the end supports and hold the rail

in position into place and fix them with a touch of solder. Again, check photographs, some wagons had small fixing brackets others had the larger triangular type that always supported the outer end of the lower handrail. Don't worry too much if you do not get everything perfectly aligned. prototype photographs show that these rails got bent and bashed about Some wagons also have a short grab rail on the end side panel but many did not.

The remaining work focuses on the chassis. There is a stiffening piece that joins the two coal chutes in the bottom of the wagon which on the prototype was a length of angle iron. On the model I dispensed with the fold up part in the kit and substituted a length of 2mm x 2mm brass angle instead. If you prepare the etched part in the kit by sharpening the half-etched fold line then it is relatively easy to hold and bend in the vice. The next step is to fit the 'V'-hangers. The rivets on the sole bars indicate their position. With the 'V'-hangers in place, the brake gear can be fitted. There are two brackets which angle out and fix the brake gear to the inner chassis frame. The safety loops can

Close-up of the brake lever with guide drilled 0.5mm to open up the pin holes.

be folded up first into a 'U'-shape then bend the last 5mm of the legs over so that they can be soldered to the underside of the chassis. Doing this is quite unobtrusive and gives a secure anchorage.

I did the brackets or the door operating mechanism next. These are placed just either side of the 'V'-hangers. I put both brackets to one side, then using a length of 0.9mm wire with the bracket for the other side threaded onto to it, I used this to line up and locate its position. The door operating handles can be fitted at this stage and the wire trimmed back almost flush with their surface.

The brake lever guide comes next. I drilled the half-etched holes through with a 0.5mm drill which does not take more than a few minutes to do and enhances the appearance of this part of the model. The guides fold up easily enough and I soldered them to the solebar and also to the last side stanchion on the wagon body for additional security.

I fitted the cast 'W' irons and axle box castings next. These need drilling with a 2.5 mm drill to take a Slater's wheel bearing. The bearing needs to fit so that its rim is level with the surface of the casting. Before fitting I cleaned up the castings with a wire brush and used the edge of a file to ensure that the top edge which fits on the solebar was neat and true. The bottom edge of the solebar was tinned with 145° solder, the casting put in place and 70° solder applied after a generous application of flux.

The heat from the iron will travel through the brass and draw the 70° solder under the casting. Hold the casting long enough for the solder to chill properly or the joint will crack open. If you have taken care to get the chassis straight and true, you should have no problems getting all of the wheels to sit level on a flat surface. I use a piece of plate glass but a piece of plastic coated chipboard will do just as well.

The brake lever can now be bent to shape and positioned and end steps soldered into place at the end with the vertical grab rail which incidentally should be at the end opposite to the brake lever guide. To complete construction the coupling strengthening plate and buffer shanks are soldered to the headstocks. I used a variety of types of buffer on the batch of

wagons I am building which can be obtained from Prestige Models or Slater's. Similarly the 'Instanter' type couplings can be sourced from the same suppliers.

I should mention that as I go along I clean the model at the end of every modelling session. This prevents the unnecessary build up of flux residue and grease the removal of which is an aid to cleaning off any surplus solder with a fibre glass scratch brush.

With construction complete, the model is given a through wash to remove any traces of flux and grease. I find that giving the model a scrub with an old toothbrush while it is immersed in a bowl of hot water with one of the propriety lime scale removers dissolved in it, good for this final clean up. After a through rinse, I run a wire brush in a mini-drill over the wheels which 'spin dries' them, thus preventing rusting. The model is put aside in a box in the airing cupboard or other warm place for a couple of days to dry.

The first coat of paint is an etching primer. I use 'Acid 8' from Halfords but there are others available. I always give this coat two days to dry thoroughly and it gives a good key for further coats of paint. The next coat is grey primer, from the same source and left to dry overnight. I then painted the solebars, wheels, etc, black, again with a Satin Black aerosol. I simply masked off the body parts I did not want painted black roughly by holding a piece of card in front of them. As the wagons were going to be finished in a weathered condition the final paint coats were going to be brushed on I did not require a particularly neat finish at this stage.

When 'weathering' I find that photographs are essential not to

What it looks like underneath.

The other side of the completed wagon showing the variations in rusting that was common on the prototype.

slavishly copy but to act as a guide as to how the prototype really appeared. From observation it becomes apparent that the edges of the side stanchions and the top edge of the wagon body soon showed signs of rusting, tipping coal into the wagon would soon erode paint away from these surfaces. The sloping parts of the wagon seem to be more susceptible to rusting than the upper panels and it is possible to find photographs of wagons where some panels are in poor condition yet adjacent ones show little sign of rusting. Similarly evidence of repairs and re-plating can be found and this can range from a patch on part of a panel to whole sections of bodywork.

Following techniques described in Martin Welch's book *The Art of Weathering*, I did the inside of the wagon first. This was painted in washes of mainly matt black, a little silver, and dark grey with touches of red oxide, mid brown and orange introduced mainly to the top parts of the wagon. There are few photos of the insides of wagons and I know memory plays tricks but I do not recall these wagons being 'rusty' on the inside. No doubt they were but the abrasive effects of 20 tons of coal sliding through them plus the coal dust adhering to the surface left the interior relatively rust free.

With the interior painted and dry, attention can turn to the outside and I first painted in black rectangles for the wagon load and number. With these dry they were masked off and

using only three shades from red oxide through, mid-brown to orange, I stippled a mix of the these colours onto the surfaces I wanted to appear 'rusty'. A little talcum powder stippled into the wet paint will add a degree of texture to the surface which can be later dry brushed and colour washed to give a quite convincing appearance of rusty metal. I use a cheap hogshair brush with the bristles chopped down to about 6mm long for this job, your expensive sable brushes will not last five minutes.

When these areas are thoroughly dry, leaving them overnight is best, paint over them with blobs of latex masking fluid. I used 'Maskol' but Precision Paints do a similar product. Don't spread this too thinly or you will not find it under the top coat of paint. This is left for about 20 minutes then brush painted over with a fairly liberal top coat of BR Freight Grey. This topcoat must be left to dry overnight and harden. Now comes the fun bit, plucking the 'Maskol' off with a pair of tweezers. This will create the effect of the rust blistering through the paint work and because you have left the top colour to harden you will get the effects of the torn edges to the paint where you have pulled the Maskol off.

When I have got all of the Maskol off I brush the surface with a dry toothbrush to get rid of any bits and further erode the surfaces. To finish, dry brushing with dark grey with a bit of silver introduced into the paint

can give a metallic highlight as well as washing thin coats of your rust colours over the rusted areas, into corners around rivets etc. To get a convincing appearance takes time and a bit of practice and a lot of patience. I never do more than ten minutes of weathering at a time and always leave things to dry especially if I am washing thinned colours on, before moving to the next stage otherwise you will undo all of the previous work. Final steps are to put the buffer heads in and fit the couplings which I usually treat to a dip in a chemical blackening before giving a highlight with a little paint. A final light dusting with the airbrush loaded with 'frames dirt' and 'weathered black' softens in the colours quite nicely.

This is not a kit for the beginner nor would I recommend it to anyone who wants an exact representation of a particular diagram of these wagons, the DJH/Piercy wagon is better for that. However, the DHJ/Piercy kit is more time consuming to build and I personally do not like the way that cast white metal components have been used where brass might have been better. As described the M&M kit has a number of shortcomings but if you are prepared to accept a degree of compromise, and like myself you need a number of hopper wagons that strike a balance between weight, robustness and appearance to run in a rake then this kit offers an ideal alternative. With the editor's permission, I will look at some of the more major variations that can be built from this kit in a future article.

Useful contacts:

■ M&M Models
22 Plantation Court,
41 Plantation Road, Poole,
Dorset BH17 9LW
Tel: 01202 695447

■ John Taylor (Profile Milling)
Moor End cottage, Steep Lane
Sowerby, Halifax HX6 1PE
Tel: 01422 839538

■ Prestige Models
8 Woodshires Road
Longford, Coventry CV6 6AA
Tel: 02476361881

■ Slater's Plastikard
Temple Road, Matlock Bath
Matlock, Derbyshire DE4 3PG
Tel: 01629 583993

Dymchurch Station circa 1935. No.2 *Northern Chief* is being replenished. It appears to be hauling a three-coach special, possibly for The Model Railway Club. Note the 1934 full brake, the oak cask water butt and the former overall roof at the station. **Captain W F Kelly - Author's Collection**

Across the Marsh from Gallows Corner to Dungeness Point

Michael C Shaw celebrates 80 years of the Romney, Hythe and Dymchurch Railway. Photographs as credited.

All great enterprises have to start with an idea, a dream in this case! R H Fuller, a young assistant at Bassett-Lowke's famous showroom at 112 High Holborn, recalled a conversation around 1918-19 between Grand Duke Dmitre Pavlovitch of Russia, a cousin of Czar Nicholas II, and the millionaire playboy Count Louis Zborowksi, heir to the Astor fortune and later the 'Racing Count' – a Brooklands and international racing ace of the '20s. These two unusual men, still in their twenties, had a dream-like vision of a miniature main line railway, double

tracked and signalled, with one third scale express locomotives, fast passenger and freight trains, and all the other paraphernalia that makes a working railway.

First locomotives ordered

Count Louis' fortune was based on owning much of New York's financial district and it enabled him to build a large 15" gauge line around his estate, Higham Park, Bridge (near Canterbury, Kent), for which he ordered two 'Pacific' locomotives, LZ1, later *Green Goddess* on the RHDR and LZ2, later *Northern Chief*

on the same railway. Some of the track is still on the site of the estate, being used as fence posts along the left-hand side of its driveway.

An association with racing driver Captain John Edward Pressgrave Howey, who also had a 15" gauge line on his estate, was set up and these two friends looked for a site for the railway. Sir Herbert Walker, General Manager of the Southern Railway, suggested a route between New Romney and Hythe, as there was the possibility of connection with the Southern's branch lines to New Romney and Hythe. This was an era of the electric tramway and the rapidly developing motor bus, and Sir Herbert wisely saw the possibilities for the tourist and holiday development of the area.

Henry Greenly appointed

Sadly the Count, like his father 20 years before, was killed on October 19, 1923, along with his mechanic, during practice for the Italian Grand Prix. Captain Howey, having inherited a fortune from his families' business interests in Australia, therefore decided to go it alone and, at Sir Herbert's bidding, build a line from New Romney to Hythe. Howey wasn't one to let the grass grow under his feet, and immediately set about purchasing land and putting in place a Light Railway Order, supported by the Southern Railway. By doing this, he stole a lead on local opposition, without the need to ask for public subscription and before obtaining permission of any sort, either under the Light Railways Act of 1896 or under local consents. He set the brilliant Henry Greenly to build the railway; Greenly and Herbert Walker had already met during the Great War at the Royal Aircraft Factory (later RAE). Work was already under way

when Howey decided to make the line double tracked, making savings by using ex-WD 'trench' light railway rail.

The line opened officially on July 16, 1927. Howey immediately put in hand a 5½ mile extension, initially double track, tearing down his recently completed terminus at New Romney, the Light Railway Order for this being confirmed on July 27, 1928. The RHDR now stretched from Hythe (Gallows Corner), through its main base at New Romney, over the shingle of St Mary's Bay and onto Denge Marsh to Dungeness Point.

Millionaires don't have to make choices dictated by budget. In addition to the original 'Pacifics', Howey ordered two new Gresley lookalike 2-8-2 locomotives for use on aggregate traffic on the highly graded route to the Southern Railway's Sandling Junction from Hythe (which was never built).

There was also talk of joining the railway up with the 2' 0" gauge Rye & Camber Tramway, something that the Army very nearly carried out during World War II.

1930s holiday boom

The RHDR settled down to its work of taking happy holidaymakers along the

coastal strip, with its holiday camps, chalet parks (some of which were old railway carriages and tram bodies)

Hythe Station also circa 1935, once again Northern Chief *is being watered, the locomotive can still be seen on the same duties today, albeit with a larger tender. The oval windows in the full brake can be seen in this picture - prior to the 1970s all trains had a guard.* **Captain W F Kelly - Author's Collection**

and some fine sandy beaches.

It prospered, new coaches and refreshment facilities had to be provided in spite of the Captain himself, who seemed rather taken aback that his private dream had proved so popular to the general public. He built a branch to a gravel pit and began transporting aggregate and another branch ran to the War Department's Sound Mirror detection system, near Maddieson's Holiday Camp at St Mary's Bay.

Two new locomotives were ordered from the Yorkshire Engine Company (later part of Leyland Motors). These were 'Pacifics' with standard boilers, but were built to a Canadian Pacific outline, with Vanderbilt bogie tenders.

Howey closed his grand station hotel at Hythe pretty soon after opening the line and sold it to private interests. The café at Hythe is now very much a local institution, and after several rebuilds, just like the locomotives, is still doing good business. Howey was forced, by public demand, to do something about the refreshment facilities at the Dungeness loop end of the line, and so a restaurant was constructed, still there today, which is very welcome on a wet and windy day on Denge Marsh, as there is very

little protection from the weather!

Howey converted a Rolls Royce Silver Ghost motor car he just happened to have lying around into a lightweight railcar, and put it into service hauling the limited stop 'Bluecoaster Limited' with new Pullman coaches built by

Clayton in 1934.

War service
During World War II, the railway continued to operate a daily service, though reduced to the winter timetable. The line became heavily used as holidaymakers reluctantly

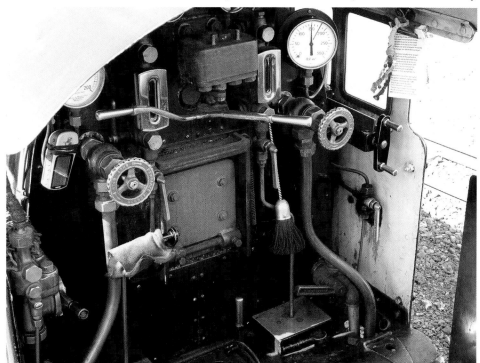

Inside the tidy cab of No.2 *Northern Chief*. It seems hard to believe these locomotives have been in service so long, they are kept in superb condition. No room for a fireman though, its a bit snug just for the driver! **Richard Wilson**

No.3 *Southern Maid*, appropriately currently painted in malachite green, has just arrived at Dungeness with a fairly full train. **Richard Wilson**

gave up their chalets and holiday camps, which overnight became military bases. The first troop train was run on September 5, 1939, the nightly leave trains for Hythe and return became legend, often double headed with all available rolling stock being used.

With the Dunkirk evacuation, the civilian population was also evacuated from this coastal area and from June 1940 the RHDR became a military railway, the 4-8-2 *Hercules* and two former Ravenglass & Eskdale bogie wagons that had been used on aggregate trains were armoured and equipped with two Lewis guns and a Boyer anti-tank rifle (later replaced by a Bofors gun). This train remained in steam at all times until autumn 1941. The armoured trains offensive activities were accredited with losses by the Luftwaffe.

Unfortunately much of the lines interlocking was smashed by a mystified Canadian unit and the double track section from New Romney to Dungeness suffered as 'PLUTO's (Pipe Line Under The Ocean) inland terminals and pumping stations were established - initially bogie well wagons were used - but as time ran out use was made of tracked

vehicles which caused damage to the track. The pipeline eventually supplied Allied forces with fuel, allowing them to liberate Western Europe after 'D' day in 1944. This section of line was relaid as single track post-war.

Post war

The Hythe - New Romney section was de-requisitioned during spring 1943, but the railway was not released to Howey until July 1945, when he was allowed back into the still restricted area. The line received very little damage from the enemy, and German and Italian POWs were used to repair any damaged sections. After much hard work, the least damaged section between Hythe and New Romney was reopened on March 1, 1946 by thc Mayors of the two Cinque Ports, which was followed by two heavy snowstorms.

To Captain Howey's astonishment, the railway was overrun with crowds of people, so more hard work was needed to have the railway ready for them for the Easter holidays. Due to the lack of stock, Howey purchased the Duke of Westminster's Eaton Hall line and stock. The now singled section from the MPD at New Romney was opened to Maddieson's Camp (St

No.2 *Northern Chief* stands ready to depart Dungeness station. The size of the replacement bogie tenders fitted to the first three locomotives can be appreciated in this photograph. **Richard Wilson**

No.9 Winston Churchill, in an approximate LMS lake livery, arrives at New Romney station from Dungeness. The line singles shortly after passing under the Station Road bridge in the background. **Richard Wilson**

the railway had the best publicity it could have for its first full season as a complete service.

During the 1940s and '50s the line boomed, despite a tailing off in the Kent Coast as a holiday destination. Captain Howey spent as little money as he could on the line, and last drove *Green Goddess* during the summer of 1957, aged 70. I met him around this time and greatly embarrassed my father by demanding to see his Rolls Royce railcar, with the bonus of being shown around the loco shed - and his new Jaguar sports car too! I must have been a pretty confident pre-school child - Howey didn't like talking to the junior public - but I had done my homework, my first interview in fact!

Decline and resurrection
Howey died on September 8, 1963, aged 77. His wife died in 1972, and with both their children dead, two retired bankers, S H Collins and J E Scatcherd, bought the line on July 1, 1964. The RHDR had not been designed to outlive its creator and owner. Greenly had done a reasonable job, but nothing lasts for ever and major repairs mounted.

Eventually, a group of 21 Folkestone businessmen purchased the line on

Mary's Bay) by mid 1946, and the rest of the line though to Dungeness was officially opened by the comedians and movie stars Stan Laurel and Oliver Hardy. Their antics were duly filmed, photographed and recorded,

Locomotives					
Number	Name	Arrangement	Works Number	Builder	Build date
1	Green Goddess (LZ1)	4-6-2	15469	Davey Paxman & Co	16/11/1925
2	Northern Chief (LZ2)	4-6-2	15470	Davey Paxman & Co	16/11/1925
3	Southern Maid	4-6-2	16040	Davey Paxman & Co	20/04/1927
4	The Bug	0-4-0	Modified	Krauss, Munich	1926
5	Hercules	4-8-2	16041	Davey Paxman & Co	20/04/1927
6	Samson	4-8-2	16042	Davey Paxman & Co	20/07/1927
7	Typhoon	4-6-2	16043	Davey Paxman & Co	19/05/1927
8	Hurricane	4-6-2	16044	Davey Paxman & Co	20/07/1927
9	Winston Churchill	4-6-2	2295	Yorkshire Engine Company	18/05/1931
10	Dr Syn	4-6-2	2294	Yorkshire Engine Company	25/03/1931
11	Black Prince	4-6-2		Krupp, Essen	1937
12	John Southland	Diesel-Hydraulic Bo-Bo		TMA Engineering	1983
14	Captain Howey	Diesel-Hydraulic Bo-Bo		TMA Engineering	1989

The driver of No.11 *Black Prince* has a brief exchange with the driver of No.9 *Winston Churchill*, whilst the train waits to depart New Romney for Dungeness.
Richard Wilson

May 31, 1968 and had no choice but to make essential repairs to rolling stock, permanent way and engineering structures. The possibility of transferring the line to the site now occupied by the Torbay Steam Railway was considered, as well as reducing the length of the existing line, and even complete closure.

A group led by Sir William McAlpine eventually took over the RHDR in February 1972, with the objective of restoring, maintaining and developing the railway in line with Howey and Zborowski's original concept.

Two diesels have now been constructed for the line, while the original contractor's loco *The Bug* was located, restored and brought back to the RHDR in 1978. One of three German 'Pacifics' brought to England was rebuilt for use on the railway and named *Black Prince*. The Romney, Hythe & Dymchurch Railway Association has gradually played a greater part in the line's development, purchasing shares in the operating company and providing help when and as required. The railway has new signalling, a new MPD and the stock is in the best condition ever.

The railway has had to find the funds for providing three of its ungated level crossings with barriers, following the sad circumstances of two drivers being killed when their locomotives were struck by careless motorists, terrible events, which could have been much worse.

This fine little railway goes from strength to strength, it is one of the few main line railways left in the world operating just as it was built to do, with all of its original locomotives.

Further Reading

One Man's Railway
J B Snell and David St John Thomas
David & Charles 1986

The Marshlander
The Journal of the RHDR Association

The World's Smallest Public Railway
O J Morris
Ian Allan 1946

The Line that Jack Built
G Freeman Allen
Ian Allan 1963

Information

The Romney Hythe & Dymchurch Railway runs between Hythe and Dungeness and is a 15" gauge, 13½ mile long, mostly double track, 'main line in miniature'. A return journey takes approximately two hours 20 minutes and costs £11.20 (children 3-15 years travel at half fare). An excellent museum, model railway, restaurant and gift shop can be found at New Romney station. For information Tel: 01797 362353 email: info@rhdr.org or visit: www.rhdr.org.uk

Location

By Car: Access to all stations *via* A259, Hythe Station three miles from M20 Junction 11

By Bus: from Ashford, Canterbury, Hastings, Rye, Folkestone and Dover by Stagecoach, Kent & East Sussex, Tel: 08702 433711

By Rail: To Folkestone Central, Hastings or Rye

By Coach: National Express service 021 between London and Hythe.

ABOVE: *Northern Chief* heads around the return loop across Dengemarsh at Dungeness, Kent, in August 1998 showing the unique landscape of the area. The distant cottages indicate the coastline. **All Michael C Shaw**

The second of the Davey Paxman Pacifics (LZ2) No.2 *Northern Chief* waits for the signal for Dungeness with a full head of steam on a wet July day in 1997.

INSET: The Armoured Train, reconstructed in 1990, photographed in July, 1994.

Interesting headboards are a feature of the Romney Hythe & Dymchurch Railway - No.9 *Winston Churchill* is seen while taking part in 'VE Day' anniversary celebrations at New Romney in the summer of 1995.

Krüpps-built German Pcific No.11 *Black Prince* takes water at New Romney in 1998.

The author's brother, Bob, views two Romney, Hythe & Dymchurch trains at Dungeness, 1952. **Peter D Page**

Choices

Peter J Page discusses choosing a prototype for your layout.
Photography as credited.

A visit to a good general model railway exhibition, or the study of the model railway press, will reveal a wide variety of approaches to railway modelling. One of the factors in this variety is the choice of prototype. I have previously argued in the pages of *British Railway Modelling* that observation and understanding of the real thing is necessary for credibility (see *BRM*, October 2004). The present article flows from the following observations:

Even within a small geographical compass it can be possible to find a huge variety of inspiration in the real thing, much of which variety can be captured by 'ordinary' modellers, and there are large areas of prototype inspiration which are under-explored by railway modellers.

If we are going to enjoy railway modelling, we need to take an approach that appeals to our personal interests, abilities and resources. It is natural (and, for ordinary mortals, advisable) that most newcomers to the hobby will follow one of the 'mainstream' strands in the early days and produce what one might term a 'generic' layout. The vision and excitement will be to get something running and gain experience. However, even while that early experience is being gained, there is time for 'armchair modelling', hours when we can read and think more widely about prototype possibilities and consider new layout projects.

If we want to give our layouts a bit of originality, one of the things that those of us who have gained a bit of experience can do is to look at the

possibilities in the less well explored corners of our hobby. This is what I am doing with 'Fantasy Park' (see *BRM* November 2003) and a smaller related project. I have chosen to go in one direction, but it is a constant source of surprise to me just how much there is to be modelled which is widely, if not completely, neglected. Some of those relatively neglected areas, such as early railways, may require quite highly developed research and technical skills, but there are others well within reach of anyone prepared to do even just a little bit more than 'shake the box'.

Originality does not have to be extreme, but it does mean getting inspiration from sources other than other people's models. Drawing inspiration from the real thing is the obvious course, and one that also helps us to make our models credible. If we understand what we see and discover, we can distil the essence of a prototype and produce a believable fiction, which may be as close to the truth as a biography or as 'freelance' as a good novel or play.

Prototype variety, a local example

As a reminder of just how much variety there is in prototype railways for us to model, Table 1 lists some possibilities from Kent and East Sussex alone - note, however, that the list is not intended to be exhaustive. The bibliography at the end of the article lists some further reading related to this table. Some of the prototypes will be more difficult to model than others, but even if one sticks with standard gauge public lines which can be modelled with little or no scratch-building, there is huge variety. Each line has its own traffic and traction patterns, and those patterns change over time.

To take a more specific example, I was brought up in Maidstone, which is served by two separate double track lines. When I was a boy in the 1950s the town was the end-of-electrification point on both lines, so even in my home town I could observe four different traffic and traction patterns, each of which might inspire a distinctive model. Those patterns were different from what my father would have seen before the 1939 electrification, and they have changed again since, most notably as a result of the further electrification of the early 1960s and, in the case of the line through Maidstone East, as a consequence of the Channel Tunnel.

In the 1950s the older South Eastern Railway line along the Medway valley saw fairly heavy freight traffic, including coal for the paper and cement industries of the lower Medway Valley and North Kent. With easy gradients, trains of 50-60 wagons were common. Maidstone West goods yard was large enough to have its own shunting locomotive, and there was a short freight only branch across the river to Tovil. South of Maidstone West towards Paddock Wood the passenger service was rural in nature and normally provided by steam powered push-pull trains. In the other direction through Maidstone Barracks towards Strood the passenger trains were third-rail electric providing a half-hourly service through a more industrial area.

Freight traffic on the former London, Chatham and Dover Railway

line through Maidstone East was then much less prominent than in the Medway valley. Trains were shorter because of the heavier gradients, and they tended to be more mixed in composition. Maidstone East goods yard, although quite extensive, was shunted by the daily pick-up freight which, if memory serves me correctly, would have left with about a dozen wagons. Hourly local passenger third-rail electric trains ran west towards London, and there were just a few morning and evening extras for commuters. Local passenger services east towards Ashford were steam hauled, but I never knew push-pull working on that route. This line was Boat Train Route 2, and saw an irregular pattern of main

line passenger trains, steam-hauled throughout. These ranged from occasional workings of 'The Golden Arrow' or 'The Night Ferry', hauled by Pacifics and diverted off one of the other two boat train routes, to relief and excursion trains being handled by smaller 4-4-0s (eg: Classes D1, E1, L and L1) whose crews must have cursed the climb up Bearsted bank immediately after the speed restricted curves through Maidstone East station.

In OO at least, all four of these traffic and traction patterns could be replicated in model form, in essence if not in detail, using ready-to-run and kit products from the trade. As inspiration for models the two involving 2-HAL EMUs on local

Mother takes two future railway modellers for a ride on the amusement park railway at Folkestone, 1956 - because of the small size of the cars this may be a prototype best suited to large scale modelling. **Peter D Page**

TABLE 1: Prototypes from Kent and East Sussex

STANDARD GAUGE
'Traditional' main lines, including:
- London-Tonbridge-Ashford-Dover (ex-SER - includes an interesting coastal section between Folkestone and Dover)
- London-Tonbridge-Hastings (ex-SER - unusual trains in pre-electrification days because of restricted clearances in tunnels)
- London-Chatham-Dover/Thanet (ex-LC&DR - electrified as far as Gillingham before World War II)
- London-Brighton/Eastbourne (ex-LB&SCR - electrified throughout before World War II)

Channel Tunnel Rail Link

London Suburban lines, such as:
- North Kent line *via* Dartford to the Medway Towns

Secondary routes
- Double-track lines such as Swanley-Maidstone-Ashford-Canterbury-Thanet or Tunbridge Wells-Lewes-Brighton
- Largely single track lines such as Tunbridge Wells-East Grinstead-Three Bridges or Tunbridge Wells-Eastbourne.
- Folkestone Harbour Branch - double-track with steep gradient and severe restrictions on the locomotives which could be used in steam days.

'Traditional' branch lines of very varying character, such as:
- Dunton Green-Westerham
- Gravesend-Grain/Allhallows (including Port Victoria and, later, refinery traffic)
- Sittingbourne-Sheerness (including lift bridge over the Swale)
- Paddock Wood-Hawkhurst
- Appledore-New Romney/Dungeness (now nuclear flask traffic)

The Canterbury & Whitstable Railway (very early)

Light Railways, including:
- Sheppy Light Railway
- East Kent Light Railway - with colliery traffic and Richborough port traffic at various times
- Kent & East Sussex Light Railway - with modern preservation movement involvement

Cliff Railways, Folkestone, 1959 - the two pairs of cars are of different designs. **Peter J Page**

Port and dockyard railways at Chatham (Royal Navy), Dover (worked by British Railways in the 1950s) and elsewhere

Colliery systems in East Kent (Snowdon, Tilmanstone, Betteshanger and Chislet)

Mountfield gypsum mines

Industrial railways serving cement, paper and other industry in North Kent and elsewhere

The Bluebell Railway and other preserved railways

NARROW GAUGE AND MINIATURE RAILWAYS
- Romney, Hythe & Dymchurch
- Rye & Camber Tramway
- Hastings Miniature Railway
- Passenger railway at Maidstone Zoo - very basic (petrol?) tractor and passenger car, no points
- Chattenden & Upnor Railway - Naval/Military
- Military railways on Lydd ranges for moving targets, etc.
- Sittingbourne & Kemsley Railway - originally an extensive industrial system serving paper industry, now a preserved line.
- Industrial railways serving cement making, quarrying, sand extraction, brick making and other industries.
- Sewage works, eg: at Maidstone
- Amusement park rides

CLIFF RAILWAYS
- Working on the water-balance principle - Hastings (two - one in tunnel) and Folkestone (two side by side with different pattern cars)

NOTE: This list is not intended to be exhaustive.

passenger services mixed with steam trains are seriously under-exploited from what I have seen at exhibitions and in the model press. (A similar comment might be made about the ex-SE&CR 4-4-0s, albeit that there has been a ready-to-run L1 in OO and a few kits for some of the other types.) Even within the 1950s there were changes over time, and just before the start of electric services, east and south of Maidstone, green-liveried diesel traction displaced some of the steam. Among other things, D50xx/D65xx combinations appeared working steam heated main line passenger trains. Details like that are worth looking for if you want authenticity and originality.

One station, but a variety of inspiration

Maidstone East itself is a useful source of inspiration whatever modelling era interests you (although because of the curves and the fact that the goods yards sprawled away from the running lines it has limitations as a suitable subject for an accurate model). There has been at least one article in the model railway press exploring its potential. For modelling purposes the line has good scenic breaks in a cutting to the west and a tunnel immediately adjacent to the platform ends to the east. In the relatively short distance between these 'breaks' the line runs first onto an embankment with a stone overbridge crossing the SER Medway Valley line, then spans the River Medway on a brick viaduct with a girder bridge over the river itself. The main part of the station is east of the river and packed into the short space between the viaduct and the tunnel.

This is a station which has changed much over time. It originally opened in 1874 as a terminus of a branch from Otford to the west. In 1884 the line was extended to the LCDR terminus in Ashford. Only after the formation of the SECR Joint Management Committee in 1899 did it become a through route linking in to the ex-SER lines through Ashford to the Channel Ports. Between the two World Wars the girder bridge was replaced to allow the heaviest locomotives to use the line (1927), and the small locomotive depot closed. Electrification from the west arrived in 1939. Prior to the extension of electrification westwards in 1961 the track layout was extensively altered and a new signal box built. In 1993 there was a further major

Horse shunting at Whitstable Harbour, 1932 - such a simple scene, yet almost impossible to recreate as a working model. **Peter D Page**

I have offered Maidstone East as one real location that offers a wealth of inspiration. Whilst I should be pleased to find that I have inspired someone to follow one of the modelling avenues I have hinted at, there is a more general lesson. There will be a prototype location that you know as well as I know Maidstone East. Why not think about the modelling choices which it offers you? You may be surprised to find out how varied they are.

How about electric trains?

If you've stuck with me thus far, you will have noticed that I've referred far more to electrification than to diesel traction. Electrified railways in general are a major area where the inspiration of the prototype seems to me to be under-exploited. I'm not

track alteration in connection with the Channel Tunnel opening, whilst there have been other, lesser, changes over the years. If you want to model 'Essence of Maidstone East' there are thus at least half a dozen ways you could do it, ranging from the obscurity of the mid-Victorian terminus to the intense operation of the period between the opening of the Channel Tunnel and the opening of the new high speed Channel Tunnel Rail Link.

Any of those interpretations could make distinctive models. Indeed, the opportunity to mix 'Eurostars', Channel Tunnel freight, and 'Heritage' EMUs in a setting drawn from life may be one of the easiest of those under-exploited areas of our hobby to explore.

Preparations for track alterations at the eastern end of Maidstone East station associated with the extension of electrification to Ashford. Photo taken September 24, 1961, works carried out October 15, 1961. **Peter D Page**

The revised track layout at Maidstone East, August 31, 1963, with what had been a loop siding transformed into a reversible through road. Further major alterations to the track layout were undertaken in the 1990s in preparation for the advent of Channel Tunnel traffic. **Peter D Page**

an expert in the field, but I don't see why there shouldn't be more models based on prototypes such as the London, Brighton & South Coast Railway's overhead London Suburban electrification from the early years of the twentieth century. If my own choices have taken me into largely narrow gauge modelling, it's probably because I've got vague memories of my first narrow gauge rides (at Maidstone Zoo) but none of my much earlier initiation (at the age of 15 months) into the pleasures of a ride on an electric train.

In Table 2 I have listed some of the earlier electrified lines which might be looked at as modelling subjects. Again the list is not intended to be exhaustive and I acknowledge that some of the subjects have already been tackled. Given the current availability

TABLE 2:

Some electrification schemes worth considering as modelling subjects:

Lancaster-Morecambe

Manchester-Bury (Pre-Metro)

Manchester-Altrincham (Pre-Metro)

The Mersey Railway

Glasgow Underground (4' 0" gauge - the pre-modernisation cars and operation were fascinating)

North Tyneside

LB&SCR London suburban electrification - overhead rather than third rail, converted to third rail in Southern Railway days

The Volks Electric Railway (Brighton - narrow gauge)

A modern Up train at East Farleigh where the Up and Down platforms are on opposite sides of the level crossing. The line curves quite sharply through the station here. **Bob Page**

A recent view of East Farleigh, note detail of crossing gate, timber station building and hipped roof signal box. **Bob Page**

Wateringbury - a modern view of the Down platform and station building from the footbridge. The Up platform is behind the camera. **Bob Page**

of power bogies such as the 'Black Beetle', modelling prototypes like these need not take great engineering skill, but I should admit that some of these projects would require fairly well developed research and scratch-building skills. Those skills could be learned as part of the project.

As I think back to my one return trip on the electric train from Lancaster (Castle) via Lancaster (Green Ayre) to Morecambe (Promenade), I can see that even along a single route and at a single date, the prototype electric railway may offer us a variety of inspiration. My memories of that trip are now over 40 years old, but I can see various realistic possibilities for a model. 'Essence of Lancaster (Castle)' would require only one route-specific EMU, shuttling into and out of a bay at the north eastern end of a WCML station otherwise populated by the usual suspects, 'Duchess of Abercorn' and her friends. Morecambe (Promenade) might make an interesting club project, a West Coast equivalent of the model of Scarborough presently on the exhibition circuit. This would need more EMUs and more overhead than Castle, but with the basic research done batch-building would be possible. My memories suggest that 'Essence of Lancaster (Green Ayre)' would be the best project for

Wateringbury in the 1980s, note how level crossing details differs from East Farleigh and different style of signal box.
Bob Page

Wateringbury, a late 20th century view of the former goods yard which was divided by the side road towards the level crossing and river bridge. The level crossing had a third pair of gates on this side to protect the siding that crossed the road. Drawings of all three main railway buildings here appeared in the *Model Railway Constructor*.
Peter D Page

A modern view of Yalding showing the level crossing and the utilitarian brick station building on the Up platform. The Down platform is beyond the footbridge in the background. At one time there was a camping coach parked in a disconnected siding on the left-hand side of this picture. **Bob Page**

Suggested further reading

Just to get you going I've included a short list of suggested further reading relating to Table 1. Even for the two counties covered in that table, there is much more available. If you're a steam locomotive fan who fancies a real challenge, start with pages 38-49 of *The Cement Railways of Kent* - sheer inspirational variety!

The Cement Railways of Kent
B D Stoyel and R W Kidner
(Locomotion Papers 70)
The Oakwood Press 1990
ISBN 0 85361 370 2

Industrial Railways of the South-East' compiled on behalf of the Amberley Chalk Pits Museum by Ian Dean, Andrew Neale, and David Smith
Middleton Press 1984
ISBN 0 906520 09 6

The Hawkhurst Branch
Brian Hart
Wild Swan Publications 2000
ISBN 1 874103 54 2

Strood to Paddock Wood
Vic Mitchell and Keith Smith
Middleton Press 1993,
ISBN 1 873793 12 X
(Includes further details of Yalding, Wateringbury and East Farleigh stations.)

Swanley to Ashford
Vic Mitchell and Keith Smith
Middleton Press 1995
ISBN 1 873793 45 6
(Includes further details of Maidstone East, although not the Channel Tunnel freight traffic)

Redhill to Ashford
Vic Mitchell and Keith Smith
Middleton Press 1990
ISBN 0 906520 73 8

a lone modeller or group of friends, particularly if they had more of a Midland bent than an interest in the LNWR. The electric trains would mix with steam trains on the Morecambe-Hellifield-Skipton route.

Generic or specific ?
I am suggesting that we draw our inspiration from very site-specific locations, even if we build 'Essence of' rather than an exact model. To illustrate this, I return to Kent. Yalding,

TABLE 3:

Some stations which might be worth looking at for modelling inspiration

Many of these examples could be modelled in an 'essence of' version.

Maidstone East (see text)

Hebden Bridge - modern image trains in a carefully restored 'heritage' station

Navigation Road, (on the Manchester-Altrincham line) - Metro and conventional railway each using one track (Altrincham itself would be worth looking at too, particularly if there is interest in modelling rail/bus interchange)

Killarney - a 'dead-end' station on a through line with through stopping trains either having to reverse in or reverse out - an interesting arrangement scenically and in operational terms if used on an otherwise conventional continuous run layout.

Folkestone Junction (latterly Folkestone East) - interesting layout and movements associated with boat trains to and from the harbour branch - Martello tunnel forms one natural scenic break.

Fersit Halt, West Highland Railway (open August 1, 1931, to January 1, 1935) - opened in connection with a construction camp for the Lochaber hydro-electric scheme - goods sidings interchanging with the construction camp and the 3' 0" gauge Lochaber Narrow Gauge Railway.

Chelmsford - intensive services through a station on a viaduct.

Tunbridge Wells West - almost a terminus with services westwards over four LB&SCR routes (to Eastbourne, Brighton, East Grinstead and London), but with a single track connection continuing east to the SER Hastings line, allowing through running to Tunbridge Wells Central (interesting in its own right as a cramped passenger station between tunnels) and Tonbridge.

Ladybank - junction station with railway workshops - the junction with the line coming in from Mawcarse Junction to the west faced south and was south of the station so that branch passenger trains had to reverse into the station on arrival or out on departure.

Dunbar - passenger station on a loop off the East Coast Main Line.

---

produced when the Chatham MRC used the station as inspiration for a layout. Chatham MRC is not alone in finding inspiration in Wateringbury. My brother Bob is currently tackling 'Essence of Wateringbury' in EM. such a project. His brief explanation of why he chose this subject, together with some photographs of the work in progress, accompanies this article.

In a similar way, if you are thinking of modelling, for example, the archetypal GWR branch terminus, or a location on the Somerset & Dorset Railway, it might be best to look at the real thing and model the essence of a specific example which interests you. There may be one that no one else has tackled in the way you're thinking of doing it. Even if you use the 'essence of' approach, working from a specific example is more likely to produce a credible result than bringing disparate elements together in an invented geography.

More generally, specific sites in the real thing may offer us some unusual features to incorporate into our model. In Table 3 I have set out a short personal selection of small to medium stations which offer something a bit out of the ordinary. With the exception of Fersit Halt, (which I read about in a book on the Lochaber Narrow Gauge Railway by Patrick Howat, published by the Narrow Gauge Railway Society, ISBN 0 9507169 0 1), the examples are stations I have visited. I am sure that other modellers would produce other lists. All the examples are capable of being turned into a model, at least in an 'essence of' form.

Conclusion

Even in standard gauge alone the range of choice in the prototype is so wide that every layout could have what the marketing men would call it's USP (Unique Selling Point). I think that would be a good thing, particularly if it resulted in more of the available options being modelled. There will always be some convergence of design as similar operating and space considerations lead to similar solutions, but this needn't lead to a lack of variety. If you're one of the great majority like me who will never make sheer modelling excellence their USP, the answer is to look for something that's clearly a bit different in inspiration from other people. The main source of that difference will be the sheer variety of the prototype. Because what I've written is based

---

Wateringbury and East Farleigh are three stations on the ten miles long Paddock Wood to Maidstone West line. All have a level crossing and the SER's typical staggered platforms, but their sites are very different.

Yalding, out in the flatness of the Low Weald, comes close to being the sort of station one might model if trying to distil the essence of a typical South Eastern Railway wayside station, although there are distinctive features which might be included. These include the camping coach which was there at one time and the industrial siding serving an agricultural chemical factory just south of the station.

Because of their setting and, in the case of Wateringbury at least, their

architecture, the other two stations are more interesting. East Farleigh is in the narrowest part of the Medway valley as it cuts through the Lower Greensand ridge. It is cramped by the valley side and on a significant curve. The station buildings are simple, and on a wide enough baseboard a model could include the lock and sluices on the Medway, as well as the mediaeval bridge. If you fancy a circular layout, think about East Farleigh.

Wateringbury is also on a curve, but not such a tight one. An unusual feature is the fact that one of the goods yard roads extends over the level crossing, requiring extra gates. The station building and house is ornate, but can be modelled from drawings in the late Model Railway Constructor

Why 'Essence of Wateringbury'?

Bob Page has chosen to create a model based on one of the prototype stations discussed in this article. Here he explains his choice.

'Why I based my model railway on Wateringbury could easily fill a whole article but for now I will concentrate on the basics. I wanted an EM gauge layout based on the final years of steam in Kent. It had to fit into a confined space, operate in prototypical fashion and allow for a wide variety of locomotive and train types.

I ruled out a single track branch line because study of contemporary time tables showed they would only allow a boringly small variety of trains. Lack of space ruled out a major station or line with a significant number of passenger trains over four coaches long. For me a shortened block freight of say 10-15 wagons is credible but an express passenger needs at least seven coaches.

I have fond memories of the Medway Valley line. My favourite loco is Wainwright's H Class 0-4-4 tank. I wanted a station scene that could be doctored to fit in the space available. I chose Wateringbury for the interesting architecture and unusual three-track, six-gate level crossing. By omitting most of the goods yard, I could get a scene that worked for me; although I keep exploring ideas to enable me to re-instate the yard and include the Down Home signal.

It is 'essence of' rather than an exact model so that I can change things to get a scene capturing the essentials that define the Medway Valley for me. These are a mediaeval stone bridge (Bow Bridge by the real Wateringbury station is actually an uninspiring concrete structure), a level crossing and an orchard with sheep and an oast in the background.

Even a simple model like this demands considerable research and modelling time and, after several years work, there is still much to research, learn and do. This layout will never be 'finished' but success is achieved when I am transported through time and find myself back train spotting in the Medway Valley in the late 1950s.'

N Class 31401 brings a Down excursion train through the station while H Class 31177 waits to propel its push-pull set towards Paddock Wood. **Bob Page**

The signal is clear for a Paddock Wood bound push-pull train as N Class 31401 approaches with an excursion. **Bob Page**

The ornate brick station building captures the 'Essence of Wateringbury'. **Bob Page**

on my own travels and reading, I've only touched on a tiny part of that variety in this article. I have not even begun to look at the huge potential of the narrow gauges as sources of inspiration. Whether in standard, broad or narrow gauge, exploring the sources for yourself will be fun.

Beware - loco-builder at work. Tony's workbench with everything to hand, including his 'MCP' award proudly displayed on the cabinet - no prizes for working out what those initials stand for!

Secrets of the workbench

John Emerson lifts the lid on the editorial team's work rooms.

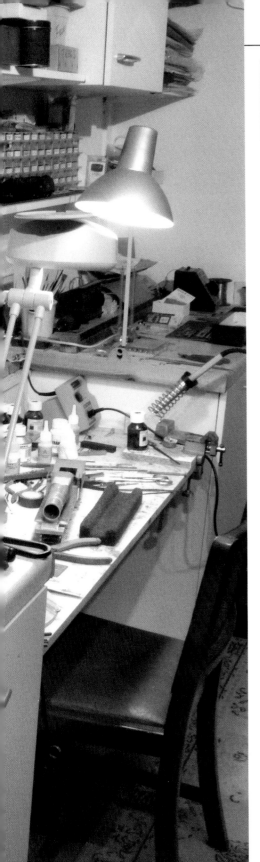

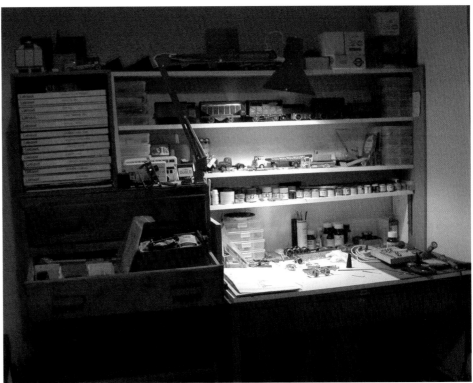

An old desk forms the basis for this workbench, the chest of drawers providing useful storage for materials, kits and other bits. The paint shelf was only temporarily in place - which explains why it is on the skew! Although the work area was quite small a lot of work was carried out - more than has been done on the new larger custom-built bench that has now replaced it. Food for thought indeed!

Somewhere, most probably in one of those Sunday colour supplements, I've seen a series of articles on authors and the rooms where the serious business of writing takes place. The photograph is often accompanied by a description of the author's personality traits, deduced from the appearance of the room by someone well-versed in 'headology'. We thought it would be fun to take a peek at the editorial workbenches.

Tony Wright's bench is seen in our heading photograph with plenty of projects in evidence, including the pair of O gauge locomotives being built as part of the 'Right Track' DVD series. The dropped section is particularly useful with a convenient test track placed at the rear of the bench. This is very obviously a loco-builders domain!

In contrast, the Editor used an old desk (above) for a variety of projects ranging from locomotives and rolling stock to buildings and signals. Paints and materials are close at hand and an old chest of drawers has been incorporated for more storage.

After seeing Tony's bench, I built a new larger workbench with kitchen base units underneath and more shelving for stock storage. Curiously I seem to have built much less on the new improved larger bench - there must be a moral there somewhere!

Beyond Hedingham

Alan Turner describes the changes made on his O gauge layout and the new branch line to Kelsey. Photography by **Ray Lightfoot**.

The branch platform at Hedingham, with the connection waiting. The nameboard was originally made for a scheme to connect with a possible exhibition branch station, since given away.

In my last article, (*BRM* December 2005), I intimated that there would be an extension from the main line to a branch of some sort.

For a while, I pondered over whether this should be to a locomotive shed and yard, using the superb turntable built by Colin Scoffin, one of our wiring gang, just as an exercise in O gauge. Sadly Colin died and his superb EM layout has been dismantled. Also, I had built a large ex-GNR hipped roof engine shed for David Hubbard, my chief wiring friend, and I rather fancied doing one for myself. At the time, locomotive storage was under the scenic village section, and shunting locomotives out from behind others by instruments and switches alone, caused some difficulties and was a chore. Apart from this, I decided I wanted to see my engines.

Experience in operating the railway also brought to light other annoying factors, while inexperienced operators could cause accidents in the storage loops hidden underneath the scenic rear of the model.

Although this area was designed and built to be removed in sections, they were heavy, it was a nuisance, and I tended rather to lose patience when forced to lift out, and sometimes repair, slight damage to the edges of the sections.

Last and not least, was the ever present matter of access to the railway room. Eight tracks over the original lifting flap was obviously far too many for good alignment. The flap had become very heavy and warped by being lifted from one side and finally became wedged down permanently. Getting trays of tea and biscuits underneath was difficult, taking them over was dangerous too, and on occasions caused damage due to the width of the model. Older or arthritic folk found difficulty and the dictates of fashions, etc, prevented some ladies from crawling underneath!

I hesitated to suggest so many changes to the railway to the friends who had done so much wiring and had given so much help. However, everyone agreed that the alterations would give improvements and all those who knew the railway voted for a branch line terminus. The feeling was that it would give operational interest in its own right, providing connecting services to and from Hedingham, and it could be operated independently into the new storage sidings, to be connected to a new loop behind the fascia.

Although the building of the branch was the main, and final, big alteration to the railway, we decided that all the other changes should be done at the same time as they were interlinked. I had decided that the storage loops should be visible and accessible from above, but from the front, hidden by a fascia. Not wanting to waste the church, vicarage and other buildings from above the loops, they had to be re-sited. The only possible place was on the end of the goods yard

The beginning of Station Approach.

beyond the lifting flap. This would mean shortening the goods yard and moving the goods shed.

Priorities decided, one morning, David Hubbard and Alan Moore felt that I ought to go and make some tea, rather than see a very large saw go through the whole layout at the platform ends of Hedingham. It sounded awful!

The section was removed and a new flap of half the width was built. The new, stronger, decently hinged lifting flap has only four tracks going across, which I think is enough for good alignment and we avoided interfering with point mechanisms. Wiring was soon reconnected and trains could run again on the main lines. The sidings extending beyond the lifting flap were removed and using a large carving knife, the goods shed, weighbridge, hut, cattle dock and accessories were taken up, undamaged, for re-use at the other end of the goods yard. The area was then cleaned up ready for the placing of buildings taken from over the storage loops. Nowadays it is called redevelopment!

With the lifting section being the only part with track, and also half its previous width, the remaining gap was bridged by a slide in section containing the blacksmith's establishment and the road through the lower part of the village, from which there is access to the new cattle dock.

By digging out the footbridge at the town end of the model and turning one end round, I was able to slightly extend the sidings, re-site the goods shed and provide a more cramped, but adequate goods yard. Access to the goods shed had to be made, the weighbridge fitted and a new footpath made to provide a route to the turned bridge.

No alterations were needed to the signalling and the advantages of all the changes have outweighed the slight loss of siding capacity. Over a period of several days, various arrangements of the salvaged buildings were tried out on the cleared site, beyond the new lifting flap. Eventually the most satisfactory grouping was with the church on a slight rise behind the signal box and the houses either side of a new road.

The only big loss was the quarry, with its own 2' gauge line, but this has been successfully incorporated

This is the only overall picture of the branch, showing the loading and cattle dock to the left, the steep approach road to the station and relationship to the village. The J6 is shunting the daily goods.

Searby's wagon awaits unloading at Kelsey's coal drops. The branch train has recently arrived.

The layout is totally usual, though its setting at the bottom of a steep road from the village is probably less so in model form. Space dictated that there would have to be the usual platform road with run round, a bay and limited sidings for coal, cattle and general merchandise.

As usual, I built everything and friends made it work.

I decided that such a small terminus should not boast an overbearing building, a small wooden single storey station would suffice. A couple of photographs of Lea station on the GN and GE line near Gainsborough provided the inspiration I needed. The GN style building was constructed as usual from artists' mounting board, with a planked surface of thin card between the framing.

I added an awning, not on the original, which does rather hide the details and nice windows. The only other feature copied from Lea is the hut with a large bell under an awning. A brick tranship shed stands at the buffer stop end, whilst near the station throat I have provided a small signal box, platelayer's hut and a corrugated iron lamp hut, the latter a gift from Derek Griffith.

on David Hubbard's railway.

With the storage loops now being open and the scenic features from above it being re-sited, actual work on the branch began. It was found possible to make a short loop from the branch in front of the storage loops, but still behind the fascia. From this came the branch proper, but with a connection back to the down main lines for continuous running of branch trains if required.

The access to the former engine storage under the village was retained for branch goods trains, if they could not be accepted at either station. Lights on the branch panel indicate track occupancy.

Also on this loop, but facing the other way, a three-way point takes trains to Hedingham, leads to two sidings for branch passenger trains and also gives access to the engine storage shelf. The diagram should make this clear. The shelf is exactly that, the spare locomotives are displayed upon it.

Minimal expense was incurred in the building of the branch terminus. Panels from a very old, solid, donated wardrobe were used for the baseboard and spare track from previous alterations was reused.

The J6 in the bay platform at Kelsey.

The N5 glides out of Kelsey tunnel. The background is from a photograph of the western edge of the Lincolnshire Wolds. It is not all flat!

At one stage, I considered making a handsome somersault bracket signal for starters, as existed at Horncastle, but as the platform becomes so narrow at the ramp end, due to pointwork, I decided on separate structures. The final exit signal, at the tunnel mouth, has a miniature arm under the main one to allow shunting into the tunnel, but not authorisation to proceed along the branch. Trains in both directions on the branch stop automatically before entering the stations.

At Hedingham, pulling off the signals for yard or branch platform restores current if the route is clear. At Kelsey, the station controller takes over for entry. Fencing all along the front of the branch layout serves as a safety feature at the edge of the baseboard in case of a derailment. The steep road down from the village, past the 'Great Northern' public house, makes a very attractive scenic feature and there is separate road access to the cattle dock and small loading platform. The 'grass' banks behind the station site are made from old towels, fixed on to a paper and card base with PVA adhesive and brush painted with acrylics. It is necessary to avoid textured patterns or looped pile of some towels. The trees need some work and more will be provided, along with suitable undergrowth, when I get round to it.

For easy removal, the bank is made in short sections.

All of the 'wooden' buildings are in the standard green and cream. After seeing Garth Patrick's Clayton steam railcar standing in the terminus in its very attractive cream and green livery, I really fancy making one for myself, in spite of the fact that the last was withdrawn just before my period. This is not a concern, if I like something.

I regret not having fitted point rodding at both stations when first built. It would have been so much easier to get the runs right before adding so many obstructions, now access has become difficult.

As always, I have reasons for making particular structures or naming businesses, shops or stations. For the branch I chose the name Kelsey as my late wife was born at North Kelsey.

The branch has added tremendously to the interest, providing real connections with Hedingham, or being worked on its own, to and from the storage sidings.

I can now see the spare engines on the locomotive shelf, which makes changes very easy.

The storage loops are hidden by the fascia, but are easily accessible.

Dedicated branch passenger stock, in the form of the ex-GNR articulated triplet set, non-corridor GER and

GNR bogie and GNR six-wheeled vehicles, all scratch-built, appear behind the C12, N5 and A5. The J6 is most commonly seen on goods trains, though the J11, more rarely the J50, and the Sentinel sometimes appear.

Small detail improvements or additions are made occasionally, when thought of. Bits of straw sticking out from cattle wagon floors or on cattle docks, or the corners of open wagons, the odd bucket, bicycle or garden tool, the addition of a pool of water (varnish) on a sagging wagon sheet suggest real life. Some of the trees will be improved. If I find a suitable cheap watch, this could be fitted on the church tower, but then this is just fiddling.

Although I have too much stock, I do from time to time find interest in making something a little bit different, whilst some vehicles can be improved or in some cases replaced.

O2 Class 3491 and 'Crab' 2823 have been added and B3 Valour is in hand. I may build a D2 next winter as another branch engine.

The passage of time has shown that no more can be done to Hedingham and Kelsey, and the layout is as satisfactory as the space allows. Obviously we could always use more space for train storage, but in my case there is no way this could happen. Already I have

The platform end at Kelsey, showing tranships shed, scratch-built wagons (from 1mm ply) and the 'Great Northern' public house at the top of the station approach.

Close up of the C12 arriving at Kelsey. The J6 rests in the bay to leave the station clear for the C12 to run round its train and leave first.

concerns over accommodation when the family visits, as only one spare room is available now and there is a second grandchild!

As regards operation, I prefer my friends to operate the layout, while I am content to just watch the trains go by.

With the Editor's permission I will deal further with the buildings, scenics and some of the more interesting rolling stock in due course.

Above: GCR D9 6014 comes to a halt at Kelsey. The loco is super power for the branch, but in my defence, a well known photograph exists of a GCR Atlantic on a branch train at New Holland!

Below: Platforms end at Kelsey showing tranship shed, scratch-built wagons (1mm ply) and the 'Great Northern' public house at the top of the station approach.

Above: N5 ready to leave for Hedingham. Locomotives are from kits but everything else is scratch-built.

Below: The C12 and triplet set arriving at Kelsey. Coal siding on the right. No.4506 is a beautiful runner, but visually the least satisfactory of my models, having been built as a return favour, before I ever thought seriously about modelling in O gauge.

ORDER FORM

I would like to order (please state quantity):

- ☐ _____ Right Track 1 £15.99 each
- ☐ _____ Right Track 2 £15.99 each
- ☐ _____ Right Track 1 & 2 £30.00
- ☐ _____ Right Track 3 £17.99 each
- ☐ _____ Right Track 4 £18.99 each
- ☐ _____ Right Track 5 £16.99 each
- ☐ _____ Right Track 6 £18.99 each
- ☐ _____ Right Track 5 & 6 £33.99
- ☐ _____ Right Track 7 £18.99 each

Your Details

Mr/Mrs/Miss/Ms _____ First Name _____

Surname _____

Address _____

_____

_____

Postcode _____

Telephone No _____

Email Address _____

Payment Details

☐ I enclose a cheque for £_____ made payable to *Warners Group Publications*

☐ Please debit £_____ from my: ☐ VISA ☐ MasterCard ☐ Switch

Card Number

☐☐☐☐ ☐☐☐☐ ☐☐☐☐ ☐☐☐☐ Switch Only ☐☐☐

Expiry Date ☐☐☐☐ Start Date ☐☐☐☐ Issue No ☐☐

Signature _____ Date _____

This is a UK offer only. Offer available whilst stocks last. Please allow 28 days for delivery. Please call for overseas prices.

Please return to: British Railway Modelling Subs, Warners Group Publications, FREEPOST PE211, Bourne, Lincs, PE10 9BR

FANTASTIC READER OFFERS

Right Track 1 – Locomotive Kit Building Part 1
The first in the series, illustrating constructional aspects of the hobby features 3 locomotives - a 4F from Alan Gibson, a GWR 61xx 2-6-2T from South Eastern Finecast and an A2 Pacific from DJH. Aspects covered during the two-hours include: chassis making, quartering wheels, arranging pick-ups, making and securing coupling rods, installing motors, fitting ponies and bogies, initial body and tender construction and first steps in detailing.

£15.99

Following on from part 1, the three locomotives are taken right through to completion, prior to painting in this three-hour presentation. Part 2 focuses on: building and detailing the smoke box/boiler/firebox, fixing and drilling chimneys, detailing the cab, forming smoke deflectors and handrails, outside motion, cylinders and valve gear assembly, test running and fine adjustments.

£15.99

PART 1 AND PART 2 FOR £30.00

Right Track 3 – Painting Lining and Finishing
Covering painting, lining, lettering, re-numbering, weathering and varnishing, this full 3 hour presentation provides all you need to know to fully finish your locomotive or rolling stock. Part 3 takes you through every stage in the painting/finishing process, dealing with the most basic disciplines and then guiding you through to simple weathering and finishing. Also covering further techniques in the likes of spray painting and varnishing.

£17.99

Part 4 takes you through the many stages involved in the process of turning already-excellent models into something that little bit special. Stretching from the most simple of improvements through to the provision of a new locomotive chassis, Part 4 provides all the information you need to detail, improve, modify and personalise current examples of RTR locomotives and rolling stock to make them even better.

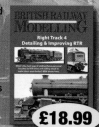

£18.99

Right Track Part 5 – Modelling Landscapes Part 1 is Introduced by Tony Wright, and presented by Barry Norman. Here he presents, the methods and techniques involved in layout design, baseboard construction, laying track, ballasting track, making landforms, laying grass and landscaping. All in all this is an essential dvd whether you're just starting out on building a layout, wishing to take your scenic modelling a step further or are already experienced in landscaping.

£16.99

Right Track 6 - Modelling Landscape Part 1-2
The second part of Barry Norman's two-part DVD, Right Track 6, explains how he creates such realistic landscapes and takes the process several stages further. He models lanes, hedges, creates water effects and makes trees from a variety of different materials and with a selection of different foliage effects. All the techniques are shown and explained in an easy-to-follow manner. Also includes some of the incredible modelling produced by the Pendon Museum team.

£18.99

PART 5 AND PART 6 FOR £33.99

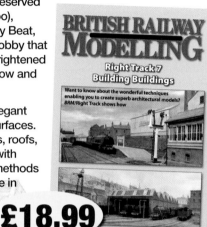

BRITISH RAILWAY MODELLING INVITES YOU TO

THE LONDON FESTIVAL of RAILWAY MODELLING

In Association with The Model Railway Club

29th & 30th March 2008

Alexandra Palace LONDON

Kindly sponsored by **HORNBY** · **GRAHAM FARISH** · **BACHMANN** BRANCH-LINE

In Association with **THE MODEL RAILWAY CLUB**

Presented by the Publishers of

BRITISH RAILWAY MODELLING **TRACTION**

COME ENJOY A FANTASTIC DAY OF RAILWAY MODELLING

- 40 working British, Continental and American layouts for you to see
- Over 100 trade stands to stock up on all those essentials
- BRM Specialist Trade Village for those harder to source items
- Clubs, demonstrations & displays – pick up some great modelling tips!
- Children's modelling area (5 – 14 yrs)
  Sponsored by Freestone Model Accessories

OPENING

Sat 10am – 5.30pm
Sun 10am – 5pm
Doors open at 9.45am for pre-booked ticket holders

Disabled Access ♿

HOW TO GET THERE

Travel by rail to Alexandra Palace Station or by under ground to Wood Green and then direct to the venue by *FREE* shuttle bus. *FREE* parking available on-site.

Book on-line at www.brmodelling.co.uk
or call the ticket hotline: 01778 391180 (Mon – Fri 9am – 6pm)

THE LONDON FESTIVAL OF RAILWAY MODELLING BOOKING FORM 2008

Title _____ Forename _____ Surname _____

Address _____

_____ Town _____

County _____ Postcode _____

E-mail address _____

Daytime Telephone _____

ADVANCE ADMISSION RATES - PLEASE SEND ME:
All under 14's must be accompanied by an adult
ONE DAY ADMISSION Letters are valid for use on **EITHER SATURDAY OR SUNDAY**

_____ Adult @ **£8.00**   _____ Senior (60+) @ **£7.50**

_____ Child (5-14 yrs) @ **£3.50**   _____ Family (2+3) @ **£23**

BRM/TRACTION subscribers *receive a £1 discount on pre-booked adult/senior admission (Max.2)*

Subscription No. _____   Magazine_____
Subs No. must be included to qualify for discount.

_____ Subscriber rate adult @ **£7.00**

_____ Subscriber rate senior @ **£6.50**   **TOTAL DUE £** _____

On-the-door admission: Adult £10.00, Senior £9.50, Child £4.50, Family £29.00

I enclose a cheque for £ _____ made payable to "WARNERS GROUP PUBLICATIONS PLC" or please debit my Credit Card **VISA / MASTERCARD / SWITCH**

INT REF: DDAY   Switch only

Card No ☐☐☐☐ ☐☐☐☐ ☐☐☐☐ ☐☐☐☐ ☐☐

Expiry Date ☐☐☐☐   Start Date ☐☐☐☐   Issue No ☐

Signature _____ Date _____

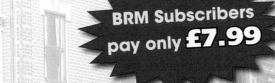